Workers and Managers in
Latin America

Consulting Editor: Phillip Hammond
Department of Sociology
University of Arizona
Tucson, Arizona

Workers and Managers in Latin America

Stanley M. Davis
Harvard University

Louis Wolf Goodman
Yale University

D.C. HEATH AND COMPANY
Lexington, Massachusetts Toronto London

Clothbound edition published by Lexington Books.

Published simultaneously in Canada.

Printed in the United States of America.

Paperbound International Standard Book Number: 0-669-74658-4
Clothbound International Standard Book Number: 0-669-84004-1

Library of Congress Catalog Card Number: 72-3745

A nuestros socios, Nancy y Shirley

Table of Contents

Workers

Managers

Introduction

On the same weekday morning Juan Arroyo and Francisco Gomez go to work. Arroyo leaves his wife, five children and three-room apartment in his worker *barrio* and takes an overcrowded bus across town to the factory where he works cutting leather. Gomez leaves his house in a new *suburbio* a few hours later and drops his two children off at school. He parks his locally manufactured Ford in the company lot and takes the elevator to his office. He busily reviews the personnel report he is to present at today's executive luncheon. Arroyo's work-group breaks for lunch at noon with five of their eight hours completed. A few workers take advantage of the two-hour *siesta* break and go home for lunch, but Arroyo lives too far away and eats in the small cafeteria the company provides for workers, chewing slowly with his plate of false teeth. Gomez is served lunch in the executive conference room and presents his report over coffee. Later in the day, Arroyo comes to Gomez's office to select the weeks for his annual vacation. While there he invites Gomez to attend his daughter's First Communion in the hope that the personnel director will take an interest in him and his family and will get to meet his unemployed cousin who has recently arrived from the *campo*.

Scenes like these are repeated daily throughout Latin America today. They are part of the world of workers and managers, the two critical human resources in the industrialization process.

In Latin America each group is known by various names. There are, of course, blue-collar laborers and white-collar clerks, ditch diggers and skilled mechanics, manuals and nonmanuals, wage earner and salaried, and union and nonunion personnel. In Spanish they may be called *obrero, empleado, trabajador, operario, maestro, capataz.* Important distinctions must also be made between workers in agriculture, in industry and in services, and between the employed, underemployed, and unemployed; but all are still workers. Workers are the soldiers in the army of industry and not the officers.

Managers are the people who run the industrial organizations. They are the ones who set the goals and direct the activity of others in order to achieve these goals. They too are known by many names: *gerente, empresario, emprendedor, hombre de negocio, dueño, patrón, administrador, jefe,* and others. Perhaps the most important distinction between the people in this group is the difference between those who build empires and those who build organizations. The former group, commonly known as *entrepreneurs,* are the ones who start with little or nothing and by their drive and innovative skills create empires. The latter group, we may call them *executives,* place greater emphasis on systematizing and explicitly defining the processes and organizational relationships needed to run these complex entities.

Modernization and the World of Work

These workers and managers are the major actors in industrialization, which itself is but part of a larger global process known as modernization. Modernization is a general term for the myriad social processes which describe the rapid changes in human affairs that have taken place since the scientific revolution. Because of the impossibility of listing all of the changes involved in this process, it is useful to compare the most salient characteristics of typical "traditional" and "modern" societies.[1]

Traditional societies are generally considered to have a majority of the population living in rural areas and engaged in subsistence agriculture; a system of social stratification that is sharply divided between a few rulers and many peasants, with little mobility between strata; a high level of illiteracy; little participation in mass media; authoritarian family structures; social systems dominated by a few multipurpose institutions; customary techniques of production handed down from father to son; and localized markets.

Modern societies, in contrast, have population concentrated in urban areas; a complex division of labor with few workers engaged in agriculture; a greater range of social strata with a more egalitarian distribution of wealth, status, and power, including increased individual mobility; high literacy rates, with emphasis on teaching pragmatic skills; wide exposure to mass media; egalitarian family structures; complex and specialized differentiation of social institutions; a sophisticated use of technology and science; and an economy based on complex commercial markets with high per capita consumption and production.

The process of modernization is characterized by the constant reorganization of *work roles*. In the first stages of the process, traditional work practices are largely transformed to fit with more productive technologies. In a sense, the continual generation of increased per capita production through the adoption of increasingly efficient technologies is both the driving and the maintaining force behind the overall process of industrialization.

To understand the pervasiveness of the impact of work on society, it is useful to divide society into three major institutional areas—*social, economic,* and *political*. The changing nature and organization of work in a modernizing society transforms human relations in all three of these areas.

In the social sphere, a son's desire to take up his father's occupation or to set out on his own can fragment or cement relations between the generations of a family. Social relations may also change on the job. Modern bosses find it increasingly difficult to maintain traditional, personalistic relationships with workers, and increasingly limit their contact to activities functionally related to their work.

---

[1]It must be remembered that these descriptions are "ideal types." This means that they list generalized characteristics and that any given society will have a mixture of attributes, some more traditional and others more modern. A society modernizes as more of its institutions take on the group of characteristics described below as "modern."

The economic organization of the firm is also transformed. Managers discover that competition and rising costs require the rationalization of productive techniques—both with respect to the organization of technology and personnel. Workers find that traditional artisan skills no longer provide job security, but that their success in the market depends on the ability to efficiently fit into an increasingly complex division of labor.

In the political arena, power is no longer exclusively wielded by a small oligarchy, but now must be shared among a larger number of people and interest groups, including the military, the church, political parties, industrialists, trade unions, and so on. For workers a new political consciousness develops. Managers no longer hold absolute power over their lives and are now to be bargained with through unions. On a national level many workers see that their interests and those of the middle class are represented by separate political parties—and they organize and vote accordingly.

The impact of the reorganization of work on each of these institutional areas is represented by a separate section of this book. Part One, The Socio-Cultural Setting, describes the impact on work of the changing Latin American social structure and culture. Cultural meanings and social arrangements in Latin America make work and management very different phenomena from what they are in North America, and from what they were in Latin America in past decades.

Part Two, The Economics of Enterprise and the Worker's Situation, focuses on explicitly work-related phenomena. Employment, unemployment, labor recruitment, work conditions, wages, productivity, worker alienation, rationalization of management, the search for capital and the mechanics of industrial expansion are all discussed. Having been exposed to the social setting in Part One, the reader can in the second part get a sense of the problems the two sets of actors—workers and managers— face, as they involve themselves in the process of production. The image which emerges shows that although workers and managers are linked by the means of production, their day-to-day work problems are of entirely different orders, with workers manifesting great concern with the vagaries of management control, but managers concerned more with the economics of their firms in relation to the larger economy. In hierarchical terms, the subordinate workers are more concerned with the managerial impact on their social, economic and political lives, than is reciprocally the case— managers worry less about workers than about other necessary resources.

Part Three, Work, Management and Politics, sheds light on this bifurcation of the interests of management and labor. The triangle of management, labor, and government is brought into sharper focus. In traditional relationships, managers exercised blatantly paternalistic control over their work force. However, as industrialization proceeds, managers begin to rationalize their operations and workers begin to defend their own interests. At first governments attempted to maintain stability by enacting encyclopaedic labor codes which rigidly fixed labor and management rights and established the state as the ultimate arbiter. This state paternalism has proven inadequate in more advanced Latin American nations.

Systems of collective bargaining are now developing where labor and management attempt to resolve their differences without resorting to a political solution.

However, politics is still a vital area for both groups. The arbitrary and volatile nature of Latin American political systems requires that managers spend considerable time mending political fences external to the firm, dealing with government ministries and foreign enterprise on such issues as sources of raw materials or access to markets. Labor's involvement in politics centers more on bread-and-butter issues. Unionism is growing in Latin America, but spends more time trying to keep real wages ahead of galloping inflation than it does constructing a working-class ideology. This does not, however, mean that workers do not act in terms of their political interests. When political candidates attempt to represent working-class interests, workers increasingly perceive this and respond with their ballots.

Latin American Modernization

Use of the term "Latin America" is more common outside that geographical area than within it. Not only are differences between the various countries strongly felt, but differences based on locality and on social class are also very much a part of the diversity. Modern highway linkage between Mexico City and the Yucatan Peninsula, for example, did not take place until the mid-1950s, and to this day, the federal district and outlying provincial centers differ profoundly from one another. Food, music, dress, facial characteristics, and personalities of the people from different states of Mexico are still very pronounced, and the same may be said for several other Latin American republics. Chileans of the hot northern deserts are very distinctive from their compatriots of the antarctic Tierra del Fuego region, yet they share enough common ties to consider themselves part of the same nation. Similar differences may be noted for the Porteños of Buenos Aires and the *gauchos* of the pampas, the Cariocas of Rio and the denizens of Belem, the cosmopolitans of Lima and the Indians of the Peruvian altiplano.

These differences express themselves not only in the cultural life of the different regions and countries, but also in the strength and composition of each nation's industrial classes. The assembly-line worker in the Ford plant in Mexico City, however, probably has more in common in his work situation with an assembly-line worker in the Brazilian Volkswagen plant than do either of these men with their fellow nationals working in interior agricultural areas of Mexico or Brazil. As with the workers, the Mexican and Brazilian managers of these two automobile companies, which are almost totally local-nationals, have considerable similarities in their cultural values and social-class backgrounds.

Despite local and national differences, then, there are probably more meaningful similarities among the nations within the Latin American region than among the countries of Africa, Asia, or Europe. Therefore, while most of the readings in this volume emphasize specific countries, thus noting the diversity in the region, the major theme of this book is to underscore fundamental similarities of workers in Latin America, and of managers in Latin America; but to stress the pronounced *dis*similarity between workers and managers, culturally, socially, economically, and politically, in each country in the region.

This split has particular relevance to the process of modernization that is taking place in each of the countries. Throughout the past century the pace of modernization has been gradually increasing in Latin America. In terms of relative "modernity," Latin American nations lag far behind North America, Europe and Japan, but are considerably more advanced than most countries in Africa and Asia. The journey toward modernization is not easy, and their coming of age at a later time causes them to follow a somewhat different path.

Improved transportation and communication now links Latin America much more closely to the rest of the world than was possible for the United States in 1900 or the United Kingdom in 1850. Within Latin American nations, communications have fostered a "revolution of rising expectations" among the bulk of the population. This both speeds and slows the pace of economic development. On the one hand, people are drawn to cities and desire change with an enthusiasm which is unprecedented. On the other hand, they are more conscious of the possible benefits of modernization and expect a better life style than did their counterparts during the Industrial Revolution. These problems are further compounded by a demographic explosion which has resulted in Latin America's population growing more quickly than that of any other continent. The resulting labor surplus causes universally high levels of unemployment and underemployment. Furthermore, industrial growth is not able to employ rapidly increasing numbers of workers as it did earlier in Britain and the United States. Workers therefore do not follow the classic pattern of moving from agriculture to industry. Instead workers must be absorbed by an amorphous "tertiary" or service sector, which is usually a euphemism for a condition of underemployment.

Finally, Latin American nations face an obstacle to their modernization which was totally alien to the early experience of the United States: competition with the United States for world markets. The result is that Latin American nations would like to modernize quickly by competing on the frontiers of technology, but find themselves forced by the need to create jobs and by the economics of comparative advantage to develop in less technologically advanced and labor intensive areas.

The adjustments made by Latin American workers and managers in their organization of work will be watched with interest by both more-advanced and less-advanced areas of the world. Knowledge of Latin American development will more clearly show the early developers which parts of their histories are time- and culture-bound, and which parts belong to a more universal historical process. Less developed countries in Africa and Asia will watch closely, hoping that Latin American experiences will prove instructive as they too modernize in a world of superpowers. For both groups of nations, the reorganization of work in Latin America will bear special scrutiny. The high hopes implicit in the process of modernization rise and fall with the ability of Latin American workers and managers to use all of their will and creativity to make production and jobs increase faster than the growth of population and national expectations.

Part One

The Socio-Cultural Setting

Introduction to Part One

Worker-manager relations do not take place in a vacuum. The impacts of variations in culture and social structure must be taken into account in order to understand how work relations are constituted in specific instances. The concepts of "culture" and "social structure" are similar in that they refer to ways of describing systems of human behavior. However, they are complementary in that they utilize different building blocks in constructing their explanatory systems.

Culture refers to the social heritage of a society. It consists of all of the knowledge, values, beliefs, norms, skills and physical artifacts available to members of a society. Human behavior is cultural in that value preferences and existential beliefs are held in common by members of a single society. In areas in which there is agreement on proper behavior, norms develop and become institutionalized into subtle (and sometimes not so subtle) mechanisms of social control. Sometimes specific cultural rules such as "love thy neighbor" and taboos on incest can be observed. More often, reference is made to the general life styles which develop from cultures. Societies are described as pacific or aggressive, flourishing or decadent, democratic or authoritarian, egalitarian or paternalistic.

Cultural values generate expected rules of behavior, or "norms," when they are applied to specific situations. When norms are associated with specific social positions, such as father or manager, they are called roles. Social structure, then, is made up of networks of roles or the grouping of social positions. Thus within the social structure of the family, a man's position includes the roles of husband and father; at work his position may include the roles of manager, employee or work-mate. Roles and positions are also grouped into larger aggregates to form distinct social classes. The class structure generally includes workers in the lower and middle (sometimes described as "working") class, and managers in the middle and upper (sometimes described as "ruling") class.

The concepts of culture and social structure often overlap. Much of social structure is culturally defined, and many of the elements of culture are limited by the dimensions of social structure. One of the tasks for social scientists is to probe into this overlap and specify more precisely which elements of human behavior are culturally determined and which result from more mechanical, structural arrangements.

The reorganization of work involved in the process of modernization is an example of a situation in which it is important to separate the effects of culture and social structure. Traditional work arrangements may include the use of relatively primitive technology. The extended family here is the unit responsible for the completion of tasks, and it is connected to the larger society by a highly paternalistic authority structure. When more modern production techniques are introduced, this often involves assigning work responsibility to individual workers rather than to family groups and results in the functional differentiation

3

of roles within the family. Until recently most role differentiation has operated along sex-determined lines, with housewife and bread-winner being the most typical. The specifically changed role arrangements at work and in the family therefore represent changes in the social structure.

Within the social structure, however, different cultural definitions of role obligations can develop. Consequently, in the process of modernization, behavior more directly tied to the social structure can be transformed much more readily than can culturally determined behavior. In contemporary North America, for example, women are entering into higher economic and political positions, while cultural attitudes about woman's liberation are slower to change.

These building blocks of the setting of work—culture, social structure, work roles and life styles—are discussed in the selections of Part One. The first two articles provide thumbnail sketches of a rather successful blue-collar worker, Jesus Sanchez, and manager, Artemio Cruz. They are somewhat better off than the "average" worker or manager, but their problems and histories reflect the volatility and flavor of the Latin American world of work. The selection by Kahl outlines the most salient dimensions of Latin America's social structure, succinctly indicating how they change in the course of modernization.

Workers and Managers

The first three articles in the section on workers compare different types of work groups. Williams, Whyte and Green discuss how attitudes regarding superior-subordinate relationships differ in two distinct cultures, the United States and Peru, showing how the Peruvian preference for more authoritarian work relations generates a set of work norms that encourages paternalism rather than egalitarianism in work relations. Roles central to the work process are described by Kahl in his contrast of workers, foremen and engineers, and by Davis, who shows the different types of obligations and expectations attached to the roles of *obreros* and *empleados*.

The last three articles on workers deal with factors that directly affect their lives. Franklin discusses methods of determining minimum living standards in the United States and Latin America, and notes that minimum living standards are culturally defined. Despite the cultural relativism, however, the absolute differences between North and South American living standards are quite stark. When Franklin's statistics on living standards are examined in light of the following data on labor participation rates and demographic trends, a hope for a short-term solution for the daily problems of the families of Latin American workers disappears. Latin America's population and potential labor force are expanding at unprecedented rates, and Jones' evidence indicates that decent employment opportunities will not keep pace with such gross population changes. Increasing numbers of Latin American workers will find themselves unemployed or underemployed.

The structural and cultural context of managers in Latin America differs considerably from that of workers. In order to understand their position in the social and class structure one must observe the different types of Latin American integration in the world

5

market and the history and political economy of the various national development programs. This is the setting in which Brazilian sociologist Fernando H. Cardoso examines the growth and relative weakness of Latin American "industrial entrepreneurs." Cardoso traces the early development of export oligarchies that were closely tied to foreign economic interests and to local landed aristocracies. He goes on to show how patterns of intensive urbanization, the growth of the domestic markets, and various government programs of enforced industrialization—through import substitution—provided stimuli for the development of an indigenous entrepreneurial class in each country. This group either joined forces with government planners and basked under policies of state protection or, in other cases, continued to ally itself with the interests of foreign capital and traditional oligarchy. In either situation, however, one sees that the ascetic values, work roles and life styles of "puritan entrepreneurs" (productivity, efficiency, free competition) did not develop in Latin America.

To understand the values, roles and styles that did develop among Latin American managers, we must leave the macro level of structural analysis and look more to the cultural setting of these groups. The articles by Davis, Lipman, Hagen, Cochran and DeRossi all focus on characteristics of Latin American culture that have been par-

ticularly salient among managerial groups.

Davis examines the emphasis that is given to the whole person as distinct from the particular and singular role that he plays at work. In place of the purely contractual agreement of rewards paid for services rendered, there is a more holistic orientation and a shying away from segmentation and compartmentalization in human relations. The specifically Latin senses of individualism, personalism, and familism are also the foci of Cochran's study in Puerto Rico and DeRossi's in Mexico. DeRossi carries her work further by relating the familial values to differences in entrepreneurial motivation, in company personnel policies and in sources of financing and growth.

Lipman and Hagen study Colombian entrepreneurs in order to examine another critical dimension of economic growth: the role of deviant values and behavior in modernizing traditional societies. Working from theories originally developed by Schumpeter, these authors highlight the importance of innovative and "rational" orientations on the part of minority groups, as distinct from the orientations of the general, surrounding population.

This picture of workers and managers in Latin America begins, then, by illuminating the culture and social structure of these groups as they are changing, shaping and shaped by the processes of modernization.

1 The Work History of Jesus Sanchez

Oscar Lewis

Ever since I was little I liked to work. . . . When I left home I knew that if I didn't work, I wouldn't eat. I was about twelve when I left my father's home. I ran away without telling anyone. First, I worked at a grain mill, then as a field hand on a sugar plantation, and then as a cane cutter. It was hard in the fields and I worked with a hoe all day long in the sun. They paid one and a half *pesos* per thousand canes but I could barely cut half of that and so I earned only seventy-five *centavos* a day, not even enough for food. I was very hungry and passed whole days without food or with only one meal a day. That's why I say, I had no childhood. I worked this way for about four years.

Then I met a Spaniard who owned a corn mill. He knew I had some experience with scales and weighing and one day he said to me, "I am going to Mexico City. If you want to come, I can give you work."

"Yes, sir, I'm ready." All my baggage consisted of a little box that held my clothes. I wanted to know Mexico City as I had never been anywhere before. We took the train the next morning and arrived in Tacuba, where we stayed. After working for him for a while, he threw me out. We had a quarrel over the weights of a scale. He was looking for an excuse to throw me out. You know how people are when they see someone more ignorant and illiterate than themselves! They do what they want, no? At that time I had just come from an *hacienda* and I didn't know anything! My eyes were blindfolded. I didn't know a single street! I had already used up the little money I had. There I was without a *centavo* and not knowing a soul.

Well, as some people say, "Where everything else is wanting, God steps in." There was a man who worked in a mill nearby. He used to pass by every day. One day he saw me and told me his boss wanted me to work for his mill. That night I was standing on the street corner with my little box of clothes under my arm, without a *centavo*, without any idea of what to do. If I had had money, I would have gone back to my homeland. At that moment this man passed by as if he had fallen from the sky. He said to me, "What are you doing here?" I told him. He said, "Don't you worry. Let's go to my house and I'll find you a job." But there was that union business. The next day we went to see his boss. He told me I had to be in the union to work in his mill. I didn't even have a *centavo*. We had come from La Tlaxpana and I walked nearly to Tepito. The millers' union was

Adapted from Oscar Lewis, *The Children of Sanchez*. Copyright © 1961 by Oscar Lewis. Used with permission of Random House, Inc., and Martin Seker & Warburg Ltd.

there. They asked me how much money I had on me. When they found out, they said nothing could be done. So I went all the way back on foot, without a bit of food in my stomach. There I was back in the same situation, going hungry. That's why I sometimes scold my children, because I've always given them food and a roof over their heads.

So I started going to the grocery stores to see if anyone was looking for an errand boy or helper. I knew something about the grocery business and could wait on customers rapidly. I went from store to store with no luck. There was bread everywhere and me so hungry, you have no idea how it feels. After a few days I met a man in La Tlaxpana, a block from where I was staying. He had a grocery store. He asked me, "Do you want a job?"

"Yes, sir."

"Do you have references?"

"No, sir. I just arrived from Veracruz." I was praying to God that he give me work or something. I explained that the only man I knew had a mill nearby. He went to speak to the man and then said he would take me on trial for two weeks. The pay was fifty *centavos* a day and food. There I was the next day with my package of clothes, for I had no place to leave it. I went to work at once. I was quick, I went around as if I were on wheels. I needed work, I had to eat. Two weeks went by, then a month, then three. I was very happy. I worked from six in the morning to nine at night without rest. I ate my breakfast cold in the store, there was no time to warm it. There were many customers. I delivered orders and lugged boxes I could barely lift, cases of beer, sacks of salt.

One morning my boss brought another boy from a village and he said to me, "Hey, Jesús, come over here. This boy is going to take your place. You're no damned good, get out." With those sweet and comforting words he fired me. That's all there was to it. There was nothing to be said. The next morning I was out on the street again.

But these difficulties help one to become a man, to appreciate the true value of things. One learns what it means to earn a living with the sweat of one's brow. To grow up away from your parents helps you to become mature.

When I was at the store, I had met a boy who had a relative who was a janitor in a building downtown. I asked for a note to this man and went to see him. I showed him the note. "Sure, why not? The building is empty," he said. "Pick out any place you like and put your box there." I stayed there without a *centavo* and once more I began to look for work.

That's when I found a job in the La Gloria restaurant. They paid me twelve *pesos* a month and three meals. I went in with my package of clothes and began to do everything they asked me. I was eager to work and while lifting a heavy package I got a hernia. I went to the toilet and saw a little lump here in my groin. I pressed on it and it hurt. I went to a doctor and he told me I had a hernia. I was lucky because the doctor belonged to the General Hospital and had me admitted. Now what about my job? I spoke to the owner, a Spaniard, a decent man, a real human being. I asked permission to go and be operated. They operated on me quickly but then I did a stupid thing. After the operation it hurt near the stitches and so I lifted the bandage and touched it and infected myself. Instead of being in the hospital for two weeks, I was there for five weeks.

When I got out I went to the restaurant and found someone at my job. But the owner took me back. Yes, I've worked there for over thirty years, and I've rarely missed a day. For the first fifteen years, I worked on the inside as a general helper and learned to bake bread and make ice cream. I worked fourteen to fifteen hours a day. Later, I began to do the shopping for the restaurant and I became their food buyer. When I began to work I earned eighty *centavos* a day. Now after thirty years, I earn the minimum wage of eleven *pesos* a day. But I could never live on this wage alone.

In thirty years I've rarely missed a day of work. Even when I'm sick I go. It seems that work is medicine for me. It makes me forget my troubles. And I like my work. I like all the walking I have to do and I enjoy speaking to the market vendors. I know them all after these many years of buying fruits, vegetables, cheese, butter and meats. I look for the best buys and all that. One has to know about buying, because each fruit has its season, no? Like melons. They're getting good at this time and I can buy them. The early melons were bad. They come from different places, from Morelos, from Michoacán, Cortazar. The ones from Guanajuato are very good; also the yellow ones from Durango. The same with oranges, they come from all over the Republic. Vegetables, too. The best avocados come from Atlixco and Silao, but they send most of those to the United States. The same with tomatoes. One must observe much to learn to know fruits and to be able to buy.

I buy six hundred *pesos'* worth of food for the restaurant each day. They give me the money in the morning and I pay cash for each purchase. There are no bills or receipts. I keep my own accounts and hand in a list of expenses each day.

I get to the restaurant each morning at seven to open the iron shutters. Then I work inside for a while, have breakfast and leave for the market at nine-thirty. Two boys assist me and they cart the purchases back to the restaurant. I get back at about one-thirty and usually there is something missing, so I run to the market again. I go back to the restaurant at three o'clock, have lunch and leave about four to look after my pigs, to sell lottery tickets and to visit my daughter Marta and the children.

My work companions at the restaurant think well of me and appreciate me because I am the oldest employee in the establishment. We joke and tease a lot and this, too, is a distraction. I've always behaved myself and gotten on well with my boss. A lot of workers hate their boss and don't feel loyal, but in that respect I am well off because I know my boss holds me in high esteem. To show his appreciation he allows me to work seven days a week and all holidays, so I can increase my earnings. For years I've worked on Wednesdays, my day off. I respect my boss and I do my best. He is like a father to me.

All I do is work and take care of my family. I never go to *fiestas*. Only once, when we lived in Cuba Street, some people in my *vecindad* made a *fiesta* and I danced a little. I didn't drink much and went right home to bed. For me there are no outings, no parties, no nothing . . . only work and family.

And I have no *compadres* where I work. I consider *compadrazgo* a serious thing, a matter of mutual respect. When I needed *compadres,* I chose older people, not youths or my fellow workers. Before you know it, young people invite you to drink with them and do things together. Some even kill each other, and that is bad. When I am invited anywhere, I don't go.

2

Artemio Cruz, Manager

Carlos Fuentes

From the airport you will go to your office, crossing a city impregnated with tear-gas because the police will have just finished breaking up a demonstration in the Caballito plaza. You will meet with your editor-in-chief and discuss the front page heads, the editorials, and the cartoons, and you will feel pleased. You will receive a visit from your Yankee associate and you'll make clear to him the clear danger in these misnamed "reform" movements to clean up the unions. Afterward your administrator, Padilla, will come to your office and report that the Indians go on agitating, and you, through Padilla, will send sharp word to the manager of the *ejido,* telling him to clamp down on them, for that's what you pay him for. Oh, you will work hard yesterday in the morning. The representative of a certain Latin-American benefactor will call on you, and you will persuade him to step up the subsidy he gives your newspaper. You will phone your gossip columnist and tell her to light some squibs under that Couto who has been waging war on your interests in Sonora. You will do so much! And later, you will sit with Padilla and go over your accounts, which will be very entertaining. One whole wall of your office is covered by the map that shows the sweep and interrelationships of your business network: the newspaper in Mexico City, and the real estate there and in Puebla, Guadalajara, Monterrey, Culiacán, Hermosillo, Guaymas, and Acapulco. The sulfur domes in Jáltipan, the mines in Hidalgo, the timber concessions in Tarahumara. The chain of hotels, the pipe foundry, the fish business. The financing operations, the stock holdings, the administration of the company formed to lend money to the railroad, the legal representation of North American firms, the directorships of banking houses, the foreign stocks—dyes, steel, and detergents; and one little item that does not appear on the wall: fifteen million dollars deposited in banks in Zurich, London, and New York. Yes: you will light a cigarette, in spite of the warnings you have had from your doctor, and to Padilla will relate again the steps by which you gained your wealth: loans at short terms and high interest to peasants in Puebla, just after the Revolution; the acquisition of land around the city of Puebla, whose growth you foresaw; acres for subdivision in Mexico City, thanks to the friendly intervention of each succeeding president; the daily newspaper; the purchase of mining stock;

11

the formation of Mexican-U.S. enterprises in which you participated as front-man so that the law would be complied with; trusted friend of North American investors, intermediary between New York and Chicago and the government of Mexico; the manipulation of stock prices to move them to your advantage, buying and selling, always at a profit; the gilded El Dorado years of President Alemán, and your final consolidation; the acquisition of *ejido* farm lands taken from their peasant occupants to project new subdivisions in cities of the interior; the timber concessions. Yes, you will sigh, asking Padilla for another match, twenty good years, years of progress, of peace and collaboration among the classes; twenty years of progress after the demagoguery of Lázaro Cárdenas; twenty years of submissive labor leaders, of broken strikes, of protection for industry. And now you will raise your hands to your stomach and to your head of grayed chestnut hair, to your oily face, and you will see yourself reflected in the glass top of your desk, the image of your sick twin, as all sounds will suddenly flee, laughing, from your hearing, and the sweat of men will swirl around you and their bodies will suffocate you, and you will lose consciousness. The twin in the glass will join the other, who is yourself, join the seventy-one-year-old old man who will fall, unconscious, between the swivel chair and the steel desk: and you will be here and you will not know which events of your life will pass into your biography, or which will be suppressed and hidden; you won't know.

3

Traditional Society versus Modern Society

Joseph A. Kahl

Most social scientists dealing with Latin America have used as a tool of analysis some aspect of the dichotomy between "traditional" and "modern" society, and have analyzed the processes of transition from one to the other. For example, Redfield wrote of the contrast between "folk" society and "urban" society; Lambert used "The Two Brazils" as the title of his book; and Germani has as his subtitle the phrase "From Traditional Society to Mass Society."[1] The dichotomy is used in several ways. It refers to a classification of societies which would make Haiti traditional, Argentina modern, and Peru somewhere in between. But these authors also recognize that *within* any one of these societies, some geographical regions and some social strata are more modern than others. And they even state that within a given individual there may exist tensions resulting from the conflict between traditional and modern values.

"Traditional society" and "modern society" are abstractions, mental constructs that create simplified models in order to help us understand the central factors that explain the complexities of historical reality. They are "ideal types," in which a limited number of characteristics in "pure" form are used to develop the theoretical model.[2]

What are the characteristics that are usually used to contrast traditional with modern society? The ones which follow seem most common:[3]

1. *The Division of Labor.* The most simple index of this characteristic is

Adapted from Joseph A. Kahl, *The Measurement of Modernism* (Austin: University of Texas Press, 1968), pp. 4–6, by permission of the author and publisher.
[1]Robert Redfield, *The Folk Culture of Yucatán* (Chicago: University of Chicago Press, 1941); Jacques Lambert, *Os dois Brasis* (Rio de Janeiro: Centro Brasileiro de Pesquisas Educacionais, 1959); Gino Germani, *Politica y sociedad en una época de transición: de la sociedad tradicional a la sociedad de masas* (Buenos Aires: Editorial Paidos, 1963). Of course, the thinking of these men was influenced by earlier analysts of the modernization of Europe, such as Marx, Tönnies, Weber, and Durkheim.
[2]At this point, I use the ideal type for purposes of theory-building; later [In *The Measurement of Modernism*], I shall indicate its limitations in empirical operations, and suggest a way to move from types to variables.
[3]For a sophisticated version of the contrast between traditional and modern society in Latin America that develops the model beyond my summary statement, see Germani, op. cit., esp. Chs. III, V, and VI. Germani relies heavily on the theoretical work of Talcott Parsons. For comprehensive statements, see Bert F. Hoselitz and Wilbert E. Moore, eds., *Industrialization and Society* (Paris: UNESCO, 1963); and E. de Vries and J. M. Echavarría, eds., *Social Aspects of Economic Development in Latin America* (Paris: UNESCO, 1963).

the proportion of the labor force engaged in agriculture; traditional societies may have 70 to 80 percent of the workers tilling the soil; modern societies can get by with less than 10 percent on the farm. More subtle indices divide the nonagricultural labor force into traditional sectors, such as artisans, priests, and lawyers, and into modern sectors, such as individual workers, clerks in bureaucracies, and engineers.[4]

2. *The State of Technology*. A traditional society uses customary techniques of production, handed down from father to son. A modern society uses sophisticated engineering based upon the latest fruits of world-wide scientific research.

3. *The Degree of Urbanization*. Since modern agricultural technology permits a small proportion of the labor force to feed the remainder of the population, using a low ratio of men to land, most of the society becomes urban.

4. *The Economy*. Traditional society is based on localized markets, where much of the production is for a meagre level of subsistence, although a plantation type of crop or minerals may enter world markets. Modern society is based on complex commercial markets unifying all parts of the nation; per capita production and consumption are high.

5. *The System of Social Stratification*. Traditional society is deeply divided between landlords and peasants. Modern society has a range of statuses that reflects the range of positions in the division of labor: there are many, and the distinctions between them are not so sharp. The distribution of prestige, of income, and of power becomes more equalitarian, and the rate of mobility between strata increases.

6. *Education and Communications*. Traditional society is in the main illiterate, although the tiny elite may have a high level of humanistic and legal scholarship. Modern society is literate, there is widespread secondary education that blurs the distinction between elite and mass, and the entire system of education moves toward the technical and the pragmatic. The mass media cater to the bulk of the population, cognizant of its primary and secondary education, and they shape thought in new images that replace customary symbols.

7. *Values*. Traditional values are compulsory in their force, sacred in their tone, and stable in their timelessness. They call for fatalistic acceptance of the world as it is, respect for those in authority, and submergence of the individual in the collectivity. Modern values are rational and secular, permit choice and experiment, glorify efficiency and change, and stress individual responsibility.

---

[4]See A. J. Jaffe, *People, Jobs and Economic Development* (New York: Free Press of Glencoe, 1959), esp. Appendix D. The theory Jaffe uses is a general one, but the statistics concern Puerto Rico and Mexico.

Workers

4

Do Cultural Differences Affect Workers' Attitudes?

Lawrence K. Williams,
William F. Whyte, and
Charles S. Green

Are the principles of human relations, inferred from research in the United States, generally applicable to supervisor-worker relations in other countries? We shall present findings from a field study in Peru to indicate some of the ways in which culture affects worker responses to supervisors.

Perhaps it is because there is such a "good fit" between the notion of participative management and the democratic values of our culture that few have questioned the validity of the research conclusions supporting participative management or even explored the general applicability of the notion or its limiting conditions. Researchers are just beginning to look to such factors as personality and cultural differences for clues as to the applicability and limiting conditions for leadership theory.

To our knowledge, the first study demonstrating certain broad culturally based influences on reactions to supervisory leadership was the replication of the . . . Coch-French participation experiment in a Norwegian factory.[1] In Norway, French and his associates found that the participative approach did not elicit the same responses they had found in a U.S. experiment. Instead, they found that workers who considered participation in decision-making legitimate *did* react favorably, whereas those who had no such views of participation did not so react. These expectations, of course, grew out of their life experiences and can therefore be considered cultural products.

The Peru–United States Comparison

Our own cross-cultural study involved a comparison between two large electrical utility companies, one in the United States, the other in Peru. Parts of the questionnaire developed and used by Williams for research in the U. S. company were translated to make up a questionnaire which Whyte applied to 364 blue-collar workers and 202 white-collar workers in

Adapted from *Industrial Relations* (May 1966), pp. 105–117, with permission of the publisher.
[1] J. R. P. French, J. Israel, and D. As, "An Experiment on Participation in a Norwegian Factory: Interpersonal Dimensions of Decision-Making," *Human Relations* 13 (February 1960): pp. 3–9.

17

the Peruvian company. . . . We will . . . summarize . . . those aspects of the survey which reveal cross-cultural differences in worker attitude toward, and perception of, supervisors.

1. For both our white-collar and blue-collar Peruvian samples, we found a small but significant positive correlation (approximately 0.20) between perceived closeness of supervision and general satisfaction with the supervisor. In our U. S. company, the correlations were at about the same level, but negative (white collar—0.17; blue collar—0.23). In other words, there was some tendency for these Peruvian workers to prefer the boss who supervised them closely, whereas the U. S. workers leaned toward the one who exercised more general supervision. Similar preferences for general supervision have been reported in many U. S. studies.

2. "How much emphasis does your supervisor put on getting out a lot of work?" Here again we found a positive correlation between production emphasis and satisfaction with supervisor, and at a substantially higher level (0.39 for white-collar workers and 0.41 for blue-collar workers). The question was not asked of blue-collar workers in our U. S. company, but for white-collar workers we found a smaller but significant negative correlation (—0.20), which again is in accord with many U. S. studies. Apparently Peruvian workers find pressure for production more acceptable than do U. S. workers.

3. "Does your supervisor let his superiors know how members of his work group feel?" Interestingly a high percentage of our Peruvians checked, "I don't know" (57 percent for white-collar and 48 percent for blue-collar workers). We have no exact comparison with the U. S. here, since the alternative of "I don't know" was not offered in our U. S. company. However, U. S. workers were free to leave the question blank, and yet very few of them did so. It is our experience that U. S. workers generally think they know the answer to this question, whereas a number of Peruvians asked us, "How should I know?"

"He lets his superiors know how his employees feel only when he feels his superiors will agree with him." In the United States, when a worker checked this alternative, we could be almost certain that he would give a negative evaluation of his supervisor. Not so in Peru. Those checking this item were somewhat more likely than those who did not to give a favorable evaluation of the supervisor. On the question as a whole, in the U. S. company there was a relatively high correlation (0.58) between the supervisor's letting his superior know work-group feelings and satisfaction with the supervisor. For the Peruvian white-collar workers, there was an insignificant (0.03) correlation, while for the blue-collar workers we found an almost significant negative relationship (—0.10).

4. We used the following participation items: How often are there group meetings in which the employees can discuss things with their supervisor? If you have group meetings in which the employees can discuss things with their supervisor, do they do any good? When there is a change to be made in your job, does your supervisor discuss it with you before he

puts it into practice? How much do you and other people of your work group have to say about how things are done in your work group?

Here we did not find the reverse relationships noted earlier, but we did find marked differences in the degree of association with satisfaction with the supervisor. In the U. S. study all four items showed positive correlations of 0.50 or more. In the first three items for Peru, correlations ranged between 0.12 and 0.17 for blue-collar workers and between 0.35 and 0.37 for white-collar workers. On the last item, the Peruvian correlation approximately equalled that for the U. S. (about 0.50).

The results suggest that, although Peruvians are just as concerned as U. S. workers about having some power and influence over their work, they are not nearly so inclined to see this power and influence as being related to the participative communication practices of the supervisor.

On the basis of these results, we felt that we had demonstrated the existence of systematic cross-cultural differences in responses to industrial supervisors. The demonstration that differences exist is only a first step. We also wanted to see whether the data available from our first cross-cultural study might enable us to probe beneath the patterns observed to learn something of the way in which a culture may condition responses to organizational authority.

Findings

Table 1 presents comparisons among U. S. college students, Peruvian school boys, and Peruvian white-collar workers for the four items we used for a faith-in-people scale. On the basis of this four-item scale, we divided our 202 white-collar workers into three groups. Those who gave trusting answers to all four items we called "high trust." Those who gave two to three trusting answers we called "medium trust." Those with a score of 0 or 1 fell into our "low trust" group. Did this sorting, in terms of trust, yield differences in responses to supervisory style? Before we seek to answer that question, let us consider a dimension of organizational life that proved to be highly related to trust.

In view of the differences among Peruvian workers with regard to trust or faith in human nature, we might expect that those who were, like U. S. workers, high in interpersonal trust or in faith in people would have similar expectations with regard to man-group relationships. In other words, our hypothesis then becomes: Individuals who are high in interpersonal trust will expect and appreciate a leader-group climate which is democratic and participative as contrasted with those who are very low in interpersonal trust, who will anticipate a more authoritarian and nonparticipative climate and, therefore, will be satisfied with supervisors as long as they provide the structure in which work can be done.

We then sorted the Peruvian workers in terms of their positions on the interpersonal trust scale. A separate factor analysis of supervisory behavior

Table 4–1

Comparison of the Responses of American College Students, Peruvian School Boys, and Peruvian White-Collar Workers to Interpersonal Trust (Faith-in-Human-Nature) Items

Item	American college students (N = 2,975)	Peruvian school boys (N = 1,833)	Peruvian white-collar workers (N = 202)
Some people say that most people can be trusted. Others say you can't trust people. How do you feel about it?			
1. Most people can be trusted	81%	31%	37%
2. Can't be trusted	19	69	60
0. No answer	–	–	3
These days a person doesn't really know whom he can count on.			
1. I agree	24	48	43
2. I agree in part	8	33	45
3. I don't agree	67	18	12
0. No answer	1	1	2
Every man is out for himself.			
1. I agree	Item	48	37
2. I agree in part	not	32	29
3. I don't agree	included	20	23
0. No answer		–	–
No one is going to care much what happens to you when you get right down to it.			
1. I agree	31	41	43
2. I agree in part	9	29	36
3. I don't agree	60	30	21

and climate items was conducted for each subgroup of high-, medium-, and low-trust individuals. If our hypothesis was to be supported, separate factors should be associated with different personality types, with the factors for high-trust individuals most resembling those found in comparable United States studies.

The items used to obtain description of supervisor behavior and attitudes toward supervision reflect technical, administrative, and human relations components of a supervisory job.

Table 2 represents the first factor loadings (Quartimax rotation) as a function of the trust score. Looking first at the low-trust score respondents, it should be noted that the highest loadings on this factor relate to the supervisor's attention to training and his technical ability, followed closely by his administrative ability in planning and organization and the summary supervision satisfaction item . . . . A total of 11 items appeared in the first factor, with technical and administrative items having the highest loadings. Only factor loadings in excess of 0.40 are shown in the table.

Table 4-2

First Factor Loadings as a Function of Trust Score and Correlations with
Summary Satisfaction Item[a]

	Trust score			United States workers (N = 590)
	Low (N = 44)	Medium (N = 81)	High (N = 77)	
Summary satisfaction	0.82	0.86	0.88	0.87
Technical ability	.85	.75	.65	.68
Training	.90	.61	.73	.67
Planning and organizing	.84	.68	.70	.74
Understand work problems	.80	.73	.74	.83
Emphasis on work	.68	.46	.52	n
Stand up for employees	.66	.71	.82	.81
Discuss job	.59	.47	.55	.70
Handle people	.74	.75	.78	.85
Working with employees	.76	.60	.71	.83
Tell superior	.51	—	.58	.68
Frequency of group meetings		.55	.61	n
Discuss job change		.51	.70	.48
Say of group		.75	.68	.62
Group discussion evaluation			.52	.61
Discuss personal problems			.44	.64

[a]The table shows factor loadings in excess of 0.40.

The human relations items include understanding work problems, discussing the job, and a general question having to do with handling people. Each of these human relations items, referring to a relationship between the individual and his superior, concerns man-to-man considerations rather than man-to-group relationships.

Somewhat more positive results for the human relations items are found for the medium-trust group. On the other hand, emphasizing the work and planning and organizing, along with other technical factors, tend to receive lower factor loadings. Additional items receiving factor loadings above 0.40 reflect more emphasis on man-to-group human relations content, including having meetings and the amount of [influence] the group has about how things will be done in the work group. The important human relations dimension of discussing job changes in advance also becomes relevant in the appraisal of the superior.

And then, for those high in interpersonal trust, factor loadings in excess of 0.40 occur for two items not found in the previous two groups—evaluation of whether group discussions do any good or not and the discussing of personal problems with the supervisor. As was the case with the medium-trust group, the additional items involve human relations or consideration content. Moreover, nearly all items having a human relations content load higher on the satisfaction factor for the high-trust group than they do for the low-trust group. By contrast, for the low-trust group, items having to do with initiating structure or technical and administrative ability load higher on the general satisfaction factor than they do for high-trust respondents.

The data in Table 2, then, tend to support the hypothesis that, with greater levels of interpersonal trust, the more human relations or man-to-group functions will be anticipated and appreciated on the part of employees as they view their supervisor. Table 2 also presents the factor loadings on the supervisory items for a group of United States white-collar workers. When this is contrasted with the factor loadings on these items for the high-trust Peruvian group, it can be seen that there is a close similarity between the general supervisory satisfaction factor for Peruvian workers and for equivalent white-collar workers in the United States.

In the U. S. data, there is also an indication that items involving a human relations content and a man-to-group orientation are even more highly loaded than they are for the high-trust Peruvian group. In particular, such items as working with the employees, which has a group referent, and the conducting of good group meetings are more highly loaded for the U. S. workers than for the high-trust Peruvian group. In general, however, there is a high degree of similarity between the general satisfaction factor derived for U. S. and high-trust Peruvian workers.

Summary and Discussion

The data generally support the hypothesis that individuals with low trust, in a sample of Peruvian white-collar workers, tend to evaluate their supervisor in terms of his administrative and technical or initiating structure ability. With succeeding levels of trust, greater appreciation of human relations content does appear in relation to satisfaction with the supervisor, and the results for high-trust Peruvians are very close to those for American workers.

The greatest difference between the American workers and high-trust Peruvians was with regard to emphasis on production and closeness of supervision. Again, these data, like the findings discussed [above], support the conclusion that the values of subordinates greatly affect their evaluations of superiors, and that, in a highly distrustful society marked by authoritarianism, certain participation forms which involve man-to-group relationships will probably not be successful when they are initiated.

Our findings suggest that the uniformities reported in the U.S. literature must be seen in the context of the culture of the United States. Our democratic ideology encourages a pattern of relations which de-emphasizes the authority of the supervisor and legitimizes the direct thrashing out of differences between the supervisor and the work group.

Although much has been said about individualism in the United States, our understanding has been obscured by an ideology which fails to distinguish between the taking of individual initiative and identification with a group . . . . Our culture tends to stimulate the individual to take initiative toward change in his organizational situation, but, at the same time, the worker tends to think and act as a member of a group and to channel his initiative through the group.

The individualism of the Peruvian seems to be a different sort of phenomenon. His organizational relations tend to be polarized in relation to a more authoritarian management, which seems to result in isolation of the individual worker from his fellows. The worker does not see the work group in terms of psychological identification or of practical support to nearly the same extent as does the U. S. worker. A high faith-in-people orientation seems to go with integration of the individual into the group and confidence in being able to solve problems through the group.

5

Three Types of Mexican Industrial Workers

Joseph A. Kahl

This is a report on interviews conducted in 1958 with seventy-two male workers in a factory located a little beyond the limits of Mexico City. The factory was only seven years old and was of modern design with many of the production processes proceeding on a semiautomatic basis. The total work force was approximately 150 men, divided into four shifts: three shifts each working eight hours a day, with one shift having a rest between turns. The engineers and office staff worked only during the day, five days a week.

We interviewed six engineers, six office workers, nineteen foremen, six mechanics, eight mechanic's aides, three guards, and twenty-four semi-skilled workers. In relation to the total work force, we under-sampled the semiskilled workers and over-sampled the other groups because they were so small. This report concentrates on the engineers, the foremen, and the semiskilled workers, for they represent rather clear-cut types that suggest interesting questions about a rapidly developing industrial country. The aim here is to raise such questions, and not to prove anything.

The Data

Every one of the twenty-four semiskilled workers was born in a small town or rural village, and all except three currently lived in such towns and villages (indeed, sixteen resided in the same place where they were born). This is no doubt a result of the location of the factory: far enough from the center of Mexico City to make the forty-five minute bus ride and its cost onerous for ordinary workers, and close enough to an overpopulated rural area to draw its work force from it. Most of the men were young, in their twenties; almost half of them were married. All had received some primary school education and were literate, but none had gone beyond the primary level (sixth grade). Half of them had fathers who were farmers; the remainder had fathers who were either petty merchants or blue-collar workers.

About half of the semiskilled respondents had started their careers in their middle teens as farm laborers, often working for fathers or kinsmen.

Reprinted with permission of the publisher from *Economic Development and Cultural Change* 8 (January 1960): pp. 164–169. Copyright © 1960 by the University of Chicago Press.

Then they discovered that higher wages (about double the agricultural day-laborer rate) were available in this new industrial zone between city and country, and they took factory or service jobs—indeed, all but four had held a nonagricultural job before entering the plant we studied. In the plant they earned two dollars a day, which was a good wage in the area for men who needed no past experience but were trained on the job for the simple tasks which they performed. Forty percent of the men obtained their jobs by going to the gate and applying; sixty percent were recommended by a relative or friend who already worked for the company.

Thus the picture begins to emerge: these men were a group of young workers making the transition from agriculture to industry. Their community patterns in the towns and villages where they lived were based upon rural traditions, yet they found better economic opportunity in factory labor. They did not have enough formal education or industrial experience to have accumulated high-order skills, so they were just semi-skilled "hands."

What did they think of factory life? Most of them thought it was splendid. Let the reader eliminate from his mind the Victorian picture of dismal sweatshops: this factory was a modern plant, constructed with ample air and light, and the front gate was even adorned with a small garden. There was a shower room for the men (some even came to the plant on their day off to use it), and also a dining room where they could comfortably eat the lunches they brought with them (it included, modern touch in old Mexico, an electric griddle for the warming of *tortillas*). An eight-hour day was a very light workload compared to the long and isolated labor of the fields.

The management was Mexican, but the company was owned and supervised by a large American corporation that followed modern techniques of "human relations"; thus the workers were led rather than driven, and they received lessons in hygiene and safety which they considered a beautiful experience both for their content and for their symbolic indication of a management who cared about them. They emphasized quite firmly, the importance to them of being treated with dignity and respect by their bosses—perhaps even more than do American workers. Insofar as they were usually treated well, they concluded that they had soft jobs, decent bosses, and high pay.

Sixty-five percent of the workers had no ambitions at all to change jobs; the remainder had rather vague notions about gaining more "independence" by buying enough land to run a decent dairy or chicken farm or starting a little grocery of their own, but the lack of concrete plans for the future (or dissatisfaction with the present) suggested that most of them would remain as factory laborers until they retired. Most expected their children to follow their own path, but about thirty percent dreamed of university educations and professional careers (mostly as medical men) for their sons, even though they readily admitted that the dreams were not realistic.

The foremen were quite different in background, satisfaction, and aspiration. Twelve out of the nineteen were born in large cities, and sixteen currently lived in Mexico City and commuted to work. They were sufficiently urban in outlook to find the commuting worth the effort, and their salaries permitted them to cover the costs of urban residence and of transport, for they earned more than three times as much as the semiskilled workers. Like those workers, the foremen were young, almost all in their twenties, and half were married. Only two had stopped with primary school; five more had received secondary training, and twelve were men who started university courses in engineering but dropped out for academic or economic reasons before graduating. Only one had a father who was a small-scale farmer; four had semiskilled or skilled fathers; five had white-collar fathers; nine had business or professional fathers. Thus the predominant background was urban and middle class. About half of the foremen obtained their jobs through newspaper advertisements; the rest were recommended through friends or relatives. The majority seriously anticipated professional careers for their sons.

What did the foremen think of their jobs? Four out of the nineteen were content, as judged by their lack of firm desires to seek out another position. Fifteen wanted a change, and all for the same reason: lack of opportunity for promotion. Let the men speak for themselves:

Yes, I want to change my job in order to be more, to have more responsibility and to develop my judgment, probably in a business of my own.

This job is satisfying in that I'm making things for Mexico, not just shuffling papers. But there is a great gulf between foremen and engineers—the foremen can't progress. Except for one or two older men who are content, most foremen think of this job as just a ladder to something better.

Foremen can progress a bit, but there really isn't any future in it.

In general, the foremen had no strong complaints against their particular jobs or against the company, beyond their gripes about night shifts and the distance of the plant from Mexico City. Like the semiskilled workers, they thought it was a pretty good place to work. But they came from middle-class families or else had strong middle-class ambitions, as evidenced by their general values and by their educational attainments, and they could not obtain the standard of living they sought on their present salaries. Furthermore, they had come to expect a level of responsibility on the job which they could not satisfy working as foremen under the close supervision of graduate engineers. They were frustrated men who sought positions with other companies or wanted to start businesses of their own so that they could earn more money and have more responsibility.

The above analysis is supported by the four negative instances of contented foremen, although they were too few in number to permit of more than a hint. One of them was a man of 45, who said:

I will be here until I die or retire. I look forward to an increase in salary, but you see I'm not very well trained for many things and at my age I can't go out and get a much better job than this one.

The other three men had skilled-worker fathers, and considered their positions to be an improvement over the lives of their fathers. By contrast, most of the discontented foremen came from backgrounds that were a bit above the skilled-worker level.

Most of the engineers were also under thirty. All had university degrees. They were either born or grew up in urban environments. Four of the six came from professional and executive families; two climbed from skilled-worker backgrounds (in both instances, the fathers were intensely ambitious for their sons and carefully planned university educations for them). The engineers showed a high degree of "modern" professional attitude: they believed in hard work, technical excellence, and promotion by performance rather than seniority or "connections." All but one obtained their jobs through newspaper advertisements. They were committed to their careers and intended to shape their sons to follow similar careers.

The following quotations illustrate the attitudes of the engineers toward work, career, and planning for the future:

I think that when you are young and energetic is the time to work hard—for people like us in the middle class, work is sacred; now is the time to push. You can't just sit back and wait for things to happen, you have to learn, and to make yourself known. I want to give my sons a fine education and a career. I don't want to give them money, because in a year they might spend it all and be paupers. But if I give them a career, teach them to study hard, then that they will have all their lives and they will always live well.

I prefer this company to the government company where I used to work. In the government it is a bureaucracy, and usually promotion is by seniority instead of the way it should be by skill and performance—and once in a while promotion in the government depends on being a friend of the boss.

The three groups were sharply separated. Only one man had ever been promoted from worker to foreman, and the standard belief in the management was that the workers were not educated or sophisticated enough to hold higher jobs. Furthermore, foremen without degrees saw no chance of becoming engineers even if they had considerable engineering training and much practical experience: the line between "professional" and "nonprofessional" was absolutely clear (indeed, Mexicans use the title "Engineer" as a form of direct address just as Americans use "Doctor" when speaking to a medical man, and the title is based on the degree, not on the character of the job that is being performed). Thus we get the interesting situation where most men were satisfied at the bottom and at the top of the hierarchy in the factory, but dissatisfied in the middle.

Discussion

There are two structures in Mexican life that come together in the industrial scene: the social-class hierarchy of the local community, and the occupational hierarchy of the work world. The link between them is education.

Satisfaction or dissatisfaction with career is mainly a result of a sense of "relative deprivation" (or its opposite) which emerges from the degree of neatness of fit between the two hierarchies. Thus a man from a peasant background who moves into semiskilled factory labor feels that he is lucky to have such a good job; a man from an urban middle-class background who moves into the intermediate ranks of industry as a foreman feels blocked, but one who becomes an engineer feels satisfied and anticipates a steadily improving future.

What can we say, extrapolating from an inadequate sample based upon a single factory, that may have general significance as a guide to further research in rapidly developing countries? It appears that middle-class culture is having the hardest time articulating with the new factory system. Its traditions are based on two models: family businesses in which sons follow fathers, and professional careers based upon university educations (and these were, in preindustrial days, careers in law and medicine). As Mexican society urbanizes and modernizes, there is increasing fixation in the middle classes upon the university degree. The basic aim of families who have achieved even the barest minimum of a middle-class standard of living is to give their sons a professional education (in the past ten years, the number of university students in Mexico has more than doubled). Those who manage to acquire the coveted *titulo* can then follow a career that is understood and admired by their families and friends. But about half of those who start towards a professional degree never get it; they receive poor grades in class, or they are forced to work while they study and find the double load too high, or their families have financial troubles and need their help, and so on. They are then placed in limbo, and there is as yet no institutionalized position for them in industry. Those whose educations were in the engineering sciences drift into positions like foremen that, in an industrially more advanced society with a more complex division of labor, would be filled by men with secondary educations who are climbing up from working-class backgrounds, rather than by men who consider themselves as failures as professionals. . . . The few semiskilled workers in our factory who had ambitious dreams for their children spoke either of the role of mechanic or that of a full-scale professional; even they did not look upon the foreman's role as a legitimate aspiration.

Thus, the peasant can rather easily become a factory operative; he continues his traditional path as a hard worker without much ambition. He judges his job by the ease of the work, the manner in which his boss gives orders, and the pay. He anticipates no future promotion, and if he has any ambitions toward upward mobility, they concern his son rather than himself, for his son will have a chance for a better education. He accepts his own position as a natural result of his background.

An urban middle-class boy can readily translate the traditions of the established professions of law and medicine into a career in engineering if he happens to enjoy machinery and mathematics. It is a little surprising to note the apparent ease with which he acquires universalistic standards of corporate competition, for Mexican culture traditionally stressed the importance of "connections" as essential to a successful career. But these engineers mostly got their jobs by answering newspaper advertisements, and at least in their verbal statements, they approved of prestige and promotion according to the sole standard of proficiency, and told horrible tales of "politics" in government bureaucracies.

However, Mexico does not yet appear to have institutionalized an accepted career for the middle ranks of industrial workers. These men are neither successful members of the working class nor accepted members of a stabilized lower middle class. They are men who have failed to reach their initial goals, and they are unhappy about it. As the middle class grows in size and complexity, Mexican society will probably create a more comfortable niche for men of their type.

There is one problem that has been touched upon in this paper that should be explored further: the division of the working class into two segments, referred to above as skilled and semiskilled. In informal conversations, managers in the factory reported on in this paper and in other establishments have noted a rather sharp distinction that correlates with level of skill but is not exactly the same thing; one man called them the "dirty" and the "clean" workers, and insisted that large numbers of "clean" factory workers have only appeared in the last fifteen years. The "dirty" ones correspond to the old stereotype: men who work simply to get a minimum subsistence wage, who are apt to go on drunken sprees, who are unfaithful to their wives and unambitious for their children, who are (from the viewpoint of the managers) "irresponsible." By contrast, the "clean" workers are constantly seeking to learn new skills on the job, attempt to save their pay or to use it to improve their families' way of living, want their sons to advance, are generally "responsible" in their work behavior. It was noted above that a few of the engineers and foremen in our factory were the sons of ambitious skilled workers who fit the description of "clean" workers. It is easy to understand that the sons of such men will have educational and occupational ambitions to rise in the hierarchy, while the sons of "dirty" workers will simply repeat the lives of their fathers. But one crucial question remains unanswered: in a rapidly expanding industrial system, with the majority of lower-level industrial workers being recruited from peasant backgrounds, what turns some men into "clean" workers and others into "dirty" ones? This question is part of a larger one: what are the dynamics of social change that transform the social-class hierarchy from a rather simple structure of two or three layers with sharp distinctions between them, into a complex structure with many layers and blurred distinctions? It is not enough to say that as industry advances, the division of labor becomes more complex; we must also discover the processes which convert that economic fact into a social one, based on the values of different groups of men.

6

Empleados and Obreros

Stanley M. Davis

The most basic distinction made in the stratification system in all Mexican industrial firms is between *empleados* and *obreros*. In English, this distinction is variously known as that between nonmanual and manual, salaried and wage earner, white collar and blue collar, office worker and factory worker, nonunion and union, respectively. The distinction between these two groups in Mexico, however, has greater significance than the English terms can suggest. It is essential for understanding this culture's system of social stratification in factories and society. It draws the basic line of division in the hierarchy of a firm and reflects the social hierarchy of the society at large.

One way of describing the difference is that *empleados* generally earn more, have greater prestige, and occupy superior authority positions. From another point of view, however, the difference does not evolve around these common indices of social stratification. These are seen as reflections of a general cultural implication that *empleados* and *obreros* are different kinds of people. The former, more democratic, interpretation implies that the differences are of degree, not of a kind, and that mobility is a definite possibility. The second statement, on the other hand, is more tradition-bound and more authoritarian. It implies that the differences are natural and fixed, or at least ought to be; they are "ascribed." In reality, there is a mixture of both views involved in the distinction between *empleados* and *obreros.*

In a firm stratified according to traditional distinctions, management rules because it is "entitled to rule," as one respondent put it. Acceptance of this rule on the part of the workers also implies a traditional mentality; each party knows his place. Indeed, the barrier between the two groups is rather caste-like.

In traditional firms, especially large ones, one may think in terms of two stratification hierarchies. These two are the worlds of the *empleado* and the *obrero*. Since there is usually little possibility of crossing this line, in the traditional firm it is more meaningful to think of differences within each group as class differences, and between the two groups as caste differences. Vertical mobility within a firm is generally limited within each of the two

Adapted from Stanley M. Davis, "Managerial Resource Development in Mexico," in Robert H. Rehder, ed., *Latin American Management: Development and Performance* (Reading, Mass.: Addison-Wesley, 1968), pp. 140–145, with permission of the publisher.

hierarchies, and although this barrier diminishes with modernization, it simultaneously acts as an inhibitor to such open hierarchies.

The caste differences, however, are basically economic and cultural, not racial, and no "pure" caste system is implied. They are manifested in various ways. In one firm, for example, there were separate but equivalent bathrooms for employees and for workers, side by side; in another firm, there were separate dining rooms, also side by side, which operated identically; in a third firm, some employees refused to ride in the same company bus that brought workers to their jobs, feeling that it was beneath their dignity and status.

In less traditional firms, the separation between *empleados* and *obreros* is less sharp, and distinctions are more a matter of degree. The general notion is that management rules because it has achieved a higher level of skill, education, preparation, and the like. This is similar to, but not identical with, the conceptual contrast between "ascription" and "achievement." What is achieved is a kind of education, not an amount of education. The Spanish term *educación* refers to a general quality of culture and breeding, not unlike the Greek word *paideia,* meaning both culture and education. A very common criticism of workers is that they are *mal educado* or *mal preparado,* meaning that they have no breeding and not that they are technically untrained. The implication here is that if they had received or assimilated the broader sense of education, then their technical training would not be a problem.

Whether the difference, then, is considered one of degree and amenable to change, or one of kind and appropriate as such, in both cases there is a sense of qualitative difference between *empleados* and *obreros.* In one view the quality is considered immutable; in the other it is not.

*   *   *

From another perspective, the difference of quality is an artifact of a difference by definition. In this case, *empleado* is a shortening of the term *empleado de confianza,* often simply *confianza,* which translates "trusted employee." . . . This latter definition, made formal by the government, has affected how people think of informal status differences. Rather than emphasizing the different nature of each group, it defines *empleados de confianza* only by the feature of not being union members. It creates a legal distinction from what had been a traditional one. While previously there had been employees, a few of whom were *de confianza,* the law recognized no such distinction and thus helped strip the term of its earlier and more literal meaning. By differentiating only between *empleados de confianza* and *obreros,* the effect swelled the ranks of the former and thus reduced its traditional significance proportionately.

The change, then, from a fixed status difference to a difference by changing degree and definition had two results. Reducing the meaningfulness and expanding the membership of the *empleado de confianza* category had a democratizing effect; by weakening the traditional barriers it nourished the openness necessary for industrial advancement. By making the difference formal and legal, on the other hand, it strengthened in some cases the barrier between the two groups, thus minimizing mobility. This latter effect, however, was both weaker and more delayed. Moreover, it may be argued that it sped up the awareness, independence, and strength of labor as an organized and legitimate force.

Once the difference rests upon role definition, and is not considered within the "nature of things," basic indices of stratification are pertinent to the analysis, for they are then more determining of one's station than they are determined by it. Apart from the cases of true *empleados* and of unionized *obreros,* there are large numbers of people whose positions in the industrial hierarchy are not crystallized; each has a disproportionate mix of class, status and power.

However, despite the stratifying effect of the distinction between *empleados* and *obreros,* considerable ambiguity exists concerning the desirability of each classification for the individual worker. The case of one worker is exemplary. He was with the firm a number of years and did his job well. Management wanted to reward him, and so he was promoted to the rank of *empleado de confianza.* His work remained exactly the same and he still punched a time clock, but he no longer wore the union coveralls and he could eat in the *empleado* dining hall although he felt more comfortable with his co-workers. His earnings were now salaried rather than based on a daily wage, and he was given a slight raise. Most important of all, he gained a considerable amount of prestige by just being of *empleado de confianza* status.

When the union contract was renegotiated (every two years, by law) the disproportionate aspects of his position rose to the fore. He found that his fellow workers, who were still in the union, received a 10 percent wage increase, while he was only given an extra 200 *pesos* yearly, equivalent to less than one week's salary (less than 2 percent). Through time, his salary slowly increased in an absolute sense, but decreased relative to the cost of living and to the gains made by his co-workers. He went to the personnel department to complain and got nowhere; he could no longer go to the union representative. He was odd man out, and truly represented by neither major power group—labor or management. In effect, he had traded money and power for prestige, and he began to feel that he could not eat prestige.

[This is] by no means unique to Mexico, and other examples of disproportionate indices of stratification reveal the similarities to universal trends. Office boys, for example, have very low pay and no power whatsoever, yet by their position as *empleados de confianza* they have begun above the basic dividing line of the industrial hierarchy, and are therefore able to rise. More than likely, their fathers are from the *obrero* class, earning more than their sons and holding some power because of their seniority among the workers, but frozen at the top of the bottom half of the structure. Secretaries, too, are above the line, yet their major perquisite as *empleados* is prestige. . . .

In sum, the most striking distinction in the stratification of Mexican firms is the dichotomy drawn by the line between employees and workers. Although the line is not always clear, it is basic. While its roots are in the traditional social structure, it nonetheless represents an adaptation to the developing industrial structure. Finally, it suggests that stratification dichotomies are real, rather than oversimplifications and that they severely restrict the potential development of manpower resources. It should be noted, however, that they are more applicable to earlier periods of industrial development and become less sharp through time.

Foremen are officially considered *empleados,* yet it is common to find them punching a time clock, hanging their clothes in the same place as the *obreros,* being paid by a daily wage, and receiving wage increases proportionate to union gains. They are not union members, but many of the indices of *obreros* status are applicable to them. In many senses they are like the workers discussed above who were promoted to employee status. The major difference, however, is that they are supervisors; their job is to see that the work is carried out, but they do no physical labor themselves. As the immediate link between management and the work force, they are the key figures in maintaining a smooth rhythm in factory operations.

7

Minimum Living Standards in Latin America

N. N. Franklin

The Concept of Minimum Needs

The concept of minimum human needs evidently includes in the first place physical needs—what is necessary to stay alive and to maintain working capacity. These needs will vary with the length of the period we have in mind, but for most purposes of social policy it is long-run needs that are relevant.

Secondly, the concept of minimum needs, at least as the term is used in contemporary studies, extends beyond bare physical needs to include what are commonly called conventional or social needs. These are usually related to the established customs of a community: for example, if it is customary for members of a certain community, A, to wear shoes—even though they live in a climate in which this is not essential for health and in which people belonging to another community, B, normally go bare-foot—shoes are likely to be regarded as a social or conventional necessity for the people of community A, inasmuch as a member of this community lacking shoes might be an object of pity or ridicule. Similarly lack of a radio set or of pocket-money for beer, tobacco, hairdressing, newspapers or visits to cinemas might also set a person conspicuously apart from his or her group. There would be no scientific way of resolving differences of opinion as to what should and what should not be regarded as social or conventional necessities in different circumstances. But conceptually the notion of minimum social needs seems to be related to that of human dignity: it is held that a family should not be obliged by poverty to live in a manner that sets it apart from other families in the social group to which it belongs and that makes it unable to live according to the established customs of the community.

We may note that the distinction between physical and social needs is not always clear. A certain degree of palatability and variety of diet may be a physical need (to render the food digestible) or a conventional one. Some clothing is no doubt a physical necessity in a cold climate, but even primitive clothing usually fulfils a social rather than a biological function.

Adapted from N. N. Franklin, "The Concept and Measurement of Minimum Living Standards," *International Labour Review* (April 1967), pp. 271–298, by permission of the publisher, International Labour Office, Geneva, Switzerland.

35

Some Estimates of Minimum Needs

The concept of minimum needs becomes "operational" only if it can be given a measurable content. Attempts to measure minimum needs proceed by determining what commodities, and what quantities of each, are to be regarded as necessary. Since it is convenient to have a money measure of the cost of maintaining a minimum standard of living, investigators generally go on to price this "basket" of commodities, with a view to comparing its price with the incomes of families in the social groups with which they are concerned.

Studies in the United States. In the United States the Council of Economic Advisers has used an annual income of less than $3,000 to define families living in poverty. It is recognized, however, that this is a very crude measure and that a family's needs depend on its size and age and sex composition and also on whether it is living on a farm or in a town. Minimum incomes for families of various compositions have been worked out, based on the cost of food.[1] Food plans prepared by the Department of Agriculture have, for more than 30 years, served as a guide for estimating costs of food needed by families of different composition. The plans represent a translation of the criteria of nutritional adequacy set forth by the National Research Council into quantities and types of food compatible with the preferences of United States families as revealed in food consumption studies.[2]

Based on the cost of food at January 1964 prices, incomes estimated to satisfy the minimum needs of nonfarm families range from $1,580 for a one-person family to $5,090 for a family of seven or more (weighted average of various age and sex compositions). Estimated on a slightly more generous "low-cost" as distinct from "economy" basis, the range is from $1,885 to $6,395. The lower estimates are based on a pattern of food consumption which, though providing an adequate diet, is considered acceptable only for "temporary or emergency use when funds are low."[3]

No attempt was made in this study to estimate nonfood requirements by individual commodities. It was assumed that unless a family received an income amounting to some multiple of the cost of the "economy" food plan (or, alternatively, of the "low-cost" food plan) it would have to go without some necessary purchases. On the basis of studies of the percentage of income actually spent on food in families of different sizes, the multiple was assumed to be three for families of three or more persons, and rather more than three for families of one or two persons.

Methods Used in Latin America. In Latin America attempts to determine

---

[1]M. Orshansky, "Counting the Poor: Another Look at the Poverty Profile," *Social Security Bulletin* 28 (January 1965): pp. 3–29.
[2]See U.S. Department of Agriculture, *Family Food Plans and Food Costs,* Home Economics Research Report No. 20, November 1962.
[3]Orshansky, op. cit., p. 6.

minimum needs have mostly been made in the context of minimum-wage fixing. Most of the countries of Latin America have minimum-wage legislation covering all or substantial parts of the labor force, even though implementation in some of them seems to be lagging. And though other criteria are frequently mentioned as well, the main criterion in determining the level of the minimum wage continues to be the sum of money needed to supply a family with the goods and services considered necessary for subsistence.

This basket of goods and services is sometimes described explicitly, as in the case of laws in Argentina, Brazil, Bolivia, Chile and Paraguay; whereas in others only general definitions, such as the minimum sum necessary to satisfy the material, moral and cultural needs of the worker, may be found. A sample budget employed by minimum wage commissions in Mexico is shown in Table 1.

The translation of these categories of expenditure into specific items takes various forms.

In Mexico the Constitution of 1917 defined the major principles to be followed in fixing minimum wages, and their earliest implementation dates back to the 1931 Federal Labor Law. At present the procedure followed is that defined in the Labor Code as amended in 1962, which establishes (article 425, section D) the budget of a working-class family containing the following items: food, clothing, housing, household expenses, transportation, attendance at cultural functions, sports training of the worker, reading and education of the children.

The minimum wage for each area must be fixed every two years by special regional committees, which have to take into consideration the documentation submitted to them for this purpose. A technical secretariat is charged with supplying the regional committees with information consisting of a report on the economic conditions of the country and the region in question, economic activities, family budgets, and conditions of demand. In order to comply with this, the secretariat conducts studies and presents the results to the regional commissions together with an appraisal of the impact of the minimum wage in force.

For 1964, for instance, the secretariat compiled family budgets for the total population of all states (32 studies), for their rural population (29), their urban population (29) and for the 16 major urban areas of the country. All this was done through sample surveys conducted by the secretariat in collaboration with other government agencies. From all these budgets a selection was made of the families whose income ranges fell within the approximate level of minimum wages in force—that is, between 301 and 400 pesos[4] per month. The actual expenditure of these families on the categories and items shown in Table I was regarded as a measure of the necessary minimum expenditure.

In Brazil, where minimum wages have a shorter history than in Mexico, a somewhat different system is applied in the determination of the minimum

---

[4]One Mexican peso = U.S. $0.08.

Table 7-1

Mexico: Monthly Family Budget for Minimum Wage Purposes
(Mexico City, 1963)

Item	Quantity and unit	Cost in U.S. $	Percentage of total
All items		$58.64	100.0%
Food		*31.50*	*53.7*
Beef	5.2 kg.	3.14	
Eggs	32.7 units	1.39	
Beans	12.0 kg.	2.84	
Rice	6.6 kg.	1.63	
Sugar	9.9 kg.	1.25	
Bread	517.8 pieces	4.14	
Corn (tortillas)	36.0 kg.	2.39	
Oil	4.0 l.	2.04	
Milk	75.4 l.	9.65	
Coffee	1.2 kg.	1.18	
Salt	2.5 kg.	0.17	
Beverages	13.8 bottles	0.50	
Fruit and vegetables[a]	—	1.18	
Housing		*6.39*	*10.9*
Rental		5.08	
Electricity		1.31	
Clothing		*5.67*	*9.7*
Wearing apparel		3.03	
Footwear		2.64	
Personal hygiene		*1.68*	*2.9*
Toiletries		0.44	
Soap		0.68	
Detergents		0.56	
Other		*13.40*	*22.8*
Household fuel		1.50	
Medical expenses		4.63	
Transport		2.79	
Cinema		1.73	
Education		1.22	
Miscellaneous[b]		1.53	

Source: Comision Nacional de Salarios Minimos, *Memoria de los trabajos de 1963*, Vol. IV (Mexico City, 1964), p. 307.

[a]Estimated at 3.87 percent of expenditure on other food, cigarettes, matches, candles, and sundry household items.

[b]Includes newspapers, haircuts.

expenditure budget. The concept of a minimum wage was set forth in legislation of 1936, which defined it as the minimum sum necessary to satisfy the worker's normal needs for food, clothing, housing, health care and transportation. Further legislation widened the scope to include the needs of the family as well, but in practice only the needs of the workers themselves are considered.[5] As implemented, it is considered as a subsistence wage in that it is supposed to cover only the material requirements for the subsistence of the worker. The minimum wage covers all occupations and varies with regional differences in cost of living. The regional commissions fixing minimum wages are required to justify or document their decisions (article 107 of Law No. 5452 of 1 May 1943). Their work is preceded by substantial analysis of certain economic indicators which include production, consumption, trade, banking, public finance, national income and cost of living—all of this on a regional basis for each of the 22 minimum wage regions.

Article 81 of the Labor Code clearly stipulates that the minimum wage shall be the result of the addition of the necessary daily expenditures of an adult worker on food, housing, clothing, health and transport, and it adds that the first item (food) should have a value equal to the cost of the list of goods *necessary* for the daily nutrition of the worker. To arrive at the specific items (in the "food" group only) the technical secretariat chose a food basket upon the recommendation of nutritionists. It was this, rather than the normal or typical expenditure pattern, which served as a basis for choosing the specific items and the quantities of them. It is expressly provided that foodstuffs of equivalent nutritional value may be substituted whenever local habits or supply conditions so require.

For other items (non-food) only global sums of percentages are included, as derived from expenditure and income surveys . . .

*   *   *

From this brief survey of attempts to determine and measure minimum needs, three facts seem to emerge—and would emerge more clearly if space permitted a more extensive survey.

First, notwithstanding the difficulties of attempting to give practical content to the concept of minimum needs, efforts to do so have been made and continue to be made, in many countries. These efforts are evidently considered to serve useful purposes . . .

Secondly, there are enormous differences in the results of attempts to measure minimum needs in different countries, and even in the same country at different times. Estimates of the cost of satisfying minimum needs range from about one-third more than the estimated cost of a minimum diet to more than three times this cost—and some minimum diets are much more austere than others.

Thirdly, these differences are partly explained by a historical evolution in the treatment of minimum needs. In the earliest attempts to measure them, and in some more recent attempts in poor countries, the emphasis was placed largely on biological or physical needs; but as living standards rise, increasing emphasis is placed on social or conventional needs. This has been paralleled by a similar evolution in other areas of social policy.

---

[5]There is also a family allowance payable along with the regular wage, according to Law No. 4266 of 1963. See Délio MARANHÃO, *Direito do trabalho* (Rio de Janeiro, Getulio Vargas, 1966), pp. 92–93a.

For example, laws or regulations governing hours of work, minimum age of admission to work and holidays with pay, formerly based largely on considerations having to do with the physical efficiency of workers, are now increasingly based on social considerations. . . .

8

Labor-Force Participation Rates in Latin America

U.S. Bureau of Labor Statistics

Since 1900, the labor force in most countries in Latin America and the Caribbean has declined steadily as a percent of total population. This decline has been caused primarily by migration of rural families to urban centers. Another important factor has been the increasing youthfulness of the population.

Often, in rural areas, the whole family is counted as part of the labor force because each member has some duties on the farm. When these families move to cities, the children usually attend school and the wife becomes primarily a housewife, so neither group is included in labor-force enumeration. Male unemployment is more prevalent and more easily measured in urban than in rural areas. Some unemployed are not counted in the labor force if they have not sought employment in the time prescribed by a given survey. The resulting underenumeration of the unemployed is more common in cities than in the country. Labor-force participation rates of men over 60 years of age also have been decreasing as the retirement age has been lowered. More men are eligible for retirement benefits in urban areas, where they work for salaries, than in the rural sector where retirement benefits are rare.

Another important factor in the declining labor-force participation rate has been the increasing youthfulness of the population. Birth rates between 1900 and 1960 were about 40 to 45 per 1,000 inhabitants, but the death rate decreased from about 28 per 1,000 in 1900 to about 9 per 1,000 in 1960. The low death rate reflects a decline in the infant mortality rate and, to a lesser degree, greater longevity among older people.

The percent of Latin Americans and islanders under 15 years of age has increased greatly in recent years. Most of these nations measure their labor force as those economically active above a certain age, usually about 14. As the average age of the population is lowered, overall labor-force participation rates decrease. The broadening base of the age pyramid of the population in these developing countries is opposite to the trend in most developed countries, where declining birth and mortality rates in recent years have increased the average age of the population.

One factor slowing the decline in the labor-participation rates is increased economic activity of the female population. Prejudice in Latin America against women working is eroding while employment opportunities

Adapted from U. S. Bureau of Labor Statistics, *Labor Developments Abroad* (August 1970), pp. 34–36, by permission of the publisher.

41

Table 8-1
Labor Force Participation Rates in Selected American Republics for Selected Years

Country	Year	Labor-force participation rate	Country	Year	Labor-force participation rate
American Republics	1920	36.5%	Guyana	1946	39.9%
	1930	36.0		1965	27.0
	1950	35.2	Haiti	1950	56.4
	1960	33.5		1965	56.9
Argentina	1914	40.0	Honduras	1940	34.3
	1947	40.6		1961	30.1
	1960	37.6	Jamaica	1943	40.8
Barbados	1950	46.7		1960	40.7
	1960	38.0	Mexico	1910	37.1
Bolivia	1950	50.3		1950	32.4
	1967	50.0		1967	31.5
Brazil	1900	46.9	Nicaragua	1920	31.8
	1966	32.0		1950	31.2
Chile	1920	35.8		1966	32.0
	1966	30.7	Panama	1940	36.7
Colombia	1938	52.5		1950	35.0
	1951	33.4		1967	30.8
	1964	29.4	Paraguay	1950	32.9
Costa Rica	1950	34.0		1966	34.0
	1963	29.6	Peru	1940	39.9
Dominican Republic	1920	22.7		1966	31.5
	1950	38.7	Puerto Rico	1968	29.7
	1967	30.7	Trinidad and Tobago	1940	40.7
Ecuador	1950	37.6		1966	34.0
	1966	32.0	Uruguay	1940	40.7
El Salvador	1950	35.2		1955	36.4
	1967	32.0		1963	39.2
Guatemala	1950	34.7	Venezuela	1941	32.2
	1968	30.7		1950	33.9
				1966	31.0

have been increasing, especially in the tertiary sector—services, utilities, communications, and government employment.

The accompanying table gives labor-force participation rates in Latin America and the Caribbean in selected years between 1900 and 1968. The data do not have a common statistical base but come from many sources, including the regular census and sample surveys. As a result of the variations in sources a detailed statistical analysis is impossible. In most nations and in the region as a whole, however, rates declined between 1900 and 1968. For any individual year the age of the labor force may vary. For example, in Brazil in 1960, the labor force included the economically active 10 years old and over, but by 1968, the minimum age had been increased to 14. The minimum age used as a "cutoff" point for the labor force varies from 7 years in Guatemala in 1964 to 15 years in the Dominican Republic in 1960.

Underutilization of Manpower and Demographic Trends in Latin America

Gavin W. Jones

Recent Demographic Trends in Latin America

Latin America is at present experiencing the most rapid expansion of population and labor force ever recorded over such a large area in the history of mankind. It is hardly surprising that such an expansion, occurring as it is simultaneously with far-reaching structural changes in the economy, is bringing with it serious problems of unemployment and underemployment.

The dominating force behind recent demographic trends in Latin America has been the rapid decline in levels of mortality, especially in countries where these levels were still high or moderately high at the end of the Second World War. Declining mortality, combined with high and more or less constant levels of fertility, has resulted in an acceleration in rates of population growth: the average annual rate of growth in Latin America climbed from 2.3 percent in the 1940s to 2.8 percent in the 1950s and has now reached 2.9 percent, a rate of growth which, if continued, would double the population in 24 years. Growth is considerably slower than the average in temperate South America (Argentina, Chile and Uruguay), where birth rates are low, and in Bolivia and Peru, where death rates are relatively high.

The most rapid growth has been in the number of children, with the result that the population of working age (15 to 64 years) has become a smaller proportion of the total population (about 54 percent in 1960–63).[1] Because of the declining activity rates,[2] especially for young males under 25, the percentage of the population in the labor force has declined even more than the percentage in the labor force age groups. Only 33 percent of the population is currently in the labor force, the lowest percentage for any continent. The labor force thus bears a heavy, and increasing, burden of dependency.[3]

But whereas from the point of view of dependency the labor force has grown too slowly, from the point of view of finding opportunities for pro-

Adapted from *International Labour Review* (November 1968), pp. 451–469, by permission of the publisher, International Labour Office, Geneva, Switzerland.

[1]Carmen A. Miro, "The Population of Latin America," *Demography* 1 (1964): pp. 28–30.

[2]The activity rate of any group in the population is the proportion of that group that is economically active (i.e., working or looking for work).

[3]The dependency ratio is the ratio of the economically inactive population to the working population.

45

ductive employment it has grown too quickly. The population aged 15 to 64 has been growing at an accelerating rate (by 25 percent during the 1940s, then by 30 percent during the 1950s, and by an estimated 32 percent during the 1960s), and although the growth of the labor force has probably been somewhat slower than this because of declining activity rates, it has nevertheless been extremely rapid (an estimated 26 percent in the 1950s and 29 percent in the 1960s), and opportunities for productive employment have not been able to keep pace.

The Changing Structure of Employment

The rapid growth of the labor force in the past two decades has brought about great strains in the employment market, and these are reflected in important changes in the distribution of employment among industries. The development of Latin American agriculture has been slow, and agriculture remains a sector of extremely low productivity. For example in Mexico the agricultural labor force in 1960 represented slightly over 54 percent of the total labor force but agriculture contributed only around 17 percent of the gross domestic product. The structure of land ownership, notably the "latifundio-minifundio complex" (large estates controlling much of the land and other resources, linked organically to a large number of very small holdings, which are dependent on them for land, employment and other means of production and livelihood) has long been an obstacle to rapid agricultural progress. Agricultural output has barely kept pace with population growth because the number of agricultural workers has grown more slowly than the total population and output per worker has increased only slowly.[4] As yet there has been no "technological revolution" in Latin American agriculture to cut manpower requirements drastically. Hence agriculture has been able to absorb rather large numbers of new workers, partly on newly opened land and partly on the minifundios created by splitting up agricultural properties, but with low levels of productivity and, almost certainly, high levels of underemployment. The absorption of labor by agriculture has been a case of "static expansion"—neither rapid enough to forestall the townward migration of large numbers of workers nor at a sufficiently high level of productivity to make agriculture a "growth sector" in the Latin American economy.

Statistically, the story has been as follows. Although the number of workers in agriculture has continued to increase—from 26.9 million in 1950 to 31.6 million in 1962—the proportion of the work force in agriculture has fallen from 53.2 percent in 1950 to 46.4 percent in 1962 (see Table 1). Agriculture absorbed only 27 percent of the increase in the labor force in 1950–55 and again in 1955–62. As might be expected, manpower absorption by agriculture was lowest in the more highly urban-

---

[4]United Nations, Economic Commission for Latin America, *Economic Survey of Latin America, 1964* (E/CN.12/711/Rev.1), 1966, p. 44, table 31.

Table 9-1

Latin America: Estimated Distribution of Active Population by Economic
Activity, 1950-1962, and Gross Product Per Worker, 1950 and 1962[a]

Economic activity	Distribution of active population (percentage)				Gross product per worker (1960 dollars)	
	1950	1955	1960	1962	1950	1962
All activities	100.0%	100.0%	100.0%	100.0%	$ 891	$1,140
Agricultural sector	53.2	50.1	47.5	46.4	394	501
Non-agricultural sectors	46.8	49.9	52.5	53.6	1347	1,578
Mining	1.1	1.1	1.0	1.1	3922	6,820
Manufacturing	15.5	14.3	14.3	14.1	1160	1,825
Factory	6.9	7.1	7.4	7.4	2069	3,146
Artisan	7.6	7.2	6.9	6.7	326	364
Construction	3.8	4.5	4.8	4.8	1116	896
Basic services[b]	4.2	3.7	5.2	5.4	1706	1,851
Commerce and finance	7.8	8.5	9.2	9.4	2057	2,243
Government	3.3	3.5	3.7	3.8	1945	1,785
Miscellaneous services	9.6	11.0	12.0	12.7	868	777
Unspecified activities	2.5	2.3	2.3	2.4	(694)	(652)

Source: I.L.O., Eighth Conference of American States Members of the International Labour
Organisation, Ottawa, September 1966, Report II: *Manpower Planning and Employment
Policy in Economic Development* (Geneva: I.L.O., 1966, mimeo., pp. 51-52, tables XVII
and XVIII.

[a]Excluding Cuba and the Dominican Republic.

[b]Utilities, transportation and communication.

ized and rapidly urbanizing countries and highest in Central America,
where 53 percent of the increase in the labor force went into agriculture
[see Table 1].[5]

Nonagricultural activities absorbed 73 percent of the increase in the
labor force between 1950 and 1962. However, the more dynamic industries
—mining, manufacturing (excluding artisan production), construction,
and basic services such as electricity, water supply, transportation and communications—accounted for only one-quarter of the increase. Factories,
for example, absorbed only 9 percent between 1950 and 1960, and even
less afterwards, which led to a decline in their share of total employment.
It appears that well over half of the increase in the labor force is still being
absorbed by the activities characterized by relatively low productivity:
agriculture, artisan manufacturing, petty retailing, domestic services and
"miscellaneous services." As shown later in this paper, part of the apparent
increase in employment in these sectors is in reality an increase in "disguised underemployment."

[5]Agriculture absorbed 6 percent of the increase in the labor force in Uruguay and Chile,
11 in Venezuela, 17 in Colombia, 25 in Brazil, 35 in Mexico and 37 in Peru. See United
Nations, op. cit., p. 38.

One reason why the higher-productivity industries are still providing relatively little extra employment is that most of these industries are not in the nature of things, very labor-intensive. Most of them, however, are somewhat flexible in their factor proportions and have probably been forced to veer away from labor in their factor mix because of the shortage of trained manpower. Around the mid-1960s less than 5 percent of the Latin American labor force had had secondary education and less than one-fourth had completed six grades of elementary school.

Closely related to the movement out of agriculture has been the large-scale migration into the towns, which has transformed Latin America from a mainly rural region into one in which half the population was estimated to live in towns with more than 2,000 inhabitants in 1965. This continuous movement raised the population growth rate in urban areas to 4.5 percent a year in the 1950s and perhaps even higher in the 1960s. . . . In comparison with most other parts of the world, industrialization in Latin America is lagging in relation to the degree of urbanization achieved, and the movement into the towns tends to result simply in the transfer of underemployment from a rural to an urban setting. . . . While this situation remains there will be a "balanced growth" of unemployment and underemployment in both rural and urban areas. The widely recognized noneconomic attractions of the towns and the forces making for a high wage floor in urban industries [will] swing the pendulum toward differentially high unemployment in urban areas.

Trends in Unemployment and Underemployment[6]

There are serious defects in the coverage and methodology of employment and unemployment statistics in Latin American countries, and very few countries have continuous information on the changing situation in employment markets. In countries where precise data are lacking, some individuals

---

[6]Underemployment can be defined in a number of different ways. The Meeting of Experts on Measurement of Underemployment, convened by the International Labour Office in 1963, identified the following major categories of underemployment but recognized that they do not necessarily cover all aspects of the problem:

"(a) *visible underemployment,* which involves persons involuntarily working part time or for shorter than normal periods of work;

(b) *invisible underemployment,* which exists when a person's working time is not abnormally reduced but whose employment is inadequate in other respects such as
  (1) when his job does not permit full use of his highest existing skill or capacity;
  (2) when his earnings from employment are abnormally low;
  (3) when he is employed in an establishment or economic unit whose productivity is abnormally low.

Underemployment in the situations (b) (1) and (2) above is sometimes referred to as *disguised underemployment* while that in situation (b) (3) above is described as potential underemployment."

From I.L.O., Eleventh International Conference of Labour Statisticians, Geneva, 1966, Report IV: *Measurement of Underemployment: Concepts and Methods* (Geneva, I.L.O., 1966), p. 16.

and institutions are nevertheless in a position to make a rough assessment of the seriousness of unemployment and underemployment.

There seems to be unanimous agreement that the incidence of unemployment is high, both in the countries with precise data and in those with only vague information. For example estimates of unemployment submitted to the Organization of American States by a number of Latin American countries indicate that current unemployment ranges between 5 and 11 percent of the total labor force—and these, if anything, would tend to be low estimates because governments do not like admitting to high levels of unemployment.

Table 2 shows the rates of unemployment in Latin American countries as recorded in censuses held between 1960 and 1964. Only very limited significance can be attached to these figures, since differing definitions of "unemployment" and methods of measuring it were probably applied in the inquiries. For example it is inconceivable that the differences in unemployment rates in Mexico and Venezuela—both countries experiencing rapid economic development—are as wide as they appear. Again, in most countries listed in the table, unemployment rates for males are higher than for females. Yet in three countries—Argentina, Honduras and Panama—female unemployment rates are approximately double the male rates.

Table 9-2
Latin America: Percentage of Unemployed Persons in the Economically Active Population and Estimated Percentage of Urban Workers Who Were Underemployed, 1960-1964

	Unemployment			Estimated urban underemployment
Country and year	Both sexes	Male	Female	
Argentina (1960)	2.7%	2.1%	4.7%	7.0%
Chile (1960)	6.7	7.2	4.9	28.0
Colombia 1964	4.9	5.1	4.1	
Costa Rica (1963)	7.0	7.8	4.5	
Ecuador (1962)	4.3	4.7	2.4	
El Salvador (1961)	5.4	5.6	4.1	21.0
Guatemala (1964)	1.5	1.4	1.5	
Honduras (1961)	7.8	7.0	12.5	
Mexico (1960)	1.6	1.7	1.1	
Panama 1960	11.2	9.4	18.1	20
Peru 1961	2.7	2.8	2.5	25.0
Uruguay (1963)	12.0	12.6	10.2	
Venezuela (1961)	13.7	14.7	9.4	

Note: Persons seeking work for the first time are counted as unemployed.

Sources: *Manpower Planning and Employment Policy in Economic Development,* (Geneva: I.L.O., 1966, mimeo), pp. 55-58; Instituto Interamericano de Estadistica: *América en cifras, 1963,* Vol. II: *Situación demográfica. Estado y movimiento de la población* (Washington, D.C.: Unión Panamericana, 1964), table 201-11; unpublished data supplied by the Pan American Union and the Statistical Office of the United Nations.

In the Latin American setting underemployment tends to be a more serious problem than overt unemployment. This is true not only in rural areas but also to a considerable extent in urban areas. In effect, the lack of more productive employment opportunities has created an abundance of "fringe" occupations, in which those who cannot find more productive employment can eke out a living—petty hawking, shoe-shining, personal service, and so forth. Some data on urban underemployment are presented in Table 2, showing that underemployment rates exceed 20 percent in the cities of Chile, El Salvador, Panama and Peru. Rural underemployment is even more difficult to measure, but one can infer that it is serious in many areas from the prevalence of very small farms.[7] In Mexico (where the recorded rate of unemployment was low in 1960) a 1959 study of underemployment in agriculture conducted by the Mexican Department of Agrarian Affairs revealed that over half of Mexico's agricultural workers were employed for only 145 days or less a year.[8]

The data in Table 1 strongly suggest that underemployment in Latin America was worsening up to the early 1960s. It shows that a growing percentage of the labor force was working in industries—construction and government and miscellaneous services—in which output per man actually declined between 1950 and 1962. The organization of the construction industry is generally defective in Latin America, a great deal of unskilled labor is employed at the low wage levels, and government construction programs are often as much concerned with soaking up unemployment as with the actual building program itself. For similar reasons, and because of a shortage of funds for modernization, government services also employ labor in excess of the technological requirements. Finally, "other services" is a miscellaneous group that tends to absorb the surplus workers who cannot find employment in other activities.

The Economic Commission for Latin America, while admitting that underemployment is very difficult to measure, claims that "it would be no exaggeration to estimate that in many Latin American countries underemployment affects 30 or even 40 percent of the total labor force."[9]

---

[7]It is a rule of thumb that a farm of less than 2 *hectares* cannot fully employ an average farm family.
[8]Arthur F. Neef, *Labor in Mexico* (BLS Report No. 251; Washington, D.C.: U.S. Department of Labor, Bureau of Labor Statistics, 1963), pp. 39–40.
[9]United Nations, op. cit., p. 43.

Managers

10 The Industrial Elite in Latin America

Fernando H. Cardoso

The basic criterion for defining industrial activity is that of the entrepreneurs' attitude toward the market and toward the state. Any consideration of the circumstances in which markets and nations came into existence in Latin America makes it evident that the countries were brought into the world market in one of three basic ways:

(a) Through the introduction of foreign economic elements, as illustrated by the Central American plantation, the mines of Bolivia and Chile, or the oil wells of Venezuela.

(b) Through an economic system based on the exploitation of resources by local producers, as in the coffee plantations of Brazil and Colombia and the stock-breeding economies of the South.

(c) Through the enforced substitution of imported goods: this resulted in an expansion of the domestic market initially created by economic development following the second type of integration into the foreign market.

In the first two of these types of development there is a very clear connection between a dominant local class ("political" in the first case, "landowning" in the second) and the representatives of the central economies. These political classes, or oligarchies, seem to have been both a means and a condition of emergence as a nation. The connection between the market (which was *foreign,* and which had existed, as we have seen, from the very earliest days of Latin American history) and the local interests was mediated through the state, which was itself controlled either by the nonproductive local oligarchy or by the landowning producers, to the exclusion of the other classes and social groups. Reference to the nation (the whole body of society) was in the nature of a recourse to outside pressure, for the purpose of bargaining with foreign groups in the case of situation (a), or to provide the agricultural classes, in the case of situation (b), with the political instruments they required, in an international trial of strength, to bargain over quotas and export prices.

Therefore, only the third case of the integration of the Latin American countries in the world market (situation c) appears to provide conditions in which the industrial entrepreneurs and merchants could emerge as the protagonists of national development. According to the previously mentioned theory, prevalent in Latin America, which draws an analogy between the course of development in Europe and the United States and that in the developing countries, the groups of entrepreneurs, as representatives of the urban and industrial economic classes, should have lent impetus to industrialization and national development and turned into the avant-garde groups in Latin America. This interpretation assumes a dual analogy with the original circumstances of development—it assumes the modernization originated among "puritan entrepreneurs" (in the style of Weber) and that the autonomy of the entrepreneur class conformed to the political behavior patterns of the European-bourgeoisie during their rise to power. The significance of the first assumption is diminished by the importance of the other types of entrepreneurs in Latin America, who were in no way characterized by economic asceticism. As for the second assumption, it has not been confirmed by research.

On the contrary, the first two types of Latin American integration in the world market, though led by the traditional and landowning classes and by the state which had been created to serve those very classes, demonstrated the possibilities available to the urban industrial elite which was bound up with industrial development. The plan of development observable in the most industrialized countries of the region was decisively marked by the following successive circumstances and social pressures.

(a) Intensive urbanization, preceding industrialization, as a consequence of the favorable economic results produced during the period of development.

(b) Formation, as the result of (a), of lower-class groups who pressed for access to the market and a place in political life, through the actions of popular movements (led by Vargas, Perón, Gaetano, etc.).

(c) Formation of urban middle-class groups (civil servants, professional men, military men, civil engineers, etc.) who gained some control of the political machinery, because of the imbalance created in the traditional power structure by the *presence* of the masses, even where they were not active, during export crises. The middle classes obtained this partial control of the machinery of government whether through movements of their own (radicalism in Argentina and Chile, *Battlismo* in Uruguay, etc.) or through "anti-oligarchic" movements which, however, had the support of certain sectors of the oligarchy (*Tenentismo* in Brazil). The first type of movement appears to have been linked to a new middle class, of immigrant origin, while the second was allied to pressure groups in the traditional middle class.

(d) Within this politico-social framework, where the export oligarchies were beginning to lose their absolute dominance, the groups created by industrialization (to meet the expansion of the domestic market which had resulted from the success of textile and foodstuff exports) *began to have marginal participation in the national political system.* In fact, when the entrepreneur groups came to the fore there was already an active state organization and an established market, and the other social forces—the urban masses and middle-class groups, the oligarchies and exporters—were competing for control of the state machinery, and thus for the possibility of influencing decisions relating to investment and consumption.

(e) The "technological" sectors of the middle classes (economists, army men, engineers, etc.) appear to have been concerned about the "unbalance of power" resulting from pressure by the masses and the danger implicit in it. Once they were to some extent participating politically in the state machinery, they began to favor an industrial policy based on public investment and aimed at achieving national independence and at creating a sufficient demand for labor to offset the disruptive effects latent in mass pressure.

(f) Not until somewhat later did the entrepreneur groups take over responsibility for industrial development. Even then, they did so under the protection of the state, and therefore, with the benefit of the expansion resulting from government investment (in energy, oil, iron, and steel), which opened up new sources of profit for private investment as a substitute for imports.

This picture, applicable to the principal industrialized countries in the region (Brazil, Chile, Mexico, and with less consistency, Argentina), indicates the content and values of entrepreneur action in Latin America. In this instance, the existence of markets did not involve such values as free competition, productivity, etc., because the market was "protected" by state measures which benefited the industrialists. Similarly, our reference to society does not imply, in the conditions prevailing in Latin America, that a deliberate scheme existed for controlling the politico-social situation; much less does it imply commitment to the construction of a democratic community for the masses, on the terms usually attributed to industrial societies. In point of fact the entrepreneur groups were emerging from a comparatively marginal politico-social situation at a time when other social forces, including the traditional exporting class, the middle groups, and the masses themselves, occupied key positions already in the political game. Moreover, these entrepreneur groups found their options restricted by the ambiguity of the situation: either they joined forces with the masses to bring pressure on the state in opposition to the exporting groups, or else their chances of political and social authority might be disturbed by mass action. In some circumstances they supported the state in its development efforts; in others, they competed with the state in the attempt to wrest certain fields of investment from it, or joined with foreign capitalists because of the technological dependence characteristic of underdeveloped countries. On occasion they sponsored measures for the extension of political rights; on other occasions they allied themselves to the oligarchy and its narrow interests because, as a propertied class, they were afraid the control of the community might pass to the masses. It is essential to analyze the responses of entrepreneurs in the dependent economic systems in terms of the problems which arose, limiting their options especially because of the existence of *underdeveloped* masses of population in the countries concerned.

Three basic problems appear to be involved: In what economic and social conditions, and under the thrust of what social movements, did the modernizing entrepreneur groups emerge and take action? What tendencies and characteristics of economic action put new dynamism into the Latin

American businesses? What type of structure framed the basic choices these groups adopted with regard to social change, and to what extent did their desire to gain power dispose them to accept popular pressure on the one hand, or to placate the traditional governing classes on the other hand?

To answer these questions would require an elaborate historical and social analysis of industrialization in Latin America. On the basis of existing work, one can say that once launched, industrial growth followed a twofold pattern in almost all the countries of that region. First there was a slow growth of the handicrafts and manufacturing system, usually reinforced by the expansion of the domestic market (related, of course, to the increased exports of raw materials and the growth of towns, the latter accelerated by immigration resulting from the expansion of the export trade). Secondly, there was the rapid and increasingly dynamic process which set in whenever market conditions were favorable (war, devaluation for the protection of exports, etc.). Sustaining these stimuli depends to a great extent upon the ability of the leading groups to frame an adequate policy of investment in the basic sectors, to accept the views of the technical sectors which lay down investment policy. From the sociological standpoint the chief problem is to discover how well the social forces have taken advantage of the influences favorable to the automatic growth of the market (either in the slow, traditional manner, or with the speed produced by exceptional circumstances) to transform that process into a development policy, and the conditions in which this occurred. Did the industrial entrepreneurs create and exploit the opportunities offered by a development policy? Did it prove possible to harmonize the interests of the various dominant groups, and how great are the divergencies between the different classes participating in the development process? What form was taken by and what solution found for, the divergencies between the groups concerned in the export sector and those concerned with production for domestic market? What opposition was there between foreign economic interests and the national groups, and how was it overcome?

Here again, the answer must depend on a concrete analysis of typical social situations: the initial impulse was sometimes provided by general, widespread, and violent pressure exercised by the urban populace against the established forms of domination (Mexico). There was sometimes an alliance between the popular movements, the traditional interests, and the entrepreneur groups (Brazil under Vargas). Elsewhere, conditions approximated a phase of vigorous entrepreneur action at the economic level, including action by the exporter groups, together with comparative isolation and political antagonism of those groups in the face of mass pressure (as in Argentina under Perón). There were situations where the entrepreneurs' pressure in favor of development met with indifference from the other social groups (as in Colombia).

11 United States versus Latin America: Business and Culture

Stanley M. Davis

The Individual

Both the North American and the Latin American have a strong sense of individuality, but the word "individuality" itself means something different in each case.

On the one hand, the [North American's] notion of individuality stresses a basic equality of people. His belief is that each person has (or should have) equal rights, an equal job opportunity, and an equal chance to find his own place in the sun. Paradoxically, it is his belief in his very sameness, vis-à-vis others, that makes him distinct and defines his individuality.

On the other hand, to the Latin sense of individuality, the notion that "each person is just as good as the next" is untrue, irrelevant, and contradictory.

Each one of the hundred Latin American mechanics in a factory knows that he is not the company president's equal, but he also knows that he is distinct from the president as well as from the other mechanics. Similarly, the maid knows that she is not equal to the president's wife, but she also knows she is unique.

Notions of the unique personality and the dignity of the individual are often found in harmony with very unequal boss-worker relationships. Anthropologist John Gillin puts the point well when he says:

"The distinctive worth of each individual has nothing to do with his social position or his recognized distinction; advancement in the hierarchy may come, although not necessarily so, as the result of fulfilling one's unique potentialities. In contrast with the United States' credo, Latin Americans do not believe that all men are born 'equal.' You cannot be equal to anyone else in your inner essence when, by definition, you and everyone else are 'unique.' It is also obvious that, from the point of view of social rank, everyone is not equal."[1]

The Latin American concept of individuality serves to de-emphasize other spheres, such as the work group and the organization. For example, it is common for a Latin businessman to say that he would not want his organization to grow "too large." If there are currently 100 persons, then

Reprinted from *Harvard Business Review* (November-December 1969), pp. 88–98, with permission of the publisher.
[1]"Some Signposts for Policy," in *Social Change in Latin America*, ed. Richard N. Adams, et al. (New York: Vintage Books, 1960), p. 35.

he might say that he would not be comfortable with more than 150; if there are 300, then a future ceiling would be around 500; and with 750 people, surely 1,000 would be the outer limit of expansion.

Beyond each of these limits, he says, he would prefer to open another business or at least another factory. In fact, however, the successful Latin American businessman is more than likely to continue increasing his outer limit so that it always stays just enough ahead of the current count. Why does he behave this way?

For one thing, he reasons that when a company reaches the outer limit of expansion people become a mass of numbers and no longer are individuals. His rationale need not be confused with humanism or egalitarianism, however, for if he is an authoritarian manager he may prefer small organizations because increased personal contact affords greater control.

Another reason for idealizing size limitations is that Latin American management policy must start with the complete human being as its unit of analysis, whereas physical, technical, or financial policies can be broken down into their discrete parts. This means an emphasis on the total person and not simply on that part of him which performs a specific job function.

In contrast, the North American single-mindedness of purpose may be admired for the achievements it reaps in productivity, but it is unlikely that it will be copied. Business historian Thomas C. Cochran points this out in the contrast between two great industrial leaders, Henry Ford and Torcuato Di Tella of Argentina:

Ford represented the classic American drives for mechanization and efficiency, Di Tella the Latin interests in the all-around social man who would be family leader, business leader, intellectual, and *patron* of the arts. Both were extremely 'driven' individuals, but Ford had the singleness of purpose so usual to American entrepreneurial personality, Di Tella the more diffused ambitions of men of Latin and many other cultures.[2]

A third reason for idealizing smaller units of organization is the importance Latins attach to face-to-face relations. Business letters, office memos, and even the telephone dehumanize personal contacts. Copyrights and contracts may be legally binding, but without the handshake and the *abrazo* (embrace), the moral bond is missing and the agreement may be starting off in the wrong way.

Personalism [also] counts in Latin America, but it should not be confused with the North American meaning of the term. In the United States, the word "personal" suggests intimacy and confidentiality ("We had a very personal conversation, and I told him everything") and informality ("Everybody calls me George"). These are expressive, not instrumental, patterns of behavior, and it is not considered legitimate to use expressive relations in order to meet instrumental ends.

The Latin variant of personalism serves a very different function. The handshake and the *abrazo,* the boss's walk through the factory, and the

---

[2]"The Entrepreneur in Economic Change," *Behavioral Science* 9 (1964): p. 117.

bestowal of gifts in lieu of cash bonuses all serve the impersonal function of maintaining the economic organization. The difference is not in being more or less personal, but in what being personal means to different individuals and for what ends it is being employed.

Another variant of the Latin American emphasis on persons is the relevance of particularism rather than universalism. Take, for example, the instance of one U.S. executive in his new Latin American assignment near the border of another Latin country. On his day off, he wanted to do some sightseeing in the neighboring land, but was told by the border official that crossing into the other country would void his work permit, prohibit his reentry, violate several laws, and cause him all kinds of grief. After spending two hours discussing the matter, the North American was finally convinced about the legitimacy of the issues involved. He accepted the decision and was walking out of the border station when the same guard said to him, "But who is going to see you just walking over the bridge?" In the concrete action, the guard's behavior was determined less by the universalism of the law than by the particular person and instance.

When one company manager fails to secure the proper import permit or tariff reduction, but the other fellow gets the green light, the same principle is operating; the particular instance and individual are frequently more relevant than the abstraction and organization.

The impact of such misconceptions on performance is even clearer in the countless stories that North American businessmen tell about bribery. One U.S. metal goods manufacturer with operations throughout the area reports that, while local lawyers are essential for fixing policies within legal frameworks, it is the local manager's network of "dispatchers" and "fixers" who actually get the job done on a day-to-day basis. The fixer need not do anything illegal, but he does have to know how to expedite his task through a network of personal relations.

[The different perspectives on the individual can be seen clearly] when beginning a new job, U.S. businessmen have a tendency to ask, "What kind of an individual is that manager?" The question reflects a fundamental orientation—they work from the occupational category toward the entire person. [Latin Americans, however, generally] start with the whole person and move toward his work role. In other words, [they] reverse the above statement to ask, "What kind of a manager is that individual?"

The Group

Emphasis on a social unit with common characteristics and interests conflicts sharply with a doctrine of uniqueness and individuality. It is therefore common to hear U.S. executives on assignment in Latin America utter such generalizations as "Latin Americans don't work well in groups" and "A committee of eight ends up being eight committees of one." These kinds of comments reflect a basic difference in Latin and North American attitudes toward the importance of the group as a basic social unit.

In traditional society, the extended family is considered the most basic and stable unit of social organization. It is the locus for all economic, political, social, and religious life. It provides companionship, protection, and a common set of values with highly prescribed means of fulfilling them. This has been the historical condition in both colonial Latin America and frontier North America.

With increased technological and economic development, the North American family more and more has ceased to serve such a variety of functions. Education, religious instruction, recreational activities, and the means of securing a livelihood have all gradually passed to other groups outside of the family; and the small nuclear household of husband, wife, and two children has replaced the earlier extended family network.

In contrast, the extended family has maintained its strength in Latin culture, and, even in urban-industrial areas, it continues to serve many of the functions which have been taken over by nonfamily groups in U.S. culture. Given the strength of kin relationships, it is easy to see why Latin American enterprise represents an extension of the family system more often than a break with it. Regarding this, Paul Strassmann wrote:

The Latin American industrialist values an enterprise mainly insofar as it is a contribution to family interests, not as an achievement in itself. His first loyalty is to the family, for he has been brought up to expect continuity and stability only in his family.[3]

The intimate connection between Latin American family and business groups, which is considered natural and compatible, has two important consequences, neither of which are operative in the North American context. First, there is a reduction of the number of significant groups in which the individual operates; the work group for the Latin American businessman frequently *is* the family. Second, the individuality of the person is not threatened and his uniqueness is not compromised by his participation in such a group.

The North American, by contrast, tends to segment his relationships according to the role that he plays in each of several significant groups. Rather than differentiating roles, however, the Latin American maintains his emphasis on the total person by mediating more social dealings through the one (family) group. Others within the family group treat him in these same terms, whether they are talking about a decision to marry or to purchase new plant equipment. The family can best understand him as a totality, and it is through his relations with this one group that he can best realize himself as an individual.

In Latin America, the group thus tends to exist as a protective environment, a sanctuary in which the unique identity of each individual is valued, supported, and enhanced, rather than absorbed and assimilated into a single group identity. Common characteristics and interests are therefore insuffi-

[3]"The Industrialist," in *Continuity and Change in Latin America,* ed. J. Johnson (Stanford: Stanford University Press, 1964), p. 168.

cient though necessary bonds to keep the group together. But the appeal of membership will depend more on its guarantees of enhancing, rather than on transmuting or submerging, individuality to meet group goals.

Borrowing from a popular North American idiom, membership in a Latin American group is to be valued to the extent that it enables an individual to "do his own thing." Ideally, the group should exist to serve the interests of each member by enabling the individual to truly be himself. Thus when a group of Latin American students . . . got together to form an association, the first sentence of their charter stated that they "have come together to act as individuals in forming this association." The individual, above all, must not be compromised, and in the Latin American context the only way that a group can function effectively is by working through the individual members.

The human group functions quite differently in North America, where there is a basic belief in the efficacy of groups and cooperative spirit. Thus teamwork both becomes the basic integrating mechanism which keeps our complex society operating and provides the essential motor power for further growth. As such, we feel that people who do not work well in groups represent a threat to both the stability and progress of our society. The words we have long used to describe such individuals emphasize our attitude: they are "anti-social," "uncooperative," and "unfriendly," if not downright "unhealthy."

Understandably, when the emphasis was carried too far some 20 years or so ago, hyperbole turned into lampoon with themes such as the "joiner," the "other-directed," and the "organization man." In more recent years, however, the genius for association and the importance attached to how one gets along with people has again gained respectability, as reflected in our current themes of "organizational development" and "T-(training) groups."

T-groups have gained great prominence in North American organizational life, and so they may serve as a useful example of the way in which North Americans use the group in order to influence the individual.[4] T-groups have found their way into board rooms, training programs, and business school curricula. The ostensible purpose of a T-group is for each member of the group to attain a better understanding of how he "comes across" to others. Knowing self is achieved through understanding the group's reactions to oneself, as a group member. It is through his own interaction with the group that the individual is implicitly asked to make more cooperative personality adjustments.

Unlike group therapy, which carries the stigma of psychiatric treatment, the T-group participant is asked less to understand himself than to understand how others see him. Also, by removing the examination of personality and character from the realm of professional treatment for mental disorder, T-groups become something that "everyone" can benefit by. When the

---

[4]Chris Argyris. "T-Groups for Organizational Effectiveness," *Harvard Business Review* (March-April 1964), p. 60.

senior management of a company becomes "sold on T-groups," the social pressures to "go through one" become so great that promotion and even job security may depend on the outcome. Hesitation on the part of the novitiate is proof that he needs to be "T-grouped."

T-groups are reflective of the North American conception of the function of groups, and of how individuals function in them. In the T-group setting, the individual is asked to be himself so that others may then examine his unique qualities and comment on them constructively. T-groups are thus a cultivation of what remains implicit in most North American committees, associations, and other work groups. They are the internalization of human relations in North American managerial ideology. Added to the traditional belief that self-improvement is both possible and desirable is the extra twist that the group can help an individual to improve himself. The dislike of working in a North American-styled group, to a Latin, is that it will try to impose itself on him, rather than to protect him from such impositions.

Thus the Latin American businessman places greater emphasis on the individual in both his operating style and in his management policy. In contrast, the North American executive operating in Latin America is more likely to stress the importance of working as a group, yet this implies a very different vision of the group function. While a Latin American executive is more likely to address his energies to individuals in order to get his messages through to the group, his North American counterpart is inclined to use the group in order to get his messages through to individuals.

12

The Colombian Entrepreneur: Rationalism and Deviance

Aaron Lipman

The picture of the Bogotá entrepreneur . . . is one of dissimilarity to the general Colombian population. He is not necessarily from the group with the greatest wealth, and the . . . majority came from middle-class backgrounds in a country characterized by a comparatively small middle class. The business leaders surveyed are disproportionately represented by the foreign-born: 41 percent. As in the United States, their educational level is much higher than that of the general population. Also, as in the United States, they are city people out of proportion to the urban population of their country. In a relatively tradition-oriented society their values are rational and modern. All these factors lend support to the thesis that the Colombian entrepreneur can be regarded as the prototype of a social deviant or nonconformist. He is a bearer of exotic values and of behavior which is incongruent with the existing traditional social order. . . .

. . . The majority of our sample of business leaders shared an outstanding . . . trait which not only links them to each other more strongly, regardless of national origins, but establishes them as nonconformists in the contemporary Colombian culture. This trait was *rationalism*.

Rational action is described by Parsons in the following manner: "Men adapt themselves to the conditions in which they are placed and adapt means to their ends in such a way as to approach the most efficient manner of achieving these ends. And the relations of these means and conditions to the achievement of their ends are 'known' to be intrinsically verifiable by the methods of empirical science."[1] Traditionalism, on the other hand, refers to "the belief in the everyday routine as an inviolable norm of conduct . . . piety for what actually, allegedly, or presumably has always existed."[2] This means-ends relationship, then, is based on maximum efficiency in the rationalistic view, and on custom and habit in the traditionalistic one.

Under a system by traditional values economic roles are distributed on the basis of ascribed, rather than achieved, status; particularistic behavior dominates universalistic behavior; and economic roles are typically diffuse,

---

Adapted from Aaron Lipman, *The Colombian Entrepreneur in Bogota* (Coral Gables, Florida: University of Miami Press, 1969), pp. 45–52, with permission of the publisher.
[1]Talcott Parsons, *The Structure of Social Action* (Glencoe, Ill.: The Free Press, 1949), p. 19.
[2]Max Weber, *From Max Weber: Essays in Sociology,* ed. and trans. by H. H. Gerth and C. Wright Mills (New York: Oxford University Press, 1946), p. 296.

63

rather than specific.[3] Perhaps the distinction between rationality and tradition marks the differentiation between technologically and economically advanced countries and underdeveloped ones.[4]

Present-day economic development, under the leadership of the entrepreneur, attempts to transform social behavior toward an emphasis on modernity and rationality. "Increased personal mobility, expanding geographical frontiers, the development of market systems freed from particularistic relations, and rapid technological innovations, among other factors, necessitated greater freedom in the implementation of goals, an emancipation of goal-fulfillment from the specifications of a tradition that no longer proved adequate."[5] Economic roles become distributed on the basis of achieved status; universalistic behavior dominates; and economic roles are typically specific rather than diffuse. "Among the many complex factors that accompany the cultural and social change of long isolated peoples in our time, perhaps none is so important as that thoroughgoing alteration of tastes and values which prompts a material transformation of the society."[6]

This rationality has been recognized as having direct bearing on the productive process. For example, Moore states that "the probabilities of technical innovation vary . . . in time and space, and one major source of such variability is the unequal extensity and intensity of a rational orientation to the environment."[7] *This rational outlook was the one trait consistently shared by all the entrepreneurs in our sample, regardless of age, national origins, educational level, or social class background.* It would seem to be a basic component of the entrepreneurial orientation; it may be the very component which determines success or failure in the entrepreneurial role. For, since all the entrepreneurs in our sample were successful, and all of them manifested this orientation, perhaps this outlook is vital to successful entrepreneurship.

As one measure of rationality, a query was formulated listing the following factors: political relations, family ties, friends, luck, hard work, education, money, and honesty. The respondents were then asked to indicate how important each of these factors was in achieving success in Colombia. The following differentiation was made between traditional and rational values; political relations, family relations, friends, and luck were subsumed under *traditional values;* hard work, education, money, and honesty were considered *rational* values. . . . A significant statistical difference was found to exist between traditional values and modern values. All entrepreneurs scored a preference for rational values—money, hard work, education, and honesty. Colombian-born and foreign-born entrepreneurs who were 45

---

[3]Talcott Parsons and Neil J. Smelser, *Economy and Society* (Glencoe, Ill.: The Free Press, 1956).

[4]David C. McClelland, *The Achieving Society* (Princeton: Van Nostrand, 1961), p. 173.

[5]Seymour Lipset and Leo Lowenthal, *Culture and Social Character* (New York: The Free Press of Glencoe, 1961), p. 91.

[6]Justis M. Van Der Kroef, "The Acquisitive Urge: A Problem in Cultural Change," *Social Research* 28 (Spring 1968): p. 37.

[7]Wilbert E. Moore, *Social Change* (New York: Prentice-Hall, 1963), p. 79.

years and older scored a preference for modern values that was significant at the greater than 0.001 level with the Chi Square Test. . . . Native-born Colombians and foreign-born entrepreneurs younger than 45 years also showed a significant difference between traditional and modern values that was greater than the 0.01 level.

The older person is often thought as being more tradition-oriented than the younger person. This fact may well be true in certain areas but does not appear to be the case in the business realm. If anything, those over 45 years of age, whether native-born or foreign-born, were more rationally oriented than were those under 45 (those under 45 years of age were rationally oriented, but the difference between rational and traditional values was not as great as it appeared with those over 45). Apparently the longer the period of time spent in the role of entrepreneur, the greater the identification with that role becomes, and the more firmly embedded and internalized are the values and attitudes that go with this role.

Western Europeans are stereotypically considered more rationally oriented than South Americans. In comparison of the native-born and foreign-born entrepreneur, however, absolutely no difference was found in measuring these values. This fact adds support to the sociological dictum that a person's role strongly affects his attitudes and values. In this case the role of entrepreneur seems to have been much more important than nationality differences. A successful entrepreneur needs a rational orientation to achieve the maximum profit for his organization, regardless of his national origins. Perhaps, as was suggested earlier, rationality is an integral component of entrepreneurial success, and thus only the selectively rational Colombian nonconformist could survive the competition of the rational European in the international market.

It is equally possible that a high rationalism exists because of *selectivity;* i.e., only the rationally oriented enter the business world at all, or the business mortality rate decimates the numbers of traditionally oriented businessmen. Certainly one recognizes that, on the international market, a Colombian businessman must be rationally oriented to the competitive world market. In Colombia itself, however, a good deal of government protection of business still exists, offering a framework of traditionalism within which a businessman may still operate nationally. It is interesting to speculate whether even more rationality would be exhibited by the entrepreneur if government protection of business were terminated.

Another evidence of this rationality can be seen in the criteria for the selection of personnel. . . . Personnel [are] recruited rationally; family was reported as playing only a small part. (An interesting note is that those two entrepreneurs who mentioned family as important—both native Colombians —were working below their plant productive capacity, an implication, perhaps, that the traditional businessmen are weeded out when competing with the rational.) No difference was apparent between foreign-born or native-born in their first, second, or third choice of criteria in selecting personnel. The most frequent first choice was "educational preparation (28 percent), followed by personality (22 percent), work capacity (20 percent), and seniority (18 percent). The only significant difference that emerged in this area existed between university-trained entrepreneurs and those who had not gone to college. The former emphasized personality much more than seniority in selecting personnel; the latter stressed seniority rather than personality. The university-trained entrepreneur apparently feels that, in business, technical competence is assumed and that social competence is extremely important.

13 Innovation, Problem-Solving, and Social Change

Everett E. Hagen

One is led to the conclusion that the difference between Antiqueños and others lay not in the external conditions but in the people. And as soon as one considers this possibility, convincing evidence appears.

First, differences appear in psychological tests in which a number of Colombian business and community leaders courteously agreed to participate. The successful economic innovators of Antioquia in 1957 were so different in personality structure from a group of equally prominent community leaders elsewhere in Colombia who were interviewed and studied that they may be thought of as a different breed of men.

The group of entrepreneurs studied in Antioquia are a group of some 20 businessmen in Medellín whose careers stamp them as effective innovators, entrepreneurs of the Schumpeterian type. Not all are among the wealthiest men in the community; some are men in mid-career who started as poor men and whose wealth today, relative to Medellín innovators in general, is only moderate. The contrasting group is a group of community leaders in Popayán, a city with a present population of some 60,000 which was a cultural and political center in colonial days and the nineteenth century, and which now lives in the past, rather defensively spurning the "crass materialism" of such cities as Medellín.

One of the psychological instruments used in analyzing these men was the "thematic apperception test" or "TAT," in which simple pictures are shown to the individual one at a time. In the series usually used, one picture is of a young man and an older one; another of a young man and woman; another of a group of men around a table; and so on. Others are less commonplace. Concerning each, the respondent is asked to use his imagination to tell out of what situation the scene pictured arose, what the individuals in the pictures are thinking and feeling, and what the outcome of the situation will be.[1] In the process he tells much of his own attitudes toward life, for no interpretations of the pictures come to his mind so readily as ones which arise out of his own view of the world.

Some simple aspects of the differences between the two groups are as follows. The responses of the Medellín innovators typically embodied:

Adapted from Everett E. Hagen, *On the Theory of Social Change* (Homewood, Ill.: Dorsey Press, Inc., 1962), pp. 368–370, with permission of the publisher and the M.I.T. Center for International Studies.
[1]He is asked, that is, to tell what themes he perceives in each picture. Hence the name of the test.

67

a) a perception of a situation as a problem to be solved, b) awareness that to be solved a problem must be worked at (absence of any fantasy of magic success), c) confidence in their ability to solve it (though sometimes tension and anxiety are also present), d) a tendency to take the viewpoint of each individual in turn and analyze the situation as he might see it before suggesting an outcome, rather than to adopt a formula identification with any one type of character—with the old versus the young, the young versus the old, and so on.

. . . They manifested high need [for] autonomy, . . . achievement, and order; had a keen sense of the realities of a situation; saw the world as manageable with good judgment and hard work. The Popayán leaders gave intellectually more complex responses. They associated a picture with something in literature or the arts, philosophized about the ways of youth, were led into speculation about the course of history—but tended to see no problems in the situations pictured. Or, if they saw problems, they had formula solutions for them ("the old know best; he should listen to his father"), or visualized success without any suggestion that it would entail effort and pain. Frequently they gave the impression of running away from the possibility that they might be facing a problem, as though it made them uneasy; they veered away to some peripheral aspect of the picture. They found it easy to turn to fantasy or reverie not closely connected with reality. They showed low need [for] autonomy, achievement, and order; saw the world as not manageable, one's position as given. These differences of course were matters of degree; there was a range of response within each group with regard to various elements. If the responses were shuffled, without identification, a person examining them would not unerringly separate all of those from Medellín and all of those from Popayán correctly. Nevertheless, the net differences between the groups were striking.

It should be emphasized that what is portrayed is not a difference in personality between all Antioqueños and all Popayanese or other Colombians. The Antioqueños selected were those most apt to have creative personalities. So, however, were the Popayanese, for they were community leaders. There are undoubtedly creative individuals, some of whom have turned their talents to problems of technology and some elsewhere, in every region of Colombia. What is suggested, however, is that the incidence of creative personality is probably much higher among Antioqueños than elsewhere, and that this is an important cause of their greater entrepreneurial success.[2]

Not surprisingly, along with this creativity goes an attitude that any man worth his salt will get into business for himself—"get his own feet wet"—and make his way. A prominent Medellín executive stated that when he came home from college in the 1930s and took a salaried job with a large corporation his action in becoming merely a hired hand was looked upon

[2]An alternative explanation may be that creativity is randomly distributed everywhere but that more of the creative Antioqueños chose to exert their talents in problems of business and technology. There is no evidence in Colombian history, however, that in other regions an equal share of the population was creative in other fields.

with raised eyebrows. Many other individuals confirmed the prevalence of such an attitude.

There probably is also a regional difference in the attitude toward manual-technical work, though here my evidence is merely impressionistic. An industrialist in Bogotá, hiring 10 college graduates, put them at operating jobs in his factory for training. Within a year eight had resigned. Underlying the avowed reasons, he felt, were attitudes on the part of the individuals or their families that the jobs demeaned them. (The two who remained, interestingly, were of lower-income families.) "If they had been Antioqueños," he said, only half jokingly, "all of them, having learned the processes, would have resigned within the first year—in order to start their own competing businesses." And the head of an enterprise with operations in four centers in Colombia, himself neutral so far as regional affiliation is concerned, told me that the learning time for office and clerical detail is clearly somewhat shorter in Antioquia than elsewhere.

Finally, there is a feeling in Medellín that effective work is a social duty. I did not sense this feeling equally in Cali or Bogotá. It is felt by many Antioqueños that the man who fails to put his capital at work productively in business is somewhat lacking in the best qualities and is failing in a duty to the community. "He neither uses his axe nor lends it" is the Antioqueño phrase of disapproval. And, while the entrepreneurs in all regions are pious Catholics, both Dr. Schaw and I thought we sensed a difference in religious attitude. We thought we sensed a feeling in Medellín, not paralleled in the same degree elsewhere, of a personal involvement with the deity and a feeling that to achieve is a personal moral duty. In short, we thought we found among Antioqueños the "Puritan Ethic."

14

The Puerto Rican Businessman: Cultural Factors

Thomas C. Cochran

A number of cultural factors appear to differentiate norms of Puerto Rican entrepreneurial behavior from those of similarly placed men in the United States. Some of these come from the Puerto Ricans being closer in both time and space to a nonmobile agricultural society. The older entrepreneurs are only one generation removed from a traditional society that had preserved the aristocratic, family-centered attitudes of an earlier age. Recognition of social distinctions based on family connections and land-holdings, and reliance on the family as a source of authority and security, have been carried over into Puerto Rican industrial enterprise.

Besides being more immediate in its influence, the Puerto Rican agrarian heritage differs from that of the United States in being based on Spanish rather than on English or other northern European cultures, and in not being conditioned by a high rate of internal migration. As North Americans moved with bewildering rapidity from farm to farm, from farm to city, and from one city to another, the ties of the extended family loosened. The patriarchal father now far away ceased to be a source of help or authority and the individual was forced to rely on pragmatic relationships with relative strangers. In contrast, the size of Puerto Rico and character of settlement preserved family ties on the Island and made it easy for a father and his sons, and even his daughters, to enter into a business without sharply changing the traditional relationships.

Together with Cuba, Puerto Rico was intimately associated with Spain for almost a hundred years longer than other Latin American countries. San Juan was a center for Spanish officials of church and state. Most of the external trade was in the hands of merchants of Spanish origin who maintained close ties with families and friends in the mother country. In addition the native Indians of Puerto Rico had been too few and too weak to give the strong coloration to the later culture that occurred in most other parts of Latin America. In view of these facts and the well-recognized pressures of Spain for cultural conformity in her colonies, it is reasonable to presume that Puerto Rican culture of 1898 was more Spanish than that of Latin America in general.

But from the standpoint of this study it is not necessary to defend this proposition. According to the anthropologists who have most carefully

Adapted from Thomas C. Cochran, *The Puerto Rican Businessman: A Study in Social Change* (Philadelphia: University of Pennsylvania Press, 1959), pp. 149–154, with permission of the publisher.

71

studied these cultures, all Latin Americans tend to illustrate the attitudes of a Spanish type found among these Puerto Rican businessmen. Anthropologists also hold that Spanish characteristics have been preserved more among the upper classes than the lower. The seventy business leaders interviewed were generally from business or professional families, with a few from among the wealthy landowners, but none from the artisan or laboring classes.

The assertion that attitudes inferred from interviews in 1955 are typical of either Spanish or Latin American culture implicitly assumes one of the major hypotheses of the present study: that some of the most important traits of the hereditary culture of Puerto Rico have been only slightly modified by over half a century of relationships with the United States. This, in turn, appears to depend upon the depth and strength of some of the earlier culture patterns and limitations on the frequency and intensity of contacts with North Americans.

Certain Puerto Rican cultural traits that run counter to entrepreneurial efficiency appear to be so basically different from the traits of most North Americans that they are little affected by superficial contacts between people of the two cultures. One of the most important of these basic differences is in types of individualism. In cultures of Spanish origin individualism is manifested in a respect for the inner uniqueness of each person, and each seeks to preserve his "wholeness" against threats of being merged into or routinized by some outside group. He is averse to the restraints of teamwork or group discipline. A relatively low value is placed on external standards such as the opinion of others. Situations are appraised more on the basis of feeling than on external norms. In contrast North American individualism puts major emphasis on certain external rights and relationships within a group. There is no general fear of ceasing to be unique; in fact there is an obvious desire to conform to group attitudes.

The reciprocal respect for unique inner qualities felt in Puerto Rico has important corollaries affecting behavior. It implies high regard for the dignity of the individual regardless of his social status. Undoubtedly, this defensive attitude was increased by three hundred years of colonialism. The result has been a degree of, and respect for, *dignidad* in Puerto Rico that can interfere with business efficiency. It can hinder the disciplining of inefficient employees, diminish the willingness to take risks, and interfere with communication with strangers. This latter involves a further corollary of inner worth: it can only be appreciated through prolonged acquaintance and leisurely discussion. The salesman must really make friends with his customers. Few matters can be settled except by satisfactory interpersonal relations. This obviously interferes with the adoption of many of the impersonal practices that North Americans have thought necessary in order to do business rapidly and efficiently in large organizations.

A greater regard for social status may come in Puerto Rico either from the agrarian or Spanish heritage. It tends to make various types of prestige more desirable than money and thus defeats the operation of the "laws of the market." Another way of stating this is that, like the North American and Northern European people of earlier ages, the Puerto Ricans are not yet wholly capitalistic. This can lead to social satisfactions that lessen concentration on maximizing profit and to levels of conspicuous personal expenditure that drain away money needed for expansion or technological improvement. Social considerations may also lead to business deals based on improving family status and friendship rather than making the most money.

In addition to more preoccupation with social position than appears to be the case in the north, Latin Americans are widely held to appreciate poetry and abstract discussion more than technology and pragmatic action. While poetry and philosophy may not occupy much of the time of Puerto Rican entrepreneurs, they represent ideals of interest or tendencies of thought. To repeat the observation of Professor Gillin, "the word is valued more highly than the thing; the manipulation of symbols (as in argument) is more cultivated than the manipulation of natural forces and objects (as in mechanics). . . ."[1]

The difference between such attitudes and those of North America scarcely need illustration, but a statement from *The American Business Creed* shows the opposite position. "The whole ideology" of American business "is shaped by a certain distrust of abstract theory and systematic argument, of theorists and intellectuals. The creed prefers common sense to abstract argument, shirt sleeve economics to academic theories, the ordinary meanings of words to professional niceties of definition. . . ."[2]

The Spanish heritage conduces to a distrust of innovation that will change the economic or social order. Professor Castro noted the Spanish opposition to physical innovation, and Professor Gillin said that "ideas from abroad find more ready acceptance in the Latin American culture than artifacts and their associated techniques."[3] While North Americans have not always welcomed innovation that disturbed their own interests, their basic belief in the value of material progress has made physical innovation an essential element in the business creed. J. Frederick Dewhurst has written of North American management's receptive attitude "toward experimentation and change, toward the substitution of new products and methods for old ones, toward progress and expansion, even at the risk of disappointment and loss."[4]

These observations regarding the culture of entrepreneurs in Puerto Rico represent, of course, only certain selected traits from a highly complex whole. . . . These traits tend to differentiate Puerto Rican entrepreneurs from those of the mainland in being 1) more interested in inner worth and justification by standards of personal feeling than they are in the

---

[1]John Gillin, "Modern Latin American Culture," *Social Forces* 25 (March 1947): pp. 243–248.
[2]Francis X. Sutton et al., *The American Business Creed* (Cambridge: Harvard University Press, 1956), p. 347.
[3]Gillin, loc. cit.
[4]J. Frederick Dewhurst, "American Productivity: Cause and Effect," *Proceedings of the American Philosophical Society* 100 (October 1956): p. 438.

opinion of peer groups; 2) disinclined to sacrifice personal authority to group decisions; 3) disliking impersonal as opposed to personal arrangements and generally preferring family relations to those with outsiders; 4) inclined to prefer social prestige to money; and 5) somewhat aloof from and disinterested in science and technology.

15 Familism in Industry

Flavia Derossi

Two characteristic features of family-owned firms—the number of relatives holding executives positions and the fact that directors of the board appeared to be recruited exclusively among relatives—were used to set up an index of familism with which family businesses could be analysed.[1]

The findings from our sample of 322 firms indicate that familism is strongest in small-sized firms and in firms in the traditional sectors of activity. The percentage of familistic firms in the modern sectors is lower irrespective of their date of establishment [see Table 1]. One possible explanation of the persistence of the familistic pattern in companies founded after 1940 in the traditional branches might be that when the time came to invest in technologically advanced ventures, familistically inclined entrepreneurs did not do so, because the investment required was beyond their means, because they lacked technological knowledge or because of a lower propensity for risk-taking. One could also suggest, considering the situation from another angle, that entrepreneurs in the modern branches are forced to set up their business along more "efficient," that is, less "familistic" lines.

In both branches the degree of familism tends to diminish with increasing size [of capitalization see Table 2].

Familistic management, which has been previously described as suffering from short-sightedness in perspectives of time and social space, is also characterized by a lack of geographical vision, in the sense that their market perspective is limited: they export less and have a negative or indifferent attitude towards the opportunities offered by the Latin American Common Market.

It would seem that the persistence of traditional patterns in management endangers the survival of the company when this survival depends on the speed of adjustment to the required change.

The pitfall of family management seems to be essentially a lack of competence and vision. But an attempt can be observed on the part of owners of Mexican family businesses to widen their outlook while maintaining the essential character of their firms. A number of pressures exerted

Adapted from Flavia Derossi, *The Mexican Entrepreneur* (Paris: OECD Development Centre, 1971), pp. 97–101 and 108–115, with permission of the author and publisher.
[1]Familism was scored when, in companies with less than 12 shareholders, the board of directors consisted exclusively of relatives, and relatives were found working in the firm.

Table 15-1
Familism in Modern and Traditional Industries

		Traditional	Modern
Familistic		62%	46%
Nonfamilistic		38	54
	Total	100%	100%
	No.	(207)	(131)

on shareholders forces them to recognize that "access to managerial positions must increasingly be based on competence" as Harbison and Myers remark. Recruitment of executives on the basis of kinship is indeed ineffective and dangerous. But, the same writers continue: "And competence becomes ever more dependent upon specialized professional training and experience." However, training and experience can be acquired: "... The managerial class in the more advanced industrial societies inevitably tends to become an elite of competence, which means that education and training, rather than family ties or political connections, must inevitably become the principal avenue of access to its ranks."[2] Should one consider the social groups as having fixed and unchangeable characteristics, a replacement of the unskilled owners by the emerging group of professional managers would be inevitable. But social and human situations are not static: when a person or a group's vital interest are challenged, their capacity of adaptation to new requirements increases. Threatened with the danger of extinction or exile in a marginal social and economic position, the former "patrimonial elite" tries to transform itself into a "managerial elite." More rational business approaches which do not imply changes in ownership are tried out. This, at least, appears to be the case in Mexico, where several examples can be found of family-controlled firms managed according to modern organization methods, which seems to point out that the two conditions are not incompatible.

The best example is the case of the Monterrey industries in which the highest degree of efficiency reached in Mexico may be observed, although they are still family controlled. In Monterrey, like in other Mexican areas, the majority of firms are family-owned (61 percent), while the percentage participation of relatives in company management is the highest (80 percent against 48 percent) in the Federal District. Yet, the composition of the boards of directors shows that the participation of outsiders is widely accepted in the same proportion as in the other areas; only in 20 percent of the cases do we find boards exclusively composed of owners and relatives. In Monterrey boards meet more frequently which is a sign of decentralization in company decisions. More firms rely on debt financing in Monterrey than in the Federal District, their management thus being exposed to controls exerted by representatives of loan agencies or by new shareholders.

[2]Frederick Harbison and Charles A. Myers, *Management in the Industrial World* (New York: McGraw-Hill, 1959), pp. 79–80.

Table 15-2
Percentage of Familistic Firms in Modern and Traditional Branches,
According to Capitalization

	Traditional	Modern
Under 10 mill. pesos	71%*	69%
10–25 mill. pesos	62	48
Over 25 mill. pesos	48	31

*This means that 71% of the firms with under 10 mill. pesos capitalization, that are in traditional branches of industry, are family firms, and that 29% are nonfamily — Ed.

Another example stems out of the research itself. During the course of the first processing of the data, we came across 49 firms (almost 15 percent of the total sample) which had larger competitors at the time they began operations and which, as of 1968, had equalled or outgrown their competitors. This is not to say that the other companies in the sample had failed to expand. But the 49 showed cases of relative dramatic growth, since they had become the "giant" in their respective field of manufacturing. Among the characteristics of these growth firms one should expect to find indicators of modernization such as a total lack of familistic patterns. Instead, these growth companies were in majority family business (77 percent against the 39 percent of the remaining). Therefore, if it is true that ". . . the family firm must adapt to the requirements of modern industrial enterprise or ultimately face extinction . . . ,"[3] it is also true that the change can be achieved without drastically affecting ownership. It would be better to state that "the family basis of enterprise, as such, need not be weakened through conscious action but it does need to be modified—as it already has to a certain extent—through increasing specialization in the management and professional training of their executives, regardless of whether or not they come from the family."[4]

In semideveloped societies, the shareholder is the man who is in the best position (on account of the educational opportunities opened by his wealth) to get a good professional training. He may be motivated to acquire such skills by his growing awareness of the increasing complexity of industrial requirements. Also, in a country which is steadily modernizing, status in society does not so much derive from the possession of wealth as it does from its active management. This seems to be the case in Mexico where, at least in the business world, the rich man enjoys less status than the professional. A divorce between wealth and economic power has taken place, which has had the effect of forcing the establishment of a connection between ownership and management.

---

[3]Stanley M. Davis, "Entrepreneurial Succession," *Administrative Science Quarterly* (December 1968), pp. 402–416.
[4]A. Lauterbach, "Government and Development: Managerial Attitudes in Latin America," *Journal of Inter-American Studies* 7 (April 1965): p. 210.

Table 15-3
Motivation of Professional Choice According to Relationship to Enterprise

| | Relationship to Enterprise | | |
Motivation	Founders	Heirs	Managers
Inheritance or Monetary Reasons	32%	46%	41%
Professional Interest	12	5	28
Achievement	56	49	31
Total	100%	100%	100%
No.	(32)	(43)	(68)

For a concept of achievement, see D.C. McClelland, D.C. Arkinson, J.W. Clark, and R.A. Lowell, *The Achievement Motive,* (New York: Appleton-Century-Croft, 1953), and D.C. McClelland, *The Achieving Society,* (New York: Van Nostrand, 1961). Under this heading were collected reasons given for entering business activity such as: "personal satisfaction, feeling of challenge, risk-taking inclination, etc."

"Patrimonial management" and "professional management"[5] overlap in the case of owners having received formal management training which is often the case with heirs to a business. Here again we meet the coexistence of tradition—jobs are transmitted through inheritance—and modern patterns of organization. Both the founder of the business and his sons accept simultaneously the principle of inherited status and the necessity of acquiring specialized skills in order to be fit to hold the inherited position. In fact, who if not a member of the upper social strata, can afford to give his son the best possible training? Efforts in spreading education in developing countries have mainly concentrated on basic education, extending primary schooling to the masses. Even in a country like Mexico, where the constantly applied policy has been to expand education at all levels, there is a correlation between social class and higher education. However, it must be acknowledged that Mexico offers the example of a country where the vertical mobility from one class to another is quite remarkable. We find many businessmen coming from the middle class in Mexico. But it is also true that dramatic vertical mobility is not easily achieved. Even if we step three generations back we find very few managers of low class origin (workers and peasants).

Entrepreneurial status in Mexico is often ascribed, not achieved. People born in the entrepreneurial caste, subjected to psychological inducements of all types and pressed by family and social expectations, feel almost bound

[5]"Patrimonial management is business management in which ownership, major policy-making positions, and a significant proportion of other jobs in the hierarchy are held by members of an extended family. The effective decision-making authority is centered on the family . . . [while] professionally oriented management is enterprise management in which major policy-making positions and nearly all other positions in the hierarchy are held by persons on the basis of alleged or demonstrated technical competence rather than on relationship to a family." Harbison and Myers, op. cit., pp. 69 and 75–76.

Table 15-4
Education According to Relationship to Firm (Summary)

Education		Relationship to Firm		
		Founder	Heir	Hired Manager
No university degree		44%	21%	34%
University degree		56	79	66
	Total	100%	100%	100%
No technical degree		50%	26%	44%
Technical degree		50	74	56
	Total	100%	100%	100%
	No.	(32)	(43)	(68)

to enter the entrepreneurial career, irrespectively of their personal inclinations.

One might expect consequently that, being less motivated[6] this group would be less dynamic, and include people less fit for risk-taking ventures. But, counteracting this possible outcome, a high percentage of well-educated heirs, whose outlook is modern and who have been bred and trained to fulfill their responsibilities are, as a consequence, closer to professional managers than they are to self-made men, restor[ing] the balance.

Even when entrepreneurial status is ascribed because it is inherited, it also has to be achieved through formal specialized training, and personal ability and effort. The heirs range far above the other heads of businesses in higher education, and what is more in technical or business education [see Table 4].

The majority of heirs have studied abroad. Education and experience opportunities, more easily available to children of middle and upper classes of society, make them the best equipped to run business.

The degree of familism seems to increase in firms as heirs take over.[7] Practically, all of the firms headed by heirs (93 percent) have some relatives in the company (against 83 percent of firms headed by owners). It might seem inconsistent that young men educated in U.S. universities should not only perpetuate but reinforce a pattern of management which seems to be traditional and ineffective. It must be stressed that the influence

---

[6]Low achievement is not a characteristic particular to heirs; managers have even lower achievement motivation [see Table 3].

[7]A similar result was found in Spain by Juan Linz, "Fundadores, Herederos y Directores en la Empresa Espanola," *Revista Internacional de Sociologia,* Nos. 81, 82, 85 (1963 and 1964):

RELATIVES IN SPANISH ENTERPRISES ACCORDING TO RELATIONSHIP TO FIRM

Relationship to Firm	Relatives
Founders	66%
Heirs	78%
Managers	38%

of familism is so pervasive in Mexican firms that even managers are not spared.[8] Family and business links are not separated even when management becomes a profession. The result is that the degree of familism is not necessarily bound to diminish as firms mature. Time is not in this case an important variable.

Yet, familism can assume qualitatively different features. Because of the size of the Mexican family and the tendency of owners to bring all their sons into the firm, several brothers will fill the top positions.[9] These younger family members will differ, however, from the unskilled relatives who preceded them: they are given specialized training before being put to work. Moreover, while owner-founders tend to entrust executive position to their relatives, both heirs and managers tend to bar them from operative activities and confine them to the board. In fact, the first sign showing that the complexity of industry has been acknowledged is the recognition of the value of technical skill: an engineer has a better claim to the position of production manager than a cousin. Awareness of financial skill comes later. A group of unexperienced shareholders sitting on a board are in a position to block innovative ventures, alleging that they would require large investments, which might be risky or reduce profits, at least temporarily. The reticence towards debt financing by the most part of Mexican business illustrates this tendency.

The real drawback of family businesses, therefore, derives not so much from lack of skill on the part of its management, but on conservative attitudes adopted towards financial risks, especially when a loss of complete family control is involved.

Managers can be recruited among the stock of relatives, or hired; in the latter case, they are, to a certain extent, kept in control by the owners. New shareholders have a position which ranks higher than that of subordinates; yet, to a certain extent, they can be kept in a position of minority, at least as long as the firm is able to survive without massive investment. When this becomes necessary, and when banks step in, changes in financial structure are followed by changes in the style of top management. Such seems to have been the case at the beginning of the century in the U.S. According to Daniel Bell, the breakup of family capitalism occurred "when American industry, having overextended itself, underwent a succession of crises. Bankers, with their control of the zone and credit market, stepped in and reorganized and took control of many of the country's leading enterprises. . . . By installing professional managers—with no proprietary stakes themselves in the enterprise, unable therefore to pass along their power automatically to their sons and accountable to outside controllers—the

---

[8]It must be taken into account that 43 percent of managers hold shares in the company; their behavior tends therefore to be somewhat similar to that of the owners.

[9]A question about professions envisaged for sons had to be discarded during the pretesting of the questionnaire, because it proved time-consuming. The number of children often being 7–8, the answer was taking several minutes of the available interview time.

bankers effected a radical separation of property and family."[10] "Financial capitalism" replaced "family capitalism."

The Mexican situation appears, in this respect, in a transitory stage, or better, as a borderline case, in which the two opposite tendencies are identifiable.

On the one side, it is unquestionable that the role played by private banks in Mexican industrial development is of primary importance. Additional capital to finance expansion can be supplied by banks more easily than by private individuals (Mexicans are considered as being reluctant investors on the stock exchange—bonds being preferred to shares.) Moreover, in view of the larger amount of capital now required for industrial development, banks are more suitable sources of financing. A comparison of past and present sources of financing of the companies in our sample shows that internal financing as well as the habit of calling on shareholders, when additional capital is needed, are practices which are becoming less frequent. Debt financing, although not as yet widely practiced, is gaining acceptance [see Table 5].

Table 15-5
Past and Present – Main Source of Financing

Mode of Financing		Past	Present
Internal Financing		64%	57%
Equity Financing – Increasing Capital Contributions of Original Shareholders		15	4
– Flotation of New Issues to Public		9	4
Debt Financing		12	35
	Total	100%	100%
	No.	(136)	(138)

On the other hand, other factors must be taken into account: capital requirements are fundamental at the stage of rapid growth of the firms, when industries have to innovate and expand rapidly, in order to make up for a late start; but, once expansion has reached its cruising speed, firms might hope to carry on by relying on internal financing, so as to limit their dependence on banks.[11] In theory at least, a well-organized and modernly

[10]Daniel Bell, *The End of Ideology* (Glencoe, Ill.: The Free Press, 1960), p. 40.
[11]Daniel Bell mentions that the power of bankers "declined as the managers became able, especially in the last twenty years, to detach themselves from financial control. . . . The tremendous growth of American corporations enabled them to finance their expansion from their own profits rather than by borrowing on the money market," ibid., p. 41.

equipped firm, operating in a protected market, where labor costs are low and prices high, can hope to be profitable enough to be able to rely mainly on self-financing.[12]

Moreover, we have to consider the uncommon vitality of the family business—we have already mentioned that in Monterrey certain industrial groups have created their own "financieras," in order to draw capital from all over the country—and the close links joining the two communities, that of the industrialists and that of the bankers. In general, the importance of personal relationships in business dealings speak in favor of the hypothesis that family enterprises, of the modern rational type, will live on in Mexico.

Familism as a traditional value appears to fulfill, in modern Mexican enterprises, a function which is similar to that of traditional values in the whole society in that it mediates change and strengthens new structures.

---

[12]Many industrialists will oppose this view, pointing out that their market is limited and excludes therefore the possibility of mass production, while the low productivity of labor in Mexico raises overall costs.

Part Two

The Economics of Enterprise and the Worker's Situation

Introduction to Part Two

This part will focus on the utilization of human resources for the production of goods and services. The major theme will be the distinctness of economic concerns between management and labor. Sometimes these concerns have been antagonistic and sometimes only different. Some antagonisms are the result of disputes over salaries and types of remuneration, introduction of new technologies, rights of workers to organize, and the nature of work conditions. Other issues that are simply different, rather than antagonistic, include: for managers, access to capital, inflation, profit, competition with foreign enterprise, and government support for private-sector development; for workers, conditions relating to job satisfaction, relations with fellow employees, relations with foremen and supervisors, and the fact of simply having a job.

This is not to say that conditions which concern one group are irrelevant to the other group. However, since workers and managers must deal with substantially different social situations in their daily routines, their economic interests are distinct though interrelated and sometimes become antagonistic. From the managerial point of view, workers comprise one element in the economics of the firm. In a worker-surplus economy, as is normally the case in Latin America, they are rarely as primary a concern as scarcer resources such as capital, technology, raw materials and skilled manpower. From the point of view of the worker, management's control over the workplace is a primary concern; jobs are scarce in Latin America, high-paying jobs are even scarcer.

From the perspective of economic development, both workers and managers play vital roles. However, their contributions are somewhat indirect and ambiguous because it is a third group—government economic planners—who are mainly concerned with national development. Managers are more concerned with consolidating power and making quick profits, yet they must be influenced to plan, reinvest, and expand if development is to proceed. Workers are most concerned with holding a job and bringing home a decent wage, yet they must also be efficient producers and must balance consumption and savings.

Slawinski's historical overview of Latin America's economic structure and Clague's analysis of the determinants of efficiency in manufacturing introduce us to the economic struggles of workers and managers. When their articles are considered with demographic and productivity statistics for all of Latin America they reveal a distressing trend. Increases in productivity are barely keeping pace with increases in employment; and both employment and productivity are being pressured by population growth. It appears that capital intensive industrialization is not able to create enough jobs to absorb both natural population growth and rural-urban migration. The result is increased employment, in less productive areas such as construction and services, and corresponding increases in unemployment and under-employment. Until such trends are reversed, the process of modernization will continue to exclude the 40 percent of Latin America's population who constitute the rural and urban marginal poor.[1]

The selections that concentrate on the labor situation cover most of the problems which directly confront the worker on the job. Jose Luis Reyna's discussion of occupational mobility in Mexico shows how the nature of worker experiences and the structure of a developing nation's economy change together. Guillermo Briones reveals an inherent vulnerability of Latin American labor by showing that workers are simultaneously under-trained and overcommitted to their scarce jobs.[2] David Chaplin reports on the variety of criteria used for recruiting labor and comments on the aspects of work which create a modern labor force.

The monetary rewards of work are discussed by Goodman, Mallet, and Mesa-Lago. Goodman shows that pay, like employment, is not equally distributed across the work force, but that some groups of workers are more able to look after their interests than others. Mallet explains the workings of Latin America's complex social security arrangements and shows how it too contributes to income inequality and social stratification within the Latin American work force. Camelo Mesa-Lago explains the mechanics of unpaid labor in Cuba and attempts to evaluate its political and economic effects.

Conditions at the workplace are examined by Chaplin and Goodman. Chaplin shows how labor-management conflicts arise out of the work situation, even when the labor force is overcommitted, and Goodman shows that the different conditions imposed by labor-scarce (the United States) and labor-surplus (Chile) economies cause objectively similar work conditions to have dissimilar effects on workers' ability to feel secure and act autonomously on the job.

The tradeoff between increasing worker productivity and decreasing unemployment is another theme touched on in most of the above selections. The advanced technology of capital-intensive investment may increase labor productivity, but it may also increase unemployment by forcing out less efficient labor-intensive firms, and will certainly concentrate income in the hands of the fortunate few who manage and work the new machines. No easy solution has appeared for this dilemma, and it appears that Latin American nations can only compete in world markets when special combinations of cheap labor, abundant resources, and technical experience give them a comparative ad-

---

[1]For a discussion of productivity, employment and economic development see "Structural Changes in Employment within the Context of Latin American Economic Development," *Economic Bulletin for Latin America* 10 (October 1965): pp. 163–187.

[2]The discussion of the commitment of the labor force in industrialization was sparked by Wilbert Moore and Arnold Feldman's *Labor Commitment and Social Change in Developing Areas* (New York: Social Science Research Council, 1960). Although Moore and Feldman indicated that training and committing workers to industrial routines would be problematic, evidence from Latin America supplied by Briones and others show that workers will go to great lengths to hold on to scarce industrial jobs. They are "overcommitted."

vantage.[3] Both the strength of international competition and the small size of their own domestic markets make it appear that Latin American industrialization will be a slow process and steady employment and decent pay will continue to be scarce commodities for Latin American workers.

The composition of the Latin American work force is another area for examination. Age, sex, and migratory status are three characteristics which change during the course of modernization. Latin America's population explosion is forcing greater numbers of underage workers (usually under age 14) onto the labor market because the large numbers of children and adolescents constitute a heavy burden for the economically active population. This happens despite the fact that educational facilities have been expanding at record rates in Latin America since the 1950s. This trend is mostly noticeable in rural areas but is also evident in cities.[4]

Female participation also changes during industrialization. Although legal restrictions on pay, hours, and maternity-leave usually affect the market position of women, their participation pattern is somewhat predictable. Private domestic service must be separated from other types of female employment. When this is done it can be shown that domestic service employs fewer women as nations modernize and other types of work employ greater numbers of women.[5]

A major reason for the surplus of labor during industrialization is the massive rate of rural-urban migration. Agricultural life becomes less attractive as the man/land ratio increases and as improved communications tell of the excitement of city life. However, despite yearly fluctuations in unemployment in Latin America, this migration appears to be a constant process which does not expand and contract with job opportunities. On the individual level it appears that the major force pulling workers to the city is not job opportunities, but the number and strength of kin-mediated ties to urban situations. Once in the cities, migrants rapidly adapt to urban consumption patterns and become part of the commercialized urban world which seeks industrial jobs and wages. This and the loss of the traditional patron's protection makes migrants willing, docile and plentiful workers.[6]

The nature of Latin American work conditions is a theme which is of daily importance for the worker. The Williams, Whyte and Green article in Part One showed that authority is viewed differently by Peruvian and American workers. Smaller places of

---

[3]For a comparison of the efficiency of United States and Argentine forms see Carlos F. Diaz, "Industrialization and Labor Productivity Differentials," *The Review of Economics and Statistics* (May 1965), pp. 207–214.

[4]See U.S. Bureau of Labor Statistics, "Employment of Children in Latin America," *Labor Developments Abroad* (March 1965).

[5]For an excellent discussion of the role of female employment in modernization, see Andrew Collver and Eleanor Langlois, "The Female Labor Force in Metropolitan Areas," *Economic Development and Cultural Change* (July 1962).

[6]Migration and employment are discussed in Bruce Herrick *Urban Migration and Economic Development in Chile,* (Cambridge: M.I.T. Press, 1965); Frank W. Young and Ruth C. Young, "Individual Commitment to Industrialization in Rural Mexico," *American Journal of Sociology* (January 1966); and Guillermo Briones, "Mobilidad Ocupacional y Mercado de Trabajo en el Peru," *America Latina* (July 1963).

work, lower wages, more primitive machines, and less complex divisions of labor are also part of the world of Latin American workers. However, primitive work arrangements contribute to the low worker productivity, discussed above, and such primitive arrangements also make it difficult for workers to feel the job security or acquire the personal habits needed to adopt modern behaviors. The constant memory and fear of unemployment also redefines the meaning of work as first and foremost *staying employed,* and only secondarily being productive.[7] An undercurrent of worker alienation also runs through much of the literature, ranging from the theme of absolute personal estrangement from work, to more common dissatisfaction with specific work conditions, to systematic resistance to the introduction of technological change.[8] The problem of finding employment, however, always supersedes the problem of alienation from work.

The above helps make clear why labor ranks low in the list of economic concerns for the Latin American businessman. Managerial economics is only peripherally concerned with the economic conditions of workers. Instead, managerial preoccupations involve concern with profits, inflation, competition—particularly from foreign investors—market size, efficiency and economic planning.

Profits often get the most attention from businessmen and from those who study businessmen, in North America as well as in Latin America. Perhaps the most concise and damaging statement about Latin business' profit orientation is made by economist Albert Lauterbach who concludes that "the predominant aim . . . is very high profit without much concern for its maximization." To fully understand this means relating the profit picture to all of the other economic factors listed above. As Brandenburg points out, for example, what does a 60 percent profit mean in a country with an annual inflation of over 50 percent? Lauterbach also relates the concern with profits to the perception of high risk in committing capital to nonliquid investment in industry.

The relation of risk to profits is further explored in the paper by Chilean financial analyst, Edgardo Jurgensen. Jurgensen measures businessmen's attitudes towards risk, and finds that those who are the more risk averse tend to operate in more diverse markets on the assumption that this will increase the certainty of their profit picture.

Businessmen in North America are constantly aware of the effect of com-

---

[7]These points are discussed in John B. Knox, "Absenteeism and Turnover in an Argentine Factory," *American Sociological Review* (June 1961); Louis Wolf Goodman, "Blue Collar Work and Modernization" (Ph.D. Dissertation, Northwestern University, 1970); Jack Harewood, "Overpopulation and Underemployment in the British West Indies," *International Labor Review* (August 1960); Wilbert Moore and Arnold Feldman, *Labor Commitment and Social Change in Developing Areas,* op. cit.; and Peter Gregory, *Industrial Wages in Chile* (Ithaca, N.Y.: Cornell University Press, 1967).

[8]Articles discussing these themes include Maurice Zeitlin, "Alienation and Revolution," *Social Forces* (December 1966); William Form, "Occupational and Social Integration of Automobile Workers in Four Countries," *International Journal of Comparative Sociology* (March 1969); and Walter Phillips, "Technological Levels and Labor Resistance to Change in the Course of Modernization," *Economic Development and Cultural Change* (March 1963).

petitors on their profit picture, and they constantly seek to make their plants and administration more and more efficient. The Latin businessman is literally concerned about the same competition: that is to say, the large and successful local firms find their stiffest competition in the foreign-based multinational enterprises rather than in the multitude of mom-and-pop family firms. Examining the unsuccessful response of Brazilian entrepreneurs to competition from international firms, sociologist Peter Evans rejects the notion that the cause of the inefficiencies are rooted in Latin cultural traditions. He argues, instead, that the more successful managers have responded quite rationally to competitive pressures in uncertain environments, and that their weakened position in local industries is due to more universal economic and organizational exigencies. The absorption of small firms into larger corporate bodies is an historical process in both North and Latin America, says Evans, only in Latin America the larger corporations are foreign. His thesis provides a strong antidote to those of the "culturist" school who see inefficiencies and uncompetitiveness as endemic in the values and traditions of the society. At the same time, it will engender serious resistance on the part of those who may mistakenly read it as an acceptance of, and apologia for, the inevitable.

Foreign investment and foreign trade are also examined by Harry Wright, who concentrates on the Mexican market. Here he details the restrictions placed on the entry of foreign enterprise and on the government policies of Mexicanizing industrialization. A critical problem from Wright's point of view is not uncontrolled competition from foreign investment, but rather the limitations on growth of the local economy because of the limited market size for domestic manufactures. Here he describes Mexico's attempt to develop an export market for their manufactured goods, and the obstacles they encounter in terms of high production costs and too many producers.

One other topic that requires consideration when discussing the economics of enterprise and the industrial growth of Latin America is the area of economic planning. Here, the quality and extent of planning that goes on within private enterprise is largely determined by the stability and interest of the various governments. Mexico's long history of political and monetary stability, and the government's heavy involvement in *planeamiento,* have helped establish both short- and long-term planning orientations among managers in both the public and private sectors. Brazil, the area's other economic heavyweight, presents a very different picture. Political and monetary instability there have inhibited the serious development of short-term planning and of planning within individual organizations. Economic and business planning here tends to be more of the grand design variety, viz. the planning and building of Brazilia and the cross-Amazonian highway. As the popular saying has it, "In Brazil you can plan twenty years ahead, but not one year ahead."

From the above discussion, and as the reader turns to the selections in this part of the book, it will be seen that the distinctness of economic concerns between management and labor stands out as a dominant theme.

16 The Determinants of Efficiency in Manufacturing Industries in an Underdeveloped Country

Christopher Clague

In any poor country which has begun the process of development there will exist a modern manufacturing sector, which we may define as the collection of factories using modern machinery and employing at least ten workers. As is well known, these factories experience widely varying degrees of success in transferring or adapting advanced techniques to their own environment, and consequently the levels of efficiency achieved range from very high to very low.

The meaning of efficiency as used in this paper can be explained as follows: Suppose a given industry (say, cement) is being compared in two countries (A and B). To say that country A's efficiency in cement is half that of country B (or, alternatively, that A's relative efficiency in cement is 50 percent) is to say that, if A's workers were endowed with as much capital per man as B's workers, and if the factories in A were expanded or contracted until their average size was equal to that of B's factories, then output per worker would be half as large in A as in B.

There are many reasons why efficiency in manufacturing industries tends to be lower in underdeveloped than in developed countries. The main factors can be divided into a) management quality, b) worker skills, and c) factors external to the firm, such as the reliability and quality of input supply and the adequacy of transportation and communications facilities. The importance of these factors would be expected to vary considerably among industries. There might be certain kinds of processes that managers and workers in underdeveloped countries can perform quite well, and certain industries are less sensitive to the external environment than others. We would also expect efficiency to be affected by such factors as the rate of tariff protection and degree of internal competition.

It would be useful for policy-makers to know what products can be produced efficiently in underdeveloped countries, for efficiency is related to (although not synonymous with) cost and the ability to predict costs would be helpful in deciding which imported products to manufacture domestically and which products might be potential export items. In view of the current interest in promoting manufactured exports from underdeveloped countries, the topic takes on added interest.

Furthermore, knowledge of efficiency levels achieved in poor and rich countries in different products and under different conditions is likely to give

Adapted from *Economic Development and Cultural Change* 18 (January 1970): pp. 188–205. Copyright © 1970 by the University of Chicago Press. Used with permission.

insight into how to raise the performance in underdeveloped countries. Probably some of the factors influencing efficiency—such as the degree of protection from imports, the degree of internal competition, and the resistance of labor unions to technical change—may be under policy control, at least indirectly.

The present study attempts to throw some light on these questions by comparing the level of efficiency in eleven manufacturing industries in Peru and the United States. The research was carried out in such a way as to eliminate as far as possible the effects on efficiency of factors external to the factory.

The paper is divided into three parts. Part I contains a description of the methodology employed in the comparison of efficiency levels in the two countries. Parts II and III explore alternative hypotheses about the relation between relative efficiency and the type of technology required by different industries.

I.   Peruvian Relative Efficiency

A detailed exposition of the statistical procedure used to calculate Peruvian relative efficiency has been published elsewhere.[1] Here we shall give an abbreviated explanation designed to clarify the concept of relative efficiency. Assuming for the moment that there are no economies of scale, let us define: L = labor input per unit of output; K = capital input per unit of output; 1 refers to Peru, 2 refers to the United States; Q = Peruvian relative efficiency.

We define the Peruvian relative labor productivity as the Peruvian output per man divided by the American output per man. It can be seen that this is equal to L_2/L_1, or the American labor requirement per unit of output divided by the Peruvian. Treating capital in the same way, we may write: L_2/L_1 = Peruvian relative labor productivity; K_2/K_1 = Peruvian relative capital productivity. Peruvian relative efficiency, Q, can be thought of as a weighted average of Peruvian relative labor productivity and Peruvian relative capital productivity: $Q = a(L_2/L_1) + (1 - a) (K_2/K_1)$, where the weights a and $(1 - a)$ depend on the capital intensity of the productive process. That is, the higher the capital-labor ratio in both countries (or the average of the two countries), the greater is $(1 - a)$.

The actual calculation of a cannot be explained in a few words, and we shall not attempt it. The reader can see in Table 1 that Q lies between (L_2/L_1) and (K_2/K_1) and is closer to (L_2/L_1) the greater the labor intensity of the industry.

Some additional features of the procedure must be mentioned. Labor productivity was calculated using data for production workers only. Managerial personnel were excluded, largely because it was impossible to separate them from personnel in the sales and purchasing departments, and

[1]C. Clague, "An International Comparison of Industrial Efficiency: Peru and the United States," *Review of Economics and Statistics* 49 (November 1967): pp. 487–493.

inclusion of the entire labor force connected with the factory would have raised serious problems of the comparability of the tasks performed in the two countries.

The capital referred to above is the value of plant and equipment measured at U.S. prices. Output was measured in physical units in each country. For most of the industries studied, it could reasonably be assumed that the product in the two countries was of the same quality. Adjustments for quality differences, however, had to be made in shirts, shoes, and leather.

Some of the differences between the two countries in labor and capital productivity are due to differences in factory size. Regressions were run with U.S. data of labor productivity on factory employment. The coefficients derived from these regressions were used to "correct" the Peruvian productivity figures, that is, to show what Peruvian relative labor and capital productivity would be if the Peruvian factories were of the same size as the U.S. factories. The figures appearing in Table 1 incorporate the adjustment for factory size.

Table 16-1
Peruvian Relative Productivity and Efficiency

Industry	(L_2/L_1)	(K_2/K_1)	$(K/L)_1$	$(K/L)_2$	Q
Men's dress shirts	43.07	25.09	1,811	1,055	40.54
Men's leather shoes	51.77	64.71	2,104	2,630	53.41
Hosiery	29.47	31.32	4,028	4,281	30.07
Leather tanning	27.92	55.72	3,469	6,923	33.16
Cotton textiles	22.75	47.47	4,145	8,649	28.55
Glass containers	28.28	38.95	7,148	9,845	30.96
Tires	51.32	69.22	11,820	15,944	58.14
Raw cane sugar	81.17	74.97	23,112	21,086	80.74
Industrial chemicals	78.29	122.75	14,893	23,350	100.80
Wheat flour	59.43	83.00	17,544	24,503	71.35
Cement	30.03	137.53	20,376	93,333	87.44

Note – L_2/L_1, K_2/K_1, Q = see text; $(K/L)_1$ = Peruvian capital-labor ratio; $(K/L)_2$ = American capital-labor ratio.

I intended to eliminate from the comparison of the two countries all of the elements influencing productivity except the quality of management and direct labor. It was not possible, however, to eliminate entirely the influence of the external environment on the plants studied. In general, procurement is more difficult in Peru because 1) many materials and spare parts have to be imported, and 2) local suppliers are probably less reliable than those in the United States. Furthermore, there are probably delays in getting machines repaired. These difficulties and delays provide Peruvian factories with an incentive to hire more administrative personnel per production worker than would be necessary in the United States. Since administrative personnel were not included in the measured labor input, no bias in our procedure results from this practice. But even with more administrators, Peruvian factories probably suffer more externally caused interruptions in the production process than do American factories. In a number of plants where I collected information, the difficulties in procurement could be eliminated by calculating productivity for a "normal month" when the plant was operating at full capacity. In other cases, however, annual figures were employed, and although as far as possible full-capacity years were selected, there may have been some loss of production due to procurement and repair problems.[2]

Another possible extraneous factor is that machinery probably tends to be of more ancient vintage in Peru than in the United States. . . . To assess the likely importance of this factor, the average age of machinery in the two countries was calculated from investment series and equipment lives. The differences in average are quite small; the average difference for the ten industries for which data are available is only 1.8 years. (The reason the differences are so small is that Peruvian investment has been growing much more rapidly than American investment.)

Our measure of relative efficiency is thus clouded by ambiguity due to the age of equipment and the effects of external environment as well as possible errors in the adjustments for product quality and economies of scale. Since we are concerned with the differences among industries, however, we can take comfort in the fact that none of the differences among the groups of industries in which we are interested appear to be explained by biases in our procedure.

The most striking feature of the data is the strong correlation between capital intensity (in either country) and Peruvian relative efficiency. This result parallels the findings of Arrow et al. in a comparison of Japan and the United States and those of Diaz-Alejandro in a comparison of labor productivity in Argentina and the United States.[3] In Parts II and III we shall discuss alternative explanations for this phenomenon.

II. Latitudes and Relative Efficiency

Hirschman has advanced the hypothesis that underdeveloped countries tend to perform better in tasks that have little latitude for poor performance,

---

[2]In the face of external uncertainties, factories in underdeveloped countries tend to keep very large inventories of materials and spare parts. (For a dramatic example of this phenomenon, see the inventory-output ratios of India, The Netherlands, and the United States listed in G. K. Boon, *Economic Choice of Human and Physical Factors in Production* [Amsterdam: North Holland Publishing Co., 1964], pp. 33–34.) Since we include only fixed capital in our capital input, measured relative efficiency is unaffected by the inventory-output ratio.

[3]K. J. Arrow et al., "Capital-Labor Substitution and Economic Efficiency," *Review of Economics and Statistics* 45 (August 1961): pp. 225–250; Carlos Diaz-Alejandro, "Industrialization and Labor Productivity Differentials," *Review of Economics and Statistics* 47 (May 1965): pp. 207–214.

that is, tasks in which the consequences of poor performance are disastrous.[4] His example of the comparative performance of poor countries in airplanes and highways is well known to students of economic development. Following Hirschman, we shall distinguish four types of latitudes, and then we shall attempt to determine to what extent each of our eleven industries possesses these latitudes. The four types of latitudes are:

1. Latitude with respect to the pace of operations. The speed of some activities can be determined by setting the speed of the machine—the operative does something when the machine requires it. In contrast to these machine-paced activities, there are operator-paced tasks in which the operator can work rapidly or slowly according to his taste or mood.

In studying the actual operations performed in factories, I have found it useful to make a distinction between two types of operator-paced activities. These are routine operations, such as sweeping floors, handling materials, and putting objects in boxes or sacks, in which the speed of the work is under the control of the worker, but which require little or no skill. Then there are what I call dexterity operations, such as using a sewing machine, cutting materials to the right size and shape, accurately mixing batches of materials (in chemical, glass, and rubber factories), and operating a crane or a forklift truck, in which the speed of the operation and the care with which it is performed can be expected to vary a great deal among workers. A priori, one would expect workers in underdeveloped countries to have more trouble with dexterity operations than with either routine or machine-paced tasks.

2. Latitude with respect to quality of workmanship. In articles such as shirts, shoes, and leather goods, high-quality workmanship is required to turn out high-quality products, but if the workmanship is mediocre the products can still be sold. These industries possess latitude with respect to the quality of workmanship. In other industries (e.g., glass, tires, chemicals, and cement), high-quality workmanship is required in the mixing of ingredients, and failure to mix the ingredients accurately leads to disaster. Here we say there is little latitude for poor-quality workmanship. Finally, there are many activities (which would be classified usually as routine or machine-paced according to the pace-of-operations criterion) in which high-quality workmanship is totally unnecessary. We would expect the performance in poor countries to be relatively worse in tasks in which high-quality workmanship is desirable but not essential than in tasks in which craftsmanship is either vital or superfluous.

3. Latitude with respect to work schedules. In certain industries the intermediate products are stored at numerous points in the production process. If operations go slowly in one part of the factory for some reason (e.g., falling behind by the workers, failure of management to distribute the necessary materials, mechanical breakdown), the slowdown spreads

---

[4]Albert O. Hirschman, *The Strategy of Economic Development* (New Haven, Conn.: Yale University Press, 1958), chap. 8.

only gradually to the rest of the factory, for the "successor departments" can work for a time on the inventories of the products already turned out by the process where the trouble lies, and the supplying departments can continue to stockpile inputs to the problem process. In other industries, often called "continuous process" industries, a breakdown in one department rapidly paralyzes the plant, since intermediate products cannot be stored. In general, the greater the number of points in the factory at which intermediate products are stored, the greater the latitude with respect to work schedules. Our hypothesis is that relative efficiency, in an underdeveloped country will be lower, other things equal, the greater the latitude with respect to work schedules.

4. Latitude with respect to maintenance. The consequences of neglecting maintenance are much more serious in some industries than in others. The classification of industries according to this criterion probably overlaps considerably with that associated with latitude 3, for the consequences of a mechanical breakdown are more serious in a process in which intermediate products cannot be stored. The consequences of neglecting maintenance also depend on the type of machinery employed as well as on other factors; but I have found no way of measuring the latitude with respect to maintenance, and it will not be further considered.

The industries can be classified according to the types of latitudes they possess, and the relationship between latitudes and relative efficiency can then be examined. On the first criterion, the latitude with respect to the pace of operations, I have employed the *Occupational Wage Surveys* of the U.S. Department of Labor to separate the activities performed in American factories into dexterity, routine, and machine-paced operations. The percentage of production workers engaged in each type is given in Table 2. (Maintenance operations are also given.) A fairly complete list of the occupations assigned by the author to each category is given in Table 3.

Attention should be drawn to the classification of certain occupations. Power-truck operators were classified as dexterity workers, hand truckers as routine. Inspectors in textiles and clothing were placed in the dexterity category (the classification thus includes dexterity of hand or eye), but inspection in glass was regarded as simple enough to be classified routine. Packaging the product was normally considered a routine occupation, but workers called boxers in the clothing industries generally spend more of their time engaged in inspecting, trimming, mending, or pressing than in actual boxing and therefore were classified as dexterity workers. It should also be noted that in the absence of information on tire factories the occupational breakdown of the mechanical rubber goods industry was employed. The share of dexterity operations in the tire industry would probably be substantially smaller than the 27 percent shown for the mechanical rubber goods industry in Table 2.

Table 2 shows that the industries fall rather neatly into two groups with respect to the role of dexterity and machine-paced occupations. In the first group of four industries—shirts, shoes, hosiery, and leather—the share of dexterity occupations is at least twice that of machine-paced occupations.

Table 16–2
Industries Classified by Latitudes

| Industry | Percentage of Workers in Each Category | | | | | Latitude on Work Schedules |
	Dexterity	Routine	Machine-paced	Maintenance	Total	
Shirts, 1964	96%	3%	0%	1%	100%	Yes
Shoes, 1965	96	3	0	1	100	Yes
Hosiery, 1964	61	4	24.5	10.5	100	Yes
Leather, 1963	59.5	29	8.5	3	100	Yes
Textiles, 1963	13.5	17.5	58	11	100	Yes
Glass, 1964	7.5	63	15.5	14	100	No
Rubber, 1947	27	18	47.5	7.5	100	No
Sugar, 1956	10	38	41	11	100	No
Chemicals, 1955	5	18	57	20	100	No
Flour, 1961	3.5	66	22.5	8	100	No
Cement, 1955	4	25	51	20	100	No

Sources: U.S. Department of Labor, Bureau of Labor Statistics, *Occupational Wage Surveys* (all the industries corresponded very closely to the products listed in Table 1, except for Mechanical Rubber Goods). For cement, data taken from U.N. Economic Commission for Africa, *Cement/Nitrogenous Fertilizers Based on Natural Gas,* Studies in Economics of Industry, no. 1, 1963.

In the remaining seven industries, machine-paced occupations are at least twice as important as dexterity occupations (except in tires, where the share of dexterity operations is overstated). If the machine-paced and routine occupations were grouped together, the two groups of four and seven industries would still emerge quite clearly.

Unfortunately, information of a comparable detail and quality is not available for Peruvian factories. The percentages in different categories are probably somewhat different. One would expect a higher percentage of routine workers in Peru than in the United States, since materials handling and packaging can be done either by hand or by automatic machinery depending on factor prices. It seems likely, however, that the division into two groups of four and seven industries would still hold for the Peruvian data.

The industries possessing latitude with respect to quality of workmanship are shirts, shoes, and leather. It is worth emphasizing that relative productivities in these industries were measured for products of the same quality. Such a procedure is essential in carrying out this type of study.

I have made a simple yes-no classification for criterion 3, the latitude with respect to work schedules. The concept employed was the number of places within the productive process where the intermediate products are stored, and this number is quite large for the four dexterity industries plus textiles and quite small for the remaining six industries.

In our sample there is a strong relationship between latitudes and relative efficiency. The average relative efficiency of the four dexterity industries is 39.3 percent, as against 65.4 percent for the seven machine-paced industries.

Table 16-3

Occupations Included in Various Categories

Dexterity: Sewing machine operators, inspectors, and trimmers (shirts, shoes, hosiery); inspectors (textiles); pressers and boxers (shirts), cutters (shirts, shoes); hide manipulation operators; doffers in spinning, drawing-and-typing-in machine operators (textiles); forklift truck operators; batch mixers (glass); compounders (rubber); mixers (chemicals); liquor men (leather); cutters and hose makers and V-belt builders and trimmers (rubber); crane operators (sugar); lab assistants (chemicals, cement)

Routine: Janitors, guards, floor boys, hand truckers, laborers in material handling, tackers, (leather), battery hands (textiles), selectors and inspectors and packers (glass), cane rakers and unhookers, drum fillers (chemicals), packers (rubber, flour, cement)

Machine-paced: Knitters, weavers, colorers (leather); tenders of carding, roving, spinning, and winding machines; forming machine and lehr tenders (glass); millmen and pressmen and calendar machine operators (rubber); tenders of sugar milling and flour milling machinery; chemical operators; tenders of cement machinery (list is abbreviated because of the very large number of occupations)

Maintenance: Repairmen, carpenters, electricians, mechanics, loom fixers, card grinders (textiles); oilers, forming machine upkeepers, mold makers (glass); pipefitters, millwrights

Similarly, the industries possessing latitude with respect to the quality of workmanship and latitude with respect to work schedules are less efficient on the average than those which do not. Since, however, the categories of industries produced by the four types of latitudes almost completely overlap, it is not possible to identify which types of latitude are most important in determining relative efficiency.

Consequently we shall use the term "latitude industry" to refer to shirts, shoes, hosiery, and leather, and "nonlatitude industry" to refer to the remaining seven industries. This division places textiles in the nonlatitude group, even though it possesses one of the four latitudes, but the figures for that group will be presented both with and without textiles.

III. The Quality of Labor

Kreinen has attempted to provide a measure of labor quality through a survey of plant managers familiar with both American and foreign operations.[5] The managers were questioned about labor requirements per unit of output under similar conditions with respect to the degree of mechanization and the quality of the product. While it is true that identical conditions do not normally exist in the United States and Latin American countries, it is reasonable to suppose that the respondents were indicating what they thought labor requirements *would be* under similar conditions and that they have a good basis for judgment. In the comparison of Latin America and the United States, the median difference in labor requirement

---

[5]Mordechai Kreinen, "Comparative Labor Effectiveness and Leontief's Scarce-Factor Paradox," *American Economic Review* 55 (March 1965): pp. 131–139.

was 30 percent, i.e., 130 man-hours were required in Latin America as against 100 in the United States. . . . We propose to test the hypothesis that the correlation between capital intensity and relative efficiency is due to differences in the quality of production workers. (For ease of exposition, we shall use the terms "labor" to refer to both managers and production workers and "workers" to refer to the latter only.)

Let Q_e be the Peruvian relative efficiency calculated with the input of workers adjusted for worker quality. We have employed adjustments of 23 percent and 49 percent. Table 4 shows the average relative efficiencies

Table 16–4
Peruvian Relative Efficiency in Latitude and Nonlatitude Industries

	Q	Q_e *(23% Correction)*
Four latitude industries	39.30%	47.40%
Seven nonlatitude industries	65.43	73.05
Six nonlatitude industries (excluding textiles)	71.57	79.60

for the latitude and nonlatitude industries. . . . What stands out in the table is that the difference between the latitude and the nonlatitude industries remains quite pronounced . . . [so we must conclude that labor quality alone does not account for this difference].

So far we have been discussing a *uniform* labor quality adjustment, that is, an adjustment that is the same for all industries. It is possible that the correlation between capital intensity and relative efficiency is explained by differences in Peruvian relative labor quality in different industries. We might call this the differential labor quality hypothesis.

The distinction between the differential labor quality hypothesis and the latitude hypothesis is that the latter supposes that labor in Peru could be shifted from one industry to another without affecting (after a transitional period) the relative efficiency of the industries, while the former hypothesis supposes that a management-worker team in Peru would achieve (again, after a period of transition) the same relative efficiency in whatever industry it is located.

It is plausible that there might be a difference in management quality in Peru as between the labor-intensive and the capital-intensive industries. The greater technical complexity of the latter group of industries might deter a prospective entrepreneur from setting up a factory unless he was familiar with the technology himself or could hire a competent manager. In the technically simple labor-intensive industries, on the other hand, a less qualified manager can get by.[6] There might be some difference in

---

[6]This point was suggested to the author by Hollis Chenery.

management quality between the two groups of industries in the United States, too, but perhaps less than in Peru.

There also might be a difference in worker quality in Peru relative to the United States. Capital-intensive factories with no latitude with respect to work schedules tend to pay higher than market wages in order to attract reliable workers. The difference in worker quality between capital-intensive and labor-intensive industries may be larger in Peru than in the United States.

Until we can measure the quality of workers and managers in individual industries, we cannot distinguish empirically between the differential labor-quality hypothesis and the latitude hypothesis. I am inclined to believe, however, that the latitude hypothesis is more important in explaining the correlation between capital intensity and Peruvian relative efficiency than the differential labor quality hypothesis.

The main argument of the last two parts can be summarized in the following propositions:

1. Peruvian relative efficiency is lower in the industries possessing latitudes than in those which do not.

2. Peruvian relative efficiency is lower in labor-intensive than in capital-intensive industries. A uniform adjustment for worker quality only slightly narrows the gap in Peruvian relative efficiency between the latitude and nonlatitude industries. It seems likely that a uniform adjustment in management quality would not narrow the gap very much more.

3. One or both of the following must be true: a) Peruvian workers and managers are of higher quality, relative to their American counterparts, in the nonlatitude than in the latitude industries (the differential labor-quality hypothesis); b) Peruvian workers and managers are relatively better at nonlatitude than at latitude tasks (the latitude hypothesis).

Concluding Observations

The principal substantive finding of [this chapter] is that Peruvian relative efficiency tends to be considerably lower for industries possessing latitudes than for those which do not. This finding has somewhat discouraging implications for the prospects for exports of manufactures from poor to rich countries because the labor-intensive, easily transportable products which seem to be potential export items are fabricated in processes containing large latitudes. A reasonable hypothesis would be that American or European managers would be better able to impose the necessary disciplines than local managers in poor countries, and, if so, this consideration together with marketing considerations would provide an argument for the establishment of American or European companies in underdeveloped countries for export to the developed-country market.

17

Prospects of Structural Changes in Employment in Latin America

Zygmundt Slawinski

In the light of the long-term and recent trends noted in the structure of employment and in the average product per worker in the major economic sectors, several conclusions may be drawn concerning the socioeconomic structures of the Latin American countries and their probable evolution in the next ten years, i.e., up to 1975. More specifically, the structural changes in employment in the major economic sectors in relation to the growth of the product of each sector can be regarded as indicative of the part each sector will play in solving the fundamental problem, that is, the provision of productive employment for the future manpower available. They also serve to evaluate the extent to which labor productivity would actually grow and how far it would contribute to the growth of the gross national product.

The point deserving most attention is the role of manufacturing industry as a source of employment and personal income for workers. From the standpoint of the relative volume and structure of factory and artisan employment, Latin America's present position is like that existing in the more advanced European countries in the middle of the 19th century, or in the comparatively advanced countries at the beginning of the present century, since the artisan sector is very large and factory employment— though still limited—is growing rapidly.

However, that is where the likeness ends. The growth of the European cities kept pace with the upsurge of industry. Manufacturing employment —mainly in the factory sector—and construction employment came to represent half, or more than half, of total urban employment. By contrast, Latin American cities have developed autonomously; industrial employment represents approximately one-third of urban employment, and often even less (it should be remembered that in Latin America the factory sector absorbs a smaller proportion of industrial employment than it does in Europe).

There is another basic discrepancy between the situation in Europe and in Latin America. In the previous century, the development of factory industry all over the world was inevitably accompanied by a substantial increase in factory employment. This happened in Western Europe, where factory industry came into being. Such is no longer the case. Industrial development in the less developed countries means in large measure the adaptation of advanced techniques. Up-to-date plants are being set up

Adapted from *ECLA, Economic Bulletin for Latin America* (October 1965), pp. 182–187, with permission of the publisher.

101

which are modelled on corresponding establishments in industrialized countries. Under these circumstances, the rapid growth of industrial production does not necessarily imply a substantial increase in industrial employment. With productivity growing quickly there is less need to increase employment. The rapid increase in factory productivity is practically a worldwide phenomenon today. In spite of the prevailing doubts as to whether the application of highly productive up-to-date techniques is economically warranted in the developing countries, where there is an enormous amount of disguised unemployment and wages are low, industrial development continues to be based primarily on the setting up and expansion of this type of establishment, no priority being attached to establishments based on more primitive techniques aimed at absorbing as much of the available labor force as possible.

Under these conditions, it would not be out of place to assume, for the purpose of formulating illustrative hypotheses, that the future growth of factory productivity will be 3.5 percent annually. Since in the meantime the relative replacement of artisan employment by factory employment would also continue, the gross product per worker in the manufacturing sector as a whole would increase at an even faster rate (probably 4.4 percent annually).

If in addition the growth rate of Latin America's gross product is assumed to be 6 percent annually, i.e., a rise of nearly 3 percent in the *per capita* product between 1965 and 1975—slightly higher than the Alliance for Progress recommendations—the annual growth rate of the manufacturing product would probably have to be about 7.5 percent. This means that manufacturing employment would increase at an average rate of 3.0 percent annually, ranging from 4.1 percent for factory industry to 1.3 percent for the artisan sector. At this rate, the manufacturing sector could absorb about 3.5 million workers, 80 percent in the factory sector and 20 percent in the artisan sector. In other words, the manufacturing sector would absorb 13.8 percent of the total increase in the labor force in 1965–1975, with factory industry accounting for 11.1 percent of this proportion, compared with 13.6 percent and 9.2 percent, respectively, during the fifties.

Artisan and cottage industry employment is tending to decline in Latin America in relation to total employment, as a result of the substitution of factory production for cottage and small-scale industry, a process which has not yet been completed in several countries, and of the slow growth of authentic up-to-date artisan industry.

In short, the manufacturing sector is playing, and will probably continue to play, a limiting part in absorbing the manpower increment, even if the growth rate of the industrial product is stepped up. This deficiency of the manufacturing sector makes it necessary to seek other sectors as additional sources of employment for a great many workers. This is a highly complex problem and entails the adoption of simultaneous action in several sectors in order to achieve a new type of balance in employment.

A second point relates to the relatively limited labor-absorption capacity of the two other highly dynamic sectors of the economy: mining and basic services. Formerly predominating in the structure of these sectors were the small enterprise and the own account worker, which permitted the employment of a relatively large number of persons. The fact that mining, energy production, transport and communications are now utilizing modern techniques, which are likely to progress rapidly, means that, as in the factory sector, the vigorous development of these branches of activity is not accompanied by a major increase in the labor force. It should not be forgotten, however, that the overall increase in employment in basic services, particularly in various branches of transport, conceals the growth in Latin America of a marginal labor force which would have no place in more advanced communities. Thus, the slow growth of productivity in basic services would be attributable more to the unwarranted increase in employment than to a lack of technical progress.

To sum up, it may be inferred hypothetically that mining and basic services might in future contribute to making good the lack of productive employment, though on a more limited scale than before. Thus, mining might absorb no more than 0.5 percent of the total increase in the labor force in 1965–1975, as against 0.8 percent during the fifties. Basic services might absorb only 7.5 percent of the total, since in 1950–1960 it absorbed 8.5 percent.

Thirdly, it is not difficult to foresee that the trade and finance sector is likely to play a very limited role as a source of future employment, for the following reasons: on the one hand, the trade sector in general has entered a period of technical and structural progress, and this has brought about a situation similar to the industrial revolution of the previous century, a process which has not yet ended in the Latin American countries. The introduction of supermarkets, chain stores and other innovations, together with major advances in storage and transport systems, enables a larger volume of merchandise to be handled by a smaller number of persons.

Merely by way of a hypothesis, it might be assumed that the trade and finance sector will absorb the same or perhaps a slightly higher percentage in 1965–1975. This would mean a labor absorption of 14.0 percent, compared with 13.7 percent during the fifties.

It will be deduced from the foregoing that the remaining sectors producing either goods or services would have to absorb the growing manpower surplus which could not find employment in manufacturing, mining, basic services or trade. In other words, miscellaneous services, construction and agriculture would have to develop considerably in the next few years in order to absorb a larger proportion of the natural manpower increment than before. Only thus could the Latin American countries find a new balance in the field of labor.

An all-important role in the provision of employment would be played by other services recording a very high growth rate in recent years, i.e., personal services (on both a domestic and commercial basis), public welfare services (health, education and entertainment) and various cultural services, as also in part, those relating to public administration, the judiciary, security and national defense. These present so complex a picture from the economic and social standpoint that the analysis of their development prospects is beyond the scope of the present [chapter]. However, a study of their past numerical development in different parts of the world leads to the conclusion that this sector offers definite possibilities of sustained growth. Hence, the problem lies not in the total volume of employment that can be absorbed by this sector's activities as a whole, but in the internal structure of such employment. The relevant socioeconomic policy would no doubt aim, as far as possible, at eliminating the marginal lowest-productivity personal services which, moreover, contribute nothing to the actual development of the community. Productive employment in public services is yet another problem. While in certain public activities there is a surplus of very low-productivity personnel, in others there is an evident shortage of personnel which impedes the efficient performance of important activities. Educational, cultural, health, social security and welfare, judiciary, security, economic and statistical administration, and municipal services, besides technical assistance for community development, agriculture and the marketing of consumer goods, etc., could be greatly extended affording employment to a great many workers.

The same might be said of entertainment and of personal services carried out on a commercial basis. On the other hand, a decline may be envisaged in domestic personal services. This process, which is nearing its end in the industrialized countries, will probably develop slowly in Latin America over the next few years, because of the persistent demand for this type of services by a section of the population and because of the broad sector for which it represents a sure source of employment, not easily replaced by other activities over the short term.

To sum up, since employment in the services sector has reached saturation point, it seems logical to think that in the near future it will not grow as rapidly as hitherto, and this, in turn, would enable the average product per worker to show a reasonable increase.

A rise of 4.2 million workers in "other services," including government services, during the decade 1965–1975, compared with some 4.5 million during the fifties, might be considered a reasonable working hypothesis. This volume of labor absorption would be equal to 16.5 percent of the total increase in employment in 1965–1975, as against 25.5 percent during the fifties.

These trends should seriously be taken into account in devising the public sector's budget policy and, in general, in achieving a balanced economic development in activities related to services.

Construction—quite apart from its significance in the capital formation process—would have to play a vital role in solving the future employment problem. During the fifties it absorbed about 8.6 percent of the total increase in employment while the factory sector absorbed 9.2 percent. The hypothesis might be advanced that in 1965–1975 construction will absorb about 13 percent of the total increment in employment, a higher proportion than—as previously assumed—would be absorbed by the factory sector.

The construction sector, although less complex than the manufacturing sector, is fairly heterogeneous. The technological characteristics of major public works, town planning schemes and housing construction projects differ widely. If the sector is to employ considerable numbers, it should not be highly mechanized. This criterion, which applies to the construction of dwellings and the numerous minor works scattered over the urban and rural areas, is no less applicable to major public works which lend themselves to intensive mechanization and large-scale entrepreneurial organization. However, to achieve a notable expansion of the construction industry which would provide employment for a great many workers, a basic condition would seem to be adequate supplies of cheap construction materials and equipment. This entails not only the corresponding growth of factory production, forestry and quarrying, but also production organized along better lines and a more efficient control of both quality and prices of these materials, and of the marketing and transport costs involved. Thus a close relationship exists between efficient manufacturing, transport and marketing, on the one hand, and the construction sector's labor-absorbtion capacity on the other.

The same consideration is applicable to the adverse effect of the high speculative prices of urban sites on the construction of dwellings.

In Europe, the employment policy of the construction sector was traditionally considered an important instrument in maintaining full employment. The same thing happened in the United States at the time of the New Deal in combating the Depression of the thirties. Powerful arguments militate in favor of adopting the same policy in Latin America, but within a different framework and directed mainly at stepping up overall economic development.

Lastly, it might be useful to consider the agricultural sector's role in the provision of productive employment. It would not be surprising to see in the future an important change in the accelerated growth rate of the urban population during the past few decades, when the rate of rural development and the growth of agricultural manpower steadily declined. This

Table 17-1

Latin America:[a] Hypothesis of the Evolution of the Total Population and the Economically Active Population, 1960-1975 (*thousands of persons*)

	1960	1975
A. *Total population*	*199,144*	*305,838*
1. Rural population	54.2%	48.8%
2. Urban population	45.8	51.2
B. *Active population*	*65,951*	*100,930*
1. Agricultural sector	47.7%	41.4%
2. Non-agricultural sector	52.3	58.6

Source: ECLA, on the basis of official statistics and unpublished data.
[a]Excluding Cuba.

Table 17-2
Latin America: Hypotheses of Future Evolution of Selected Indexes Related to Employment, 1960–1975, and Productivity, 1950–1975

| Sector | Employment 1960–1975 | | | | | | | Productivity 1950–1975 | |
| | Evolution of the Active Population[b] | | Percentage Distribution of Future Active Population: | | Net Increase[b] | Percentage of total increase | Growth rate | Growth rate of product per worker (annual percentage) | |
	1960	1975						1950–1965	1965–1975
Total[a]	65,951	100,930	100.0%	100.0%	34,979	100.0%	2.9%	1.9%	3.0%
A. Agricultural sector	31,480	41,830	47.7	41.4	10,350	29.6	1.9	1.9	3.0
B. Non-agricultural sector	34,471	59,100	52.3	58.6	24,629	70.4	3.8	1.7	2.0
1. Goods and basic services	16,628	27,710	25.2	27.5	11,082	31.7	3.5	1.1	3.5
(a) Mining	681	820	1.0	0.8	139	0.4	1.2	2.6	3.0
(b) Manufacturing	9,373	13,850	14.2	13.7	4,477	12.8	2.6	4.5	3.4
(i) Factory sector	4,875	8,410	7.4	8.3	3,535	10.1	3.7	3.6	4.4
(ii) Artisan sector	4,498	5,440	6.8	5.4	942	2.7	1.3	3.2	3.5
(c) Construction	3,187	6,940	4.8	6.9	3,753	10.7	5.3	0.9	2.0
(d) Basic services	3,387	6,100	5.2	6.0	2,713	7.8	4.0	0.0	2.2
2. Services	17,843	31,390	27.1	31.1	13,547	38.7	3.8	0.8	2.0
(a) Trade and finance	5,995	10,790	9.1	10.7	4,795	13.7	4.0	-0.3	2.4
(b) Government	2,419	4,200	3.7	4.2	1,781	5.1	3.7	0.5	1.5
(c) Miscellaneous services	7,899	12,860	12.0	12.7	4,961	14.2	3.3	-0.8	1.5
(d) Unspecified activities	1,530	3,540	2.3	3.5	2,010	5.7	5.7	-0.6	3.5

Source: ECLA, on the basis of official statistics and unpublished data.
[a]Excluding Cuba.
[b]in thousands

process, stemming from socioeconomic factors, has already given rise to the agglomeration of marginal population in urban areas, with the result that the low incomes prevailing there came very close to the low rural income levels. Moreover, the saturation of disguised unemployment in the cities is such as to threaten to produce large-scale overunemployment within a few years. Hence, in many cases there is no longer an economic incentive for migration from the country to the town.

On the other hand, the average *per capita* agricultural product has risen steadily in the last few decades. . . . It may be concluded that the next few years might witness an appreciable acceleration of agricultural employment and a declining rate of urban growth, accompanied by a geographical shift of nonagricultural employment prompted by the increased labor-absorption capacity of various activities allied to agriculture in rural areas.

On the basis of the above hypothesis, the agricultural sector could absorb over 31 percent of the total increase in the labor force in 1965–1975, as against only 27.6 percent during the fifties. The effect of this would be to raise the growth rate of the rural population from 1.6 percent in 1950–1960 to 2.5 percent in 1965–1975, and to reduce that of the urban population from 4.5 percent to 3.4 percent (see Tables 1 & 2).

If the agricultural sector and the rural area failed to absorb the potential manpower increment at the rate indicated above and agricultural employment went up no faster than before, there would almost inevitably be a sharp increase in the marginal labor force, concentrated chiefly in the major cities. By way of illustrating its possible magnitude, suffice it to think that marginal employment in 1965–1975 might extend to nearly 7 million persons, i.e., a net increase of over 4 million, or 16 percent of the total manpower increment.

A general conclusion to be drawn from the above analysis of the labor market's development prospects is that there is a notable imbalance in the structure of employment in most of the Latin American countries, and that a great many factors prevent a balance from being restored. It is difficult to achieve this under more or less spontaneous economic development conditions, and this enhances the need for a socioeconomic policy that will deliberately lead to the necessary structural changes, and for an intensive education policy that will conduce to a better utilization of human resources, a more equitable income distribution and a more efficient production system.

Workers

18 Occupational Mobility: The Mexican Case

José Luis Reyna

In considering the Mexican case we start from the hypothesis that economic development and social mobility are two closely related phenomena. Taking this hypothesis as a general one, we will propose others, to some extent less vague. One of them indicates that those processes not directly related to industrial [ones] will account more clearly for occupational mobility than for industrialization. At the same time we will attempt to show that Mexico's rural agricultural structure can be characterized by a high degree of rigidity, that is, that minimal chances of vertical mobility exist in it.

The actual analysis is very limited. Available data concern only one year, 1963, although mobility data refer to two generations. The units of analysis will be the thirty-two federal entities (states) which make up the Mexican Republic. The kind of mobility to be analyzed is occupational mobility.[1]

Economic Development and
Occupational Mobility

Mexico as a whole has undergone—and is still undergoing—major transformations in its social and economic structure. Gross National Product grew more than six times from 1910 to 1965. Net income per capita tripled from 1929 to 1962. Urban population . . . increased from 12.2 percent in 1900 to 37.5 percent in 1960; the nonagricultural sectors accounted in 1964 for 82 percent of the Gross Domestic Product, and, although more than 50 percent of the population was engaged in the agricultural sector, the nonagricultural sectors grew rapidly between 1925 and 1960 (from 30 to 47 percent).[2]

These changes suggest that large numbers of the active population have found, in the last decades, occupations very different from those of their parents, leaving the "rural model" and becoming incorporated in an "urban

---

Adapted from "Some Patterns of Occupational Mobility," *Social Research* 35 (1968): pp. 540–564, with permission of the publisher and author.
[1]The indicators used to systematize the mobility variables were drawn from *El VIII Censo General de Población* (México: Secretaría de Industria y Comercio, 1963). Occupational mobility data were taken from a recent study, *La Población Economicamente Activa de México* (Secretaría de Industria y Comercio, Dirección General de Muestreo [México: 1964–65]).
[2]Simposio Latinoamericano de Industrialización, *El Proceso de Industrialización en América Latina* (Santiago de Chile: CEPAL, 1966), p. 13.

occupational model." This is not to deny that Mexico is to a large extent rural and agricultural. These changes suggest the hypothesis that economic development bears an intimate relationship to occupational mobility.

This does not imply that industrialization accounts for the changes described. Although Mexico is achieving a significant degree of industrial growth in comparison with other Latin American countries, there are other factors or situations that distinguish the character of the "new model of development" from the "original" development process typical of thoroughly industrialized countries.

In another publication the author has emphasized some of the outstanding features of the new process of development.[3] One, the "tertiarization phenomenon," [refers to] rapid growth of the services sector, [slower growth in] the manufacturing sector, [and a shrinkage in] the agricultural sector. Some of the patterns shown by the processes of "original development" indicate that technological innovations and specialization grew first, and in a later phase the service sector expanded.[4] Developed countries began their self-sustained growth in the course of the Industrial Revolution.

In developing countries the salient characteristics are different: technology is not indigenous but imported, agriculture retains an important weight in the economic structure, and the tertiary (services) sector is growing very fast. This indicates that the development process in these countries neither can assume nor reproduce the various social, economic and political transformations that took place in the industrialized countries. . . . Industrial expansion to a certain degree accounted for social mobility in industrialized countries and later delayed effects that expansion (the increase of service activities) continued to increase social mobility. . . . For societies undergoing recent economic growth, occupational mobility is closely related to mobility of the individual within the social structure. Meanwhile, in developed societies the older pattern continues, so that economic development and occupational mobility can occur at different moments.[5]

*Mexico's Social Mobility in
Comparative Perspective*

Joseph Kahl's research on values and social stratification in Mexico and Brazil has shown, for Mexico, a zero-order correlation of 0.50 between the

[3]José Luis Reyna, Manuel Villa, and K. Albrechtsen, "Dinámica de la estratificación social en algunas ciudades pequeñas y medianas de México," *Demografía Economía* 1 (1967): pp. 368–394.
[4]See, for the British case, G. D. H. Cole, *Studies in Class Structure* (London: Routledge and Kegan Paul, 1961). For Latin America, see F. H. Cardoso and J. L. Reyna, "Industrialization, Occupational Structure and Social Stratification in Latin America," in *Constructive Change in Latin America,* ed. Cole Blasier (Pittsburgh: University of Pittsburgh Press, 1968), pp. 19–55; and Gláucio Ary Dillon Soares, *The New Industrialization and the Brazilian Political System,* Santiago de Chile, 1966 (mimeo).
[5]L. A. Costa Pinto, *Estructura de Clases y Cambio Social* (Buenos Aires: PAIDOS, 1964), esp. pp. 41–59. Costa Pinto points out some differences of patterns of social mobility between developed and developing countries.

occupations of fathers and sons.[6] This implies that 25 percent of the variance of the sons' occupations is accounted for by the fathers' occupations. Although Kahl's sample is not a random one, it gives an image of the rate of occupational mobility for Mexican society. . . . While occupational mobility in the United States is much higher than in Latin America,[7] occupational mobility in Mexico is nevertheless significant.

"Tertiarization," Middle-School Education
and Urbanization Effects in Relation to
Industrialization and Mobility

We are interested in determining the effects of the tertiary (services) sector, of middle-school education and of urbanization on the relation between industrialization and [occupational] mobility. We will try to test the hypothesis that those factors not directly related to industrialization are more important than industrialization itself in the explanation of vertical occupational mobility.

Industrialization Without "Tertiarization." Our hypothesis, derived from the theoretical model of "the new development," leads us to assume that, if the tertiary sector is kept constant, the relation between industrialization and upward mobility tends to decrease; this pattern is not valid for the opposite strategy. To simplify we will choose only [one] aspect of occupational mobility: upward movement. . . . The results appear in Table 1.

Table 18-1
Mexico: "Tertiarization" Effects on the Relation Between Industrialization, and Upward Mobility in the 32 Federal Entities, 1963

Constant variable	Relating	Partial correlation	Zero-order correlation
Tertiary sector	Manufacturing sector and upward mobility	0.197	0.670
Manufacturing sector	Tertiary sector and upward mobility	0.540	0.770

The tertiary sector shows a more significant effect than the manufacturing sector. The association between industrialization with upward mobility . . . tends to decrease markedly. When the manufacturing sector is controlled,

[6]Joseph Kahl, "Estratificación Social en la Metrópol y en las Provincias," *Ciencias Politicas y Sociales,* no. 37 (1964), p. 434.
[7]A zero-order correlation of 0.38 is reported by Blau and Duncan between occupations of fathers and occupations of sons. See P. Blau and O. D. Duncan, "Some Preliminary Findings on Social Stratification in the United States," *Acta Sociológica* 9 (1965): fasc. 1, 2, p. 6. See also T. Fox and S. M. Miller, "Intracountry Variations: Occupational and Stratificational Mobility," in *Class, Status and Power,* ed. R. Bendix and S. M. Lipset (New York: The Free Press, 1966), p. 576.

although there is some decrease in the association between the tertiary sector and upward mobility, . . . the decrease is not so strong as in the former case.

Industrialization Without Urbanization. In developing countries, it has been frequently said that urbanization, defined as growing urban population, fosters social inequality and changes the employment structure.[8] At the same time, it has been said that between urbanization and the emergence and growth of middle strata a high correlation prevails.[9]

The results appear to show that urbanization has a more important weight than industrialization [see Table 2]. When urbanization is controlled, and

Table 18-2
Mexico: The Urbanization Effects on the Relation Between Industrialization, and Upward Mobility in the 32 Federal Entities, 1963

Constant variable	Relating	Partial correlation	Zero-order correlation
Urbanization	Manufacturing sector and upward mobility	−0.041	0.670
Manufacturing sector	Urbanization and upward mobility	0.609	0.807

industrialization and upward mobility are allowed to vary, the partial correlation is near zero and tends to change its sign. This means that if urbanization, a fundamental factor accounting for upward mobility, is kept constant, industrialization loses its explanatory power. When the manufacturing sector is controlled, the association between urbanization and upward mobility does not undergo substantial decrease.

Industrialization Without Middle Education. It has been observed among developing countries that there is a lack of complementarity between their economic and educational aspects. Education tends to isolate itself from the economy, making up an independent institutional order, developing its own standards and ignoring external demands.[10] This may be a distinctive characteristic of these countries as contrasted with developed countries.

Education in developing countries seems to constitute a set of prestige symbols, and it can be regarded as a channel of social mobility per se. Therefore, education and upward mobility tend to be strongly associated.

[8]Luis Ratinoff, "The New Urban Groups: The Middle Classes," in *Elites in Latin America,* ed. S. M. Lipset and A. Solari (New York: Oxford University Press, 1967), p. 64.
[9]Gláucio Ary Dillon Soares, "Economic Development and the Class Structure," in *Class, Status and Power,* ed. Bendix and Lipset, op. cit., pp. 190–199.
[10]Eduardo Muñoz, "La asincronía institucional economia-educación," *Anales de la Facultad Latinoamericana de Ciencias Sociales* 1 (1964): 15.

Table 3 shows that the impact of middle education on the industrialization-upward mobility . . . relation is very great. Again, the explanatory power of industrialization disappears when education is kept constant.

Industrialization does not have a strong effect when it is controlled. This result supports the hypothesis that education is a channel of social mobility per se, having a more important role in the explanation of occupational mobility than industrialization. Therefore, it can be concluded that education is one of the most important channels of social mobility in developing countries. The above results, for the Mexican case, support to some extent this conclusion.

Table 18-3
Mexico: The Middle Education Effects on the Relation Between Industrialization, and Upward Mobility in the 32 Federal Entities, 1963

Constant variable	Relating	Partial correlation	Zero order correlation
Middle education (7 years of schooling and over)	Manufacturing sector and upward mobility	0.076	0.670
Manufacturing sector	Middle education and upward mobility	0.444	0.745

Mobility by Occupational Strata in the Mexican Republic

We will now examine occupational mobility by occupational strata; this will be helpful in order to complete, to some extent, the foregoing results.

First, we can observe the distribution of individuals based on mobility by occupational strata [see Tables 4 and 5]. Those strata that can be regarded as nonmanual workers (I–IV) present a large proportion of upward mobility during one generation. This suggests that in the last three decades, approximately, a process of renovation has occurred among these strata, and therefore in the overall class structure, partially accounted for by the effects of the Mexican Revolution and by the general characteristics of Mexican development.

Nevertheless, this does not imply lack of ascription. In many cases, it is possible to find families or individuals belonging to the higher strata and whose origins are rooted before the Mexican Revolution. They have changed their occupational activity (from *hacendados* to big entrepreneurs) without changing their real rank position; they still remain in the high ranks of stratification. This conclusion is valid, in general, for the professional and executive strata whose members constitute the elite. However, we do not deny that both strata are fed by individuals belonging to other strata (middle or lower positions).

In strata III and IV we can also observe the process of renovation, a

Table 18–4

Mexico: Occupational Mobility and Structural Flexibility by Occupation Stratum in the 32 Federal Entities, 1963 (percentages)

Son's stratum	Upward	Non-mobiles	Downward	Total[a]	Index of structural flexibility
		Mobility of sons in relation to their fathers			
I. Managers and directors, except in agriculture	63.54%	27.68%	8.76%	99.99% (281,659)	2.61
II. Professionals and technicians	78.05	20.18	1.76	99.99 (402,210)	3.95
III. Clerks and kindred people	59.09	24.28	16.62	99.99 (826,606)	3.11
IV. Salesmen	59.72	31.68	8.59	100.00 (892,757)	2.15
V. Labor force in mining	12.02	76.07	11.90	99.99 (68,681)	0.31
VI. Artisans and workers directly related to production	14.81	63.22	21.97	100.00 (2,039,502)	0.58
VII. Workers non-directly related to production	14.71	43.06	42.23	100.00 (847,306)	1.32
VIII. Labor force in agriculture (Includes hunting, fishing, etc.)	0.61	97.29	2.10	100.00 (5,050,530)	0.03
Index of structural flexibility for all strata					0.43
Index of structural flexibility excluding the agricultural stratum					1.20

[a]From these totals the percentages were extracted.

Note: The occupational scale presented is the same used by the Census Bureau. In order to justify the ranking of the eight strata, the scale was correlated with the income indicator. The results show that the higher the stratum the higher the monthly income per capita. This tendency is monotonical. The results can be found in J. L. Reyna, M. Villa and K. Albrechtsen, "Dinamica de la Estratificación social en algunas ciudades pequeñas y medianas de México," in *Demografía y Economía* 1, (1967): p. 374.

Table 18-5

Mexico: Participation of Each Stratum in Overall Occupational Mobility in the 32 Federal Entities, 1963 (percentages)

Son's stratum	Mobility of sons in relation to their fathers			
	Upward	Nonmobiles	Downward	Total
I	1.72%	0.75%	0.24%	2.71%
II	3.02	0.78	0.07	3.87
III	4.69	1.93	1.32	7.94
IV	5.12	2.72	0.74	8.58
V	0.08	0.50	0.08	.66
VI	2.90	12.39	4.30	19.59
VII	1.20	3.50	3.44	8.14
VIII	0.30	47.20	1.01	48.51
	19.03%	69.71%	11.20%	100.00% (10,409,251)[a]

[a]From this total the percentages were extracted.

tendency which can be explained by the commercial and bureaucratic expansion. These phenomena give a different character to the Mexican stratification system in comparison with past times. In these strata we can observe that one-fourth to one-third of individuals have not undergone any change; this points to the importance of these kinds of activities in past years.

We can see that downward mobility is very low in stratum II, of moderate intensiveness in strata I and IV, and relatively high in stratum III. The results indicate that there exists in stratum II an "intellectual elite" tending to keep its position. In relation with stratum III, it is possible that downward-moving individuals can be taken as an indicator that during the last decades large bureaucracies have absorbed sons of fathers in high positions.

In regard to the manual strata, it can be inferred that their upward mobility is not so important as that of the nonmanual strata, being evident in the high degree of rigidity of the agricultural stratum. However, we must not underestimate the upward mobility of manual strata since it has some significance. It may be true that a large proportion of persons here have a peasant background; this means that they are migrants. If this is true, they are undergoing the process of integration with the urban stratification system.

In strata VI and VII we have found individuals who have undergone downward mobility. This can be explained by the industrial expansion of recent years and the rapid growth of the services sector. This growth has been sponsored by sons of middle strata background fathers in an urban environment. This finding has a certain degree of correspondence with Di Tella's hypothesis.

Furthermore, if we think in terms of upward plus downward mobility (this is structural flexibility), it carries us to the tentative conclusion that within the Mexican stratification system there is a relatively high degree of flexibility. For the whole republic, excluding the peasant stratum [VIII], it appears that the proportion of mobile individuals to nonmobile individuals is 1.28 to 1. Flexibility is most significant in the nonmanual strata. For strata II and III there are more than three mobile individuals to one non-mobile individual.

A major conclusion is that the agricultural stratum accounts for almost half of nonmobility, when the whole participation of the separate strata is analyzed. Mobility in the other strata, taking into account the presence of nonmobile individuals, is relatively low, excepting in the stratum of workers and artisans. This points to the role that inheritance plays in this stratum. However, it can be said that in this stratum there is little mobility since upward mobility accounts for 2.9 percent and downward 4.3 percent; furthermore, these figures are important due to the total participation which has been observed. Strata III and IV present a relatively high degree of up-ward mobility, suggesting that middle strata tend to have a significant role in the Mexican class structure.

Conclusion

The evidence suggests that Mexico is undergoing a relatively significant degree of mobility, and indicates that . . . Mexican class structure is rela-tively flexible, tending to modernization in terms of stratification and mo-bility. . . . On the basis of this analysis, it can be stated that the processes representing nonindustrialization account for vertical occupational mobility to a greater degree than does industrialization.

This conclusion . . . appears to be due to the patterns belonging to the "new model of development."

Tertiarization, middle-level education and urbanization are phenomena that have more important weights in the process of vertical mobility and social stratification, and in accounting for the rapid expansion of middle strata, than has industrialization. From this, we can deduce that the patterns of mobility have very different features from those of the mobility patterns of developed countries.

Another conclusion points to the high degree of rigidity prevailing in the Mexican rural class structure. This can have deep future implications, since it is one of the conditions leading to crystallization of any kind of political extremism.

19 Training the Labor Force in Peru

Guillermo Briones

. . . The emerging labor force in the underdeveloped countries is largely of rural origin, which means that, apart from having little or no education it now has to face the special problems of urban and industrial life. This point is frequently made in the sociology of development, although unfortunately we do not have enough actual data to compare the many hypotheses put forward in this field. The aim of the following article is to provide some factual data about the different levels of skill of the labor force in a country now being industrialized.

The information supplied hereunder forms part of a broader study being conducted by the author in the Sociology Department of the Universidad Nacional Mayor de San Marcos in Lima, about occupational mobility and adaptation to economic and social change. It was gathered by means of interviews held with 1,096 workers in manufacturing industries situated in an area stretching between Lima and Callao, in Peru. Workers were selected by taking a stratified probability sample in the first stage from establishments employing twenty or more workers. The total number of workers in this category amounted to 49,381. Field work was carried out in October and November 1962.[1]

Education and Levels of Skill

Manpower distribution graphs reveal various social problems, two of which are felt to be of special importance. In the first place, the industrial and economic system which is the goal of the developing countries is such that it requires a far more highly skilled manpower than is now available, besides which this skill cannot be acquired quickly enough to satisfy the urgent demand for increased production. Secondly, any increase in the level of formal training, including on-the-job apprenticeship in industry, would require considerable capital which is usually quite difficult to raise from domestic sources or to provide from the traditional budgets of these countries.

From the *International Social Science Journal,* Volume XV, No. 4 (1963). Reproduced by permission of Unesco.
[1]The project was carried out with the assistance of Professor José Mejia and the collaboration of Dr. Elías Flores, both of the Universidad de San Marcos. The part concerned with the dissemination of information about occupational opportunities is being prepared by Dr. Paul J. Deutschmann, of the University of Michigan, with the assistance of the author of the present article.

Table 19-1
Years of Schooling for Factory Workers at Lima-Callao[a]

Years of schooling	Total
Primary school	
Up to 1	6.7%
2 to 3	17.6
4 to 5	49.7
Secondary school	
1 to 3	19.4
4 to 5	6.6
Total	100.0%
	(N = 1,096)

[a]This and the following tables refer to industrial establishments employing twenty or more workers.

Some of the findings of our study will illustrate this point. Table 1 . . . [shows] the educational level of factory workers in the Lima-Callao area which is the main industrial center of Peru.

First of all it will be seen that about a quarter of the workers under consideration (6.7 plus 17.6 percent) have had barely three years of primary schooling and are mostly what may be described as "potential illiterates"; 49.7 percent have gone as far as the fourth or fifth year of primary school; and at the upper level, only one out of four workers (26 percent) has had even one year's secondary schooling. . . . Furthermore, the older workers have had less schooling, the educational level being appreciably lower among those of 30 or over, who make up almost half of the 1,096 persons studied.

When these figures are viewed in relation to Peru's illiteracy rate of approximately 53 percent, the educational level among industrial workers probably compares favorably with that found in other sectors of the national economy.[2] The fact is that industry, being the most modern sector of the economy, can take its pick from the large labor force available, the ranks of which are constantly being swollen by immigration from rural areas. However, if an examination of the school attendance of these workers shows that they represent a cross-section of all categories of manual workers in industry it is reasonable to inquire whether this labor force is equal to the tasks of industrialization and economic development. The problem may be stated in the form of two questions. First, what is the extent of underqualification of manual workers in industry at present? Secondly, what leeway will have to be made up if the different stages of industrialization plans are to be carried out within the time-limits set?[3]

[2]Unesco, ECLA, United Nations, Celade, "Situación Demográfica, Economica, Social y Educativa de América Latina," *Proyecto Principal de Educación*, Unesco, Bulletin No. 13, January-March 1962, p. 63.
[3]This issue is dealt with in "The Determinants of Efficiency in Manufacturing Industries in an Underdeveloped Country," by Christopher Clague, Chapter 16 of the present volume.—Eds.

The answer to the first question, which is the only one that will be dealt with in this article, requires, first of all, a definition of the term "levels of qualification," and then a knowledge of the percentages of workers who must move up to each level during the various stages of industrialization, so that they may be compared with the actual percentages at any given moment. According to the definitions proposed in a recent report submitted to the Conference on Education and Economic Development held in Santiago, the unskilled level requires the completion of six years of primary schooling, the semiskilled level requires these six years plus two or three years of vocational training and the skilled level requires six years of primary schooling, two of secondary schooling and three to four years' vocational training. Applying these standards to the workers considered in the present study, we find that 74 percent would have to be classified in the lowest, that is, unskilled category (see Table 1). The remaining 26 percent, even though they have the general education required for the other levels, do not have the requisite vocational training, as may be seen from Table 2, giving the percentages of workers who have pursued other studies connected with their present industrial activity.

Table 19–2
Technical and Vocational Education of Workers in Manufacturing Industries of the Lima-Callao Area

Type of education	Total
Have attended some technical school or institute	1.2%
Have attended some commercial school or institute	0.9
Have attended one or more courses connected with their present work	5.5
Have attended one or more courses not connected with their present work	13.5
Have not attended any other courses	53.9
Did not reply	25.0
Total	100.0% (N = 1,096)

Table 2 shows that only an insignificant percentage—1.2 percent—has ever attended an institution of technical education and that only 5.5 percent have ever taken a course directly connected with their present industrial activity. These figures clearly indicate that workers taking up industrial employment have most inadequate formal vocational training, while at the same time they focus attention on the importance of the part that technical education has been or is playing in these countries. Incidentally, technical education, which is obviously of vital importance to economic development, is either a much neglected part of the general educational system, or else it is unable, for reasons which it would be interesting to explore, to train a sufficient number of skilled workers to meet the needs of industry.

To sum up, as regards the first question (concerning the present qualifications of workers), we have seen that, according to the criteria applied, three-quarters of the sample studied—74 percent to be precise—should, strictly speaking, be classified as "unskilled" for purposes of modern industry. The reservation "strictly speaking" is necessary as we have not considered the practical skill acquired by workers on the job. Such qualifications, of course, are very difficult to assess, but at present they should always be taken into account when comparing actual qualifications with those required for industry at a given stage of economic and technological development.

To return to Table 2, the percentages it gives indicate that many skilled jobs and occupations are filled by persons with inadequate training for the purpose. It should be remembered that this aspect of [the] situation is not usually apparent from the figures on manpower in underdeveloped countries, since they often classify workers as skilled or unskilled according to the job they are doing and not according to the skill which they actually possess.

On-the-Job Adaptation to
Modern Industrialization

It is clear that industrialization, which is new to . . . [Latin] America, is not only assimilating people who come from rural areas or from small towns and villages; in the cities themselves a gradient has been produced which extends from the most traditional sectors of the economy to the most modern, represented in this case by industry. For the great majority of industrial workers of both rural and urban origin, the change from one type of occupation to another implies a transition from a previous way of life to a new industrial and urban system with its different values, standards and status relations. . . . The two aspects of this subject discussed in the present article are the psychological consequences of the industrialization process and, more particularly, the degree of personal satisfaction derived by manual workers from the new environment in which they work.

. . . The degree of satisfaction expressed by the workers under consideration [was measured by] the question: "Generally speaking are you satisfied or dissatisfied with your present employment?" The percentages of those who claimed to be satisfied or fairly satisfied—30.9 percent and 51.6 percent respectively—are both far higher than the 17.2 percent who stated that they were dissatisfied with their work. The percentage of dissatisfaction is higher among men than among women, 19.3 percent and 11 percent respectively.

With reference to age, dissatisfaction tends to be higher among the younger groups. Thus . . . 19.4 percent of the workers 29 years of age or under stated that they were dissatisfied with their present employment, whereas the figures go down to 16.5 percent [for workers between 30 and 40 years of age] and 7.3 percent in the higher age group.

What light do [these figures] shed on the subject under consideration? First of all, the low percentage of dissatisfied individuals would seem to indicate that the workers have a somewhat complacent attitude towards their industrial work. A large portion of them are migrant workers, since only 35 percent of those in the sample were born in the Lima-Callao area, and it may be that for many of them the new environment offers more satisfaction than the limited opportunities of their former provincial or rural surroundings.

Although the above hypothesis is plausible, it should be borne in mind that a low percentage of persons expressing dissatisfaction with the work they are doing has been a constant feature of the many studies that have been conducted to date on satisfaction in employment. These percentages are much the same as those given in the present study; Blauner, for instance, reports that, in five surveys conducted and analyzed between the years 1935 and 1957, the percentage of dissatisfaction varies between 10 and 21 percent.[4] According to these figures, the labor force in the early stages of industrialization does not differ in respect to work satisfaction from workers similarly employed in countries with a more advanced economy, though the source of satisfaction may be different.

It has been pointed out in sociological literature that the concept of work satisfaction or morale is in many ways ambiguous.[5] For the sake of clarity, it is at least necessary to break the term down into some of its component parts in order to isolate the principal sources or bases of this satisfaction. With these observations in mind and in an effort to arrive at a more exact definition of those elements which go to make up the part of the worker's world formed by the factory, the individuals being studied were asked to state what aspects of their employment attracted them most. The sources indicated are shown in Table 3.

For 67.8 percent of the workers, which is the highest percentage in this table, the main source of satisfaction is the type of work they are doing, that is, the particular industrial activity in which they happen to be engaged at present. The figure is approximately the same for men and women. Next in importance (48.9 percent) comes the human element of pleasure derived from friendship with fellow workers. In this connection it should be borne in mind that for many of these workers the social system of the factory— and in a general way the whole industrial system to which they now belong —is totally different from their original environment, especially for those who come from rural areas. The important point is that the workers have a very

---

[4]Robert Blauner, "Work Satisfaction and Industrial Trends in Modern Society," in *Labor and Trade Unionism,* ed. Walter Galenson and Seymour Lipset (New York: John Wiley, 1960), pp. 339–360.

[5]An excellent discussion of this subject is to be found in Jacqueline Frisch-Gautier, "Moral et Satisfaction au Travail," in Traite de Sociologie du Travail, ed. Georges Friedmann and Pierre Naville (Paris: Librairie Armand Colin, 1961), pp. 132–157.

Table 19-3
**Principal Sources of Work Satisfaction Among Industrial Workers of the
Lima-Callao Area**

Sources of satisfaction	Total[a]
Type of work done	67.8%
Friendship with fellow workers	48.9
Wages	35.7
Prestige of the employer firm	24.7
Employers	23.3
Security benefits	9.7
Miscellaneous	7.0
	(N = 1,096)

[a]The percentages add up to more than 100 because some people gave more than one source.

positive attitude towards the greater degree of human contact and the inter-relationships which are characteristic of the industrial system, and this has a whole series of consequences when it comes to fulfilling many of the "commitments" of industrial civilization. It is likely that the value attached to the work-group is especially important in various aspects of the socialization of the workers, such as trade-union membership, solidarity, influence in labor disputes, etc.

Lastly, Table 3 shows that wages come third as a source of satisfaction . . . , 35.7 percent . . . . It would be a mistake, however, to consider this reply in absolute terms and to conclude that the wages they receive constitute a very considerable part of the satisfaction which the worker claims to derive from his job. Although their awareness of the situation has by no means caught up with reality, the workers feel that their wages form the

Table 19-4
**Principal Sources of Work Dissatisfaction Among Industrial Workers of the
Lima-Callao Area**

Sources of Dissatisfaction	Total[a]
Wages	21.9%
Schedule	8.0
Distance home to work	3.0
Type of work done	10.2
Substances worked with	6.8
Hygiene	2.1
The boss	10.4
Fellow workers	5.0
Miscellaneous	4.0
No complaints	29.1
No answer	4.2
	(N = 1,096)

[a]The percentages add up to more than 100 because some people gave more than one source.

most unpleasant aspect of their present employment. This is the conclusion reached from replies to another [question] on which they were asked to indicate those aspects of their present employment which were most disagreeable to them. [These results are shown in Table 4.]

Wage level is most frequently indicated as a source of dissatisfaction (21.9 percent), although one should note that less than one-fourth of the workers made this reply. The second highest factor is the boss (10.4 percent). In general the figures strengthen our hypothesis that, in some underdeveloped countries, adaptation to urban and industrial life styles does not imply great tensions or problems for the individuals involved in this process. It is significant that the largest percentage of responses in Table 2 was, "no complaints." Furthermore 36 percent of the recent migrants (1–4 years) gave this reply compared with the overall percentage of 29.1 percent.[6]

------

[6]This rosy analysis should be tempered by the realization that this is not a sample of all city-dwellers, but only a sample of the most successful blue-collar workers. Unemployed, underemployed and service workers were excluded from the analysis.— Eds.

20 Industrial Labor Recruitment in Peru

David Chaplin

. . . Economics and sociology share an interest in the labor market, which is popularly referred to as "Commercialization," and academically as "disenchantment" by rationalization (Max Weber).[1] The theoretical issue is: How far can this process go in any human society? How many types of services and types of people will be available at the right price? And, does this process continue unilineally during industrialization, or is it cyclical? Also, is it a unitary phenomenon or does it have concretely separable aspects which can change in opposed directions?*

The Sample

An opportunity was found to suggest answers to some of these questions in a currently industrializing society, Peru. In 1959 I examined a stratified purposive sample of 3,918 textile factory workers chosen: 1) from 13 of the largest of Peru's 40 mills, 9 in Lima, the "primate" capital, 3 in Arequipa, the next largest city, and 1 in Cuzco, a provincial city in the heart of the most Indian section of the country. 2) The mills also represented the overall distribution of spinning and weaving operations, as well as cotton, wool and rayon varieties of production. This industry is the largest and most developed branch of manufacturing. As in many countries, it has been a leading sector in industrialization. 3) Mills of the major eras of development were also proportionately represented, the oldest and the newest being

Adapted from *América Latina* (October 1966), with permission of the publisher.
*For an account of the political aspects of the Peruvian labor movement, see David Chaplin, "Peruvian Blue-Collar Workers," *International Journal of Comparative Sociology* 10 (1969); also reprinted in N. Dufty, ed., *Blue-Collar Workers* (Leiden: Brill, 1970). It should be noted that the October 1968 takeover by a military Junta has drastically changed the political constraints on unions in Peru. It is not anticipated, however, that most of the patterns suggested above will be directly affected by this change. The Junta has begun (1971) to institute an industrial community reform designed to transfer stock ownership of factories to the workers with the widely understood purpose of undercutting the union political base of the A.P.R.A. Party (a formerly radical reform party now to the right of the Junta). This program thus far has only had the effect of paralyzing investment in manufacturing with a Jugoslav style of worker control still much in doubt. The Junta is clearly unfavorable to any mass socio-political mobilization even in favor of their program.—D.C.
[1]H. H. Gerth and C. Wright Mills, *From Max Weber: Essays in Sociology* (New York: Oxford University Press, 1946), p. 51.

in the sample. In the 13 factories selected, all the currently employed workers were covered as well as all ever-employed, in one case.

Analytical Perspective

I am interested in labor mobility [and recruitment] as one type of social mobility. Within the former category I have concentrated on [milieu mobility, employer mobility, and migration] to the exclusion of the more traditional sociological concern with status mobility. My reasons for this exclusion have . . . some theoretical interest. . . . It was not due to any rejection of the validity of this major field of research, but rather to the following factors.

1. For the first- or second-generation rural migrants, such as were most of the sample of factory workers, the overriding change is one of situs. As industrialization proceeds, the urban and rural worlds in Peru have grown even farther apart, since modernization is concentrated primarily in the larger cities. Thus the question of whether a worker has moved up, down or sideways is confused in his mind, as well as that of his urban observers, by the blurred criteria of evaluation.

2. The relevance of his occupation, whatever its prestige, to his overall status is also confused by his ambivalent attitude toward the meaning of work. In the agrarian world his life status determined his occupation, whereas in an urban industrial society the opposite tends to be the case, that is, a man *is* whatever he *does* for a living. In between these stages, participation in the labor market tends to be a purely practical necessity with little relationship to the total self. His job may highly influence the worker's behavior without serving as a meaningful basis of identity. (In such societies, the independently wealthy need have no occupational identity at all, with no loss of self-image. Both rich and poor are known primarily by their style of consumption rather than their productive roles.)

3. The significance of occupations for social status is also confused by the endemic phenomenon in Peru of multiple job holding at all levels. Typically these jobs are at different prestige levels and often in different situses. Which will be revealed to the investigator depends on the subject's "definition of the situation." This "moonlighting" is made necessary by many factors, the major ones being inflation and a tendency for all classes, which are part of the urban industrial milieu, to mimic upper class norms.

A Demographic Index of Market Fluidity

. . . Although business conditions facing the textile industry fluctuated "normally," the wage level and the very substantial nonwage labor costs (40–60 percent of the wage bill) were fixed politically. They rose steadily from the onset of extensive government control in 1936 without respect to the violent shifts in the supply of, or demand for labor. [However,] a number of worker characteristics [did] fluctuate, in response to changes in supply and demand, thus providing us with a substitute "demographic" index of labor-market fluidity (or commercialization) in situations in which the wage level cannot change "normally." In fact, to the sociologist, changes in these characteristics are more significant symptoms of alterations in worker norms than the wage level could provide. The latter, after all, is presumably under the direct control of management and is in significant direct touch with labor-market factors only at the lower level entry positions, assuming, as is the case here, that seniority is a strongly established norm. On the other hand, the characteristics of workers who choose to make themselves available for employment are, of course, largely under their own control. (The only conscious managerial recruitment criteria used were 1) an aversion to female employment after 1955, and 2) a preference on the part of some Lima employers, for *serranos* (migrants from the mountains) over *Limeños,* on the assumption that the former would be more docile. For the most part, however, workers were hired "at the gate." As a result, thanks to the grapevine and chain migration effect, plants and even rooms tended to be stereotyped by barrios or urban neighborhoods, and by birthplace (among the migrants).

In the case of the plant for which records are available of all workers ever employed since its opening in 1900, the following patterns and changes among sensitive indices of mobility were observed [see Table 1].

Table 20-1
Labor Recruitment, 1900–1959

		% of Migrants	
Years	Average % female hired each year	Male	Female
1900–1920	29%	36%	30%
1921–1939	33	36	13
1940–1945	53	60	22
1946–1950	30	56	12
1951 +	12	27	–

The gradual rise in the percentage of women employed between 1900 and 1920 (29 percent) and the 1921–1939 period (33 percent) was sharply accelerated to 53 percent during the labor shortage period from 1940–1945. Thereafter the proportion of women fell sharply in the face of 1) a large surplus of workers due to postwar migration, 2) a slump in business conditions in textiles, and 3) the legally prescribed higher cost of female employment.

In addition to this change in the sexual composition of the labor force, the percentage of migrants also rose sharply during World War II as employers reached out in various directions . . . for new sources of recruits.

After the war, in spite of the flood of migrants, this factory, like most others, retrenched by releasing migrants more often than *Limeños* and preferring the latter when hiring new workers. The gradual rise in the age-on-employment of *Limeños* from 1900 to 1959 was temporarily set back by the World War II shortage while the decline in the age-on-employment of migrants was temporarily accelerated by the same market factor. This difference in the age-on-employment by birthplace can be explained as follows: the rise in the ages of *Limeños* can be considered "normal" given the prohibition of child labor and increased schooling while the higher and declining age-on-employment of migrants appears to be the result of their high rate of early career turnover, due to the acculturation ordeal. Had other personnel data been available, doubtless other worker characteristics would also have varied with changing market conditions.

Female Workers

The situation of the female worker was one of the most interesting and unexpected to come out of this study. The higher seniority and low percent of females employed in 1959 was notable. Generally, the older plants had a higher proportion of females with longer service. It turned out that all of these employers had been drastically reducing their female employment since the all-time high during World War II, due to their greater cost. If all the provisions of the labor and welfare laws are enforced, women cost considerably more than men. When this is added to their normally greater absenteeism and higher rate of turnover, they become uneconomic to employ.

Factors Affecting the "Modernity" of the Various Plants

In terms of structural factors favoring and opposing universalism, functional specificity, etc., the following were examined: the size of the labor force, the rate of turnover, the use of *compadrazgo* (god-parenthood), managerial preferences for particular types of workers, the location of the plant and the labor law, and welfare benefits.

The combination of small size and low turnover per se would tend to particularize labor management relationships (not necessarily in a pleasant fashion). Only one firm had over 500 workers (894), while the rest averaged 310. . . . Among those firms in existence longer than 35 years—thus allowing for a full range of possible seniority statuses—the median male seniority was 11 years and female 15 years.

Perhaps a more significant indicator of stability is the fact that, for the one plant for which data on all workers ever-employed was available (from 1900 to 1959) only 26 percent left voluntarily, 40 percent left due to normal attrition (died or retired) and 34 percent were fired—the latter largely during the 6-year dictatorship between 1949–1955, when management temporarily recovered some of its prerogatives.

The low rate of voluntary average annual turnover suggested by this long range figure (less than ½ of a percent per year) arises from several factors:

1. The surplus of blue-collar labor in Lima and relatively high wages and good working conditions in textiles.
2. The housing shortage which effectively immobilizes workers *within* the city.
3. Company-related benefits.
4. Advancement via seniority.
5. Lack of knowledge of alternative job opportunities and wage scales elsewhere.

In terms of sex and origin differentials, migrant males were the most stable and local females the least. Overall the low rate of turnover from the establishment of Lima's mills reveals that the often cited pattern of an era of instability in industrial labor recruitment in such countries is a feature of the usual type and location of early industrial plants. Most were mines and decentralized agricultural processing operations. Their unstable operation and closeness to rural communities inevitably complicated their recruitment of a committed industrial labor force.

Within this structurally particularizing context some managements went further in this direction. A few deliberately sought out Indian migrants from the sierra as more docile and "trainable." Beyond this policy, some executives accepted requests from workers to be the godfather of one of their children. This ancient institution used to exist largely between peers and focus primarily on the godparent-godchild tie. More recently in Latin America it is commonly found between unequals in which the subordinate is much more interested in his new compadre than in establishing a lifelong protector for his child.[2] Needless to say, such personal ties to some of their workers disrupt managerial relations with those "left outside."

The two major factors favoring "modernity" are the urban location of most of these plants and their relatively high wage level. Decentralized rural locations, one of which was observed near Cuzco, invite conquest by a pre-industrial environment.[3] They are sought either by sentimental decentralists or businessmen hoping to capitalize on cheap labor. The loss of efficiency and the subsequent externally forced wage raises make such locations a poor bargain in the long run, as the bankruptcy rate of these firms has demonstrated. The relatively high wage level in textiles roughly correlates

[2]Sidney W. Mintz and Eric R. Wolf, "An Analysis of Ritual Co-Parenthood" [Compadrazgo], *Southwestern Journal of Anthropology* 6 (Winter 1950): p. 364.
[3]For other cases where a rural or small-town location complicated efforts at industrial progress (even though this was not the lesson drawn by the authors): see Charles H. Savage, "Social Reorganization in a Factory in the Andes," Monograph no. 7 (Ithaca, N.Y.: Society for Applied Anthropology, 1964); and Manning Nash, *Machine Age Maya* (New York: The Free Press, 1958).

with a shorter social distance between labor and management which in turn is associated with a more effective diffusion of industrial norms.

Although "modern" in form, [Peru's labor and welfare] legislation fits traditional expectations of paternalism, especially since, until recently, the employer was made responsible for many of the benefits promised by the state. One could thus say that, in general, some of these workers have moved from traditional to welfare-state paternalism in one generation without an intervening "rugged individualist" phase. State-managed welfare theoretically should free workers from personalistic dependence on charitable patrons. In practice workers could hope to enjoy these benefits only by staying put in one firm *and* by being active and influential in their union.

In addition, the wage scale is prevented from reflecting market forces or labor productivity because:

a. Until 1951 no labor productivity study had ever been made in this industry. Nor has any use been made of this or a 1959 resurvey in determining wages.
b. The blue-collar workers covered in this sample were amazingly ignorant of the wages paid for comparable work at other textile mills. The union newspaper published only the skimpy average which management made available (which were predictably not given much credence by the workers in view of their source). A systematic self-survey by the Union had never been taken, not only from a lack of experience in such work, but also because of worker reluctance to reveal their pay even to their unions. Also, since interfirm mobility was very low and entry possible only at the bottom, few workers personally had had any comparative experience.

Previous Occupational Experience

The utility of previous industrial experience to employers is not a settled issue in terms of our perspective of the rationality of the labor market and of employment practices. On the one hand, employers in underdeveloped countries bemoan the shortage of skilled efficient workers. Yet they often refuse to hire experienced workers, largely, it would seem, because they are harder to discipline. Some also complain that such workers would have to unlearn bad habits and that it is easier to train fresh recruits.

Before World War II, and for some time thereafter, it was generally assumed that the acquisition of technical skills was a major labor problem in underdeveloped areas. More recent studies indicate that there are few people . . . who cannot learn how to operate machinery if sticking at the job is made rewarding in their terms.[4] Consequently, however suspect the ex-

---

[4]Clark Kerr et al., *Industrialism and Industrial Man* (Cambridge: Harvard University Press, 1960), p. 8. "Problems of turnover and absenteeism seem to be clearly more a function of the existing structure of employment than of any cultural hangover or built-in incapacity to adjust. . . . Commitment and productivity prevail where working

pressed preference of some Peruvian managers for "green" workers may be, such a policy probably does not, per se, lower efficiency given the well-established custom of hiring in at the bottom. This apprenticeship system does, of course, stereotype work habits such that subsequent efforts to change workloads and practices, even at higher pay levels, are usually resisted. There is certainly a loss of flexibility both in terms of the employer's ability to hire and fire, as well as to reorganize. Only for a brief period while new plants are being established does management enjoy a "full" prerogative in structuring the organization of production.

In spite of this uncertainty about the relevance of previous industrial experience, it is still of interest to review the data on previous employment of our sample. In terms of a developing industrial labor market it is important to determine whether workers do move directly from home and school into factories or pass through a series of nonindustrial occupations first, and whether there are differences in this respect between the sexes and between local urbanites and migrants.

Previous Occupations

Among the male workers in Lima we find that 18 percent of the *Limeños* and 18 percent of the migrants had previously worked in a textile mill with an additional 11 percent in both cases having had other industrial plant experience. Consistent with the higher age-on-employment of the male migrants only 6 percent went to work directly from "home" whereas 24 percent of Lima's males had not been previously employed. . . .

For all workers the extent of prior experience was as follows (A—any previous employment; B—previous factory employment):

	A	*B*
Lima Males	76%	29%
Lima Females	47%	19%
Migrant Males	94%	28%
Migrant Females	82%	47%

In terms of classic "entry" occupations, "other manual labor" (largely construction work for males and seamstress jobs for females), appears significant in Lima largely for male migrants.

Overall, the low proportion of workers with prior industrial experience would seem normal in view of the low median age-on-employment. Twenty-eight percent of the Lima . . . workers had previously worked in factories.

In Lima, . . . there is now an explicit managerial preference for inexperienced *serranos* (Indians from the mountains). Related to this is the fact that prior experience correlates inversely with current occupation.

conditions support them." Frank Bonilla, "The Urban Worker," in *Change and Continuity in Latin America,* ed. J. J. Johnson (Stanford: Stanford University Press, 1964), p. 197.

Workers with substantial employment experience, and hence an older age-on-employment, generally enter low-level dead-end *peon* positions. Those who eventually become weavers, on the other hand, started work no later than 20 years of age, often younger. Consequently interfirm mobility is not advantageous in the form of helping a worker accumulate a "capital" of skill. On the contrary, given the scarcity of good jobs, few workers in the relatively well-paid textile factories ever quit voluntarily.

One prior occupation never encountered was that of artisan weaver. Unlike the English case, the rural part-time weaver in Peru persists, whereas the urban artisan was eliminated even before textile mills were first established around 1900.[5]

In general, the prior employment experience of our sample is held down by management's preference for "green" workers and labor's desire for a strict seniority system regulating promotion. The resulting exclusion of workers with prior industrial experience could well be called a particularistic narrowing of labor-market extension in that each plant is deprived of benefiting from the accumulation of industrial experience on the part of recruits. On the other hand, such a "policy" thereby diffused industrial experience more widely throughout the society. It represents a type of "stockpiling" of workers with factory experience in the pool of those employed at other jobs or among the unemployed.

Factories in such countries can operate quite efficiently, as is the case in Peru cotton mills, through primary reliance on their own facilities as the first industrial experience. The more significant sociological issue remains open, however. Would an industrial labor market develop more rapidly and effectively if, when they were available, experienced workers were hired? This policy would require a higher level of labor turnover which, in the case of such a labor surplus, could lower wages. Such market fluidity, in turn, woud probably inhibit labor commitment.

Conclusions and Speculation

From our sample, and such background data as is available on Peru, the following conclusions seem warranted.

In terms of factors favoring and opposing "modernization," were a standardized scale available, this sector of the urban industrial Peruvian labor market could be classified as rather deficient. Other than its urban location and relatively high wages, most other features of its situation are relatively unfavorable to the diffusion of what are felt by U.S. social scientists to be the requisites of a fully committed industrial labor force. The workers are "overcommitted" to one firm and subjected to a number of generally nontraditional conditions beyond their own control which particularize their status. Their level of turnover is "too low," the firms are "too small," and an extreme atmosphere of *desconfianza* (lack of trust in others) leads them

---

[5]See Chapter VII of Neil J. Smelser, *Social Change in the Industrial Revolution* (Chicago: University of Chicago Press, 1959).

to focus primarily on personal (*compadrazgo*) or collective security measures at the expense of all other considerations. I am not asserting that their behavior is at all irrational, *given* their *own* goals and available means. It may well be the case, however, that like much of Europe until the 1950s, the social organization of industrial work in Peru "jelled" too soon and that a full-scale economic "takeoff" will require a disruption of current industrial organization in some respects more painful than that involved in pulling workers into industry in the first place. In fact, our evidence suggests that this earlier stage of industrial labor recruitment under the conditions described above, *is not as difficult as it is often reported to be, and that the most disruptive stage is yet to be reached in those industrial organizations already well established in such countries.*

The total picture of labor-market rationalization could be summarized as follows, partly from the data on Peru, partly from that on the U.S., and partly on the basis of conjecture. In the earliest stages of industrial labor recruitment, involving largely mines and decentralized agriculture processing plants, one finds the widest range of rural lower-class labor. This arises from the nearly total participation in work in the preindustrial setting by all the physically able. Subsequently, under the above mentioned circumstances, various categories of workers in currently developing societies will be excluded in a manner analogous to, but different from the current narrowing of the U.S. labor market in the face of automation and an aging population.

Descriptive evidence on earlier labor practices in this industry as well as situations still current in rural areas indicate that the range of services expected has also narrowed. Textile factory workers are not expected to contribute after-hours work to their employers as domestic servants, mistresses, musicians, manual laborers on other projects, etc., except in the one rural plant and in the case of a few *serranos* seeking to ingratiate themselves with their employers.

This latter narrowing of labor-market extension is, of course, linked with the other dimension, purity. In terms of expecting fewer services, the labor-management relationship has become more functionally specific. However, the low level of turnover, small size of firm, and company-based fringe benefits are countervailing impurifying forces.

21

The Unequal Distribution of Income in Latin America

Louis Wolf Goodman

This essay presents some facts about income distribution in Latin America. First the overall situation is documented and compared with that of the United States. The body of the paper then outlines a set of mechanisms which foster unequal income distribution within the working class. As a conclusion government income policies and future trends are discussed. The main purpose of this essay is to point out that income is not only unequally distributed among upper, middle, and working classes, but also *within* the working class. This income inequality among wage earners at the lower end of the economic scale produces fierce competition for scarce earnings and jobs. The search and competition among workers for these scarce resources keeps the poorest workers at bare subsistence and prevents any semblance of working-class solidarity.

Personal income is more evenly distributed across the populations of the United States and United Kingdom than it is in any Latin American country for which data exists. In the United States the wealthiest 10 percent of the population receives 30 percent of national income; the next 40 percent of the population receives 47 percent; and the lower 50 percent of the population earns only 23 percent. Corresponding figures for Colombia shows the wealthiest 10 percent with 43 percent, the next 40 percent with 37 percent, and the poorer 50 percent with 20 percent of national income.

On one level this contrast might be ascribed to overall differences in national development. In countries with a lower per capita income, relatively little is left for the bulk of the population once the small upper- and middle-income groups have taken their share. Hence 79 percent of Brazil's population falls below the national income average, while the comparable figure for the United States is only 64 percent. In 1960 Brazil's per capita income was $208 compared with the United States' $2,775.[1]

Unequal income distribution is caused by advantaged groups using their social power to gain greater income shares. Not only do upper- and middle-class groups use their power to earn more than do workers, but more advantaged workers exert whatever leverage is possible to continue to earn more than less-advantaged workers. Among the circumstances which give some workers more leverage than others are: 1) working in a more productive economic sector; 2) performing an economic function which entails

[1]See "Income Distribution in Latin America," *Economic Bulletin for Latin America* 12 (1967): pp. 38–60; and "The Measurement of Latin American Real Income in U.S. Dollars," ibid., pp. 107–142.

greater control over the means of production; 3) possessing a special skill; 4) belonging to a union; and 5) being a member of a social security system. Access to these worker sources of leverage are carefully guarded and tightly stratified in Latin American society—as will be seen in the following pages.

The more productive *sectors of national economies* have corresponding earnings. For 1970 the estimated Latin American per capita produce per worker in agriculture was $616, in manufacturing it was $2,952, and in services it was $1,583. Within the mixed service sector, trade and finance averaged $2,422, government $2,114, and the large miscellaneous services category only $901.[2] These levels of productivity parallel the income levels of the various economic sectors. In Brazil the per capita agricultural product is one-third of that of manufacturing. Thus 70 percent of the lower-income families are engaged in primary sector economic activities and two-thirds of the middle-income group (fifth to ninth percentiles) are employed in secondary activities. The services group is appropriately divided with families performing miscellaneous services falling in the lower half, many commerce and government employees in the middle sectors, and professionals in the highest 10 percent. In Mexico the per capita income for largely agricultural rural families is only 43 percent of average urban income. However, even within the same economic activity, rural workers earn less than their urban counterparts.[3]

Within these broad regional and sectional groupings, the most important factor influencing income distribution is the *economic function* fulfilled by the worker. In Mexico the 50 percent lower-income group is largely composed of agricultural workers, artisans, self-employed but "marginal" agricultural, construction and service workers, and small farmers. The middle 30 percent includes workers employed in more productive industries, self-employed workers and small owners who have a margin of security, and a number of white-collar employees. The highest 20 percent include mainly owner-entrepreneurs, a healthy proportion of white-collar employees and self-employed, and a small number of workers.[4] In many Latin American countries distinctions are made between wage earners (paid on an hourly basis), salaried employees (paid on a monthly basis), and self-employed individuals. The above data shows how this is reflected in Mexico's income distribution. Wage earners predominate in the lower half; salaried employees are clustered in middle income groups; the self-employed are split with marginal individuals (who are essentially underemployed) falling in the lower half, and professionals and owner-entrepreneurs in the highest categories.

Differences between skilled and unskilled workers are reflected in the wages paid to different skill levels in the same occupations in Buenos Aires, Argentina. Skilled electricians earned an average of 62¢ an hour in 1965 while unskilled electricians earned 45¢ an hour; skilled lathe operators

---

[2]See "Structural Changes in Employment within the Context of Latin America's Economic Development," *Economic Bulletin for Latin America* 10 (1965): pp. 165–187.
[3]See "Income Distribution in Latin America," op. cit., pp. 41–44.
[4]Ibid., pp. 44–45.

average 55¢, while the unskilled earned 46¢; skilled bakers averaged 38¢ while unskilled bakers earned 35¢. Overall the average hourly pay for all occupations was 52¢ for skilled workers, and 42¢ for unskilled. The differential is far more acute when a comparison is made of the real purchasing power of the highest paid group of skilled workers and the lowest paid group of unskilled workers in Buenos Aires. Fifteen minutes of work are required by the unskilled to buy a pound of bread, 1¾ hours to buy one dozen eggs and 44 hours to buy a pair of shoes. The skilled worker spends 8 minutes of work-time to buy a pound of bread, 55 minutes for one dozen eggs and 24 hours for a pair of shoes. Average figures for the United States in 1964 were 3 minutes for a pound of bread, 14 minutes for one dozen eggs, and 6 hours for a pair of shoes.[5]

Another characteristic of higher-income workers is that of *union membership*. It has been estimated that 9 million Latin American workers or 15 percent of the total work force were enrolled in unions in 1964.[6] The union-based ability to bargain collectively and to strike has enabled these workers to have higher earnings than their nonunion counterparts. However it is difficult to separate the effects of union membership from those of other characteristics mentioned above. Usually, studies report that higher-income workers include greater proportions of nonagricultural, urban, skilled, and unionized workers than do low-income groups. In such studies it is impossible to know if all or only some of these factors contribute to the wage differential. Nevertheless when controlled analyses have examined comparable situations, each of these factors has made a separate contribution to having income distributed unevenly among working groups.

Fringe benefits constitute another dimension of the unequal division of income. Latin American workers are insured against a wide variety of risks, including old age, disability, death, sickness, work-connected accidents, maternity and unemployment. However, only 25 percent of the 1967 labor force was able to contribute to a social security system which insured them against any of these risks.[7] Furthermore, among those insured, the amount and type of coverage varied considerably.[8] The small proportion of the Latin American work force covered by social security, and the great inequalities among those covered, are additional factors in the unequal distribution of income in Latin America.

The inequality of income distribution in Latin America is evident. However, the development of *national incomes policies* which simultaneously spur economic growth and diminish interpersonal inequality has met with very limited success. The uneven distribution of income is not only disastrous because of the privations experienced by poor families, but also because the power to consume is not sufficiently diffused within Latin Amer-

---

[5]U.S. Bureau of Labor Statistics, "Wage and Salaries by Occupation and Industry in Argentina," *Labor Developments Abroad* (May 1966), pp. 1–5.
[6]*Statistical Abstract of Latin America, 1969* (UCLA), p. 106.
[7]See U.S. Bureau of Labor Statistics, *Labor Developments Abroad* (August 1970).
[8]For a detailed discussion of this see "Trends in Latin American Social Security" by Alfredo Mallet, Chapter 22 of this volume.

ican societies to support substantial industrial growth. For factories to prosper, consumers with reasonable incomes are needed to buy their products. On the other hand, in nations with a low per capita domestic product, some concentration of income is needed to generate the savings required for capital formation.

Latin American nations have tried to balance consumption and savings through a variety of economic policies. Entrepreneurs have been encouraged to concentrate income and generate savings through greater access to credit, low interest rates, preferential exchange rates, and direct government subsidies. Consumption has been regulated by governmental controls over wages and prices. Typically an attempt is made to equalize wage and price increases so that real income does not decline among wage earners. This often takes the form of a year-end wage increase equal to the aggregate price increases of the previous 12 months. In situations of economic growth, consumption may be spurred by greater wage increases. In situations of economic stagnation, wage increases may not equal price increases, although minimum wages are sometimes fully increased to protect the poorest workers (such attention to the poor is not fully effective since minimum wage legislation is extremely difficult to enforce).

Many Latin American nations have adopted income and corporate tax policies in an attempt to redistribute income. These have been largely ineffective due to the ease of evasion of income taxes and the nature of corporate tax laws which allow payment to be passed on to the final consumer. More effective tools in the redistribution of income have been the expansion of social services by Latin American governments. Widened social security systems, increased educational and public health services and public housing programs have somewhat improved the situation of the Latin American worker. However, as mentioned above, inequities exist even among these arrangements.

The net effect of these policies has not been uniform among Latin American countries. However, since 1940 there seems to have been intermittent improvement in income distribution. The share of high-income families has declined, but the income share of the lowest 20 percent of families also appears to be shrinking—both in absolute and relative terms. The principal beneficiaries of these changes have been the middle 60 or 70 percent of families.[9] Such changes may indicate that increasing numbers of workers can share in economic development, not only at the expense of the already privileged upper class, but also at the expense of the most impoverished group of workers.

[9]"Income Distribution in Latin America," op. cit., pp. 46–50.

22 Trends in Latin American Social Security

Alfredo Mallet

The development of social security in a number of Latin American countries has been marked by pronounced disparities between the legal provisions applying to different categories of workers, by an extraordinary proliferation of extremely diverse schemes, and by the multiplicity of institutions applying them. In other countries of the region the trend has been just the opposite—towards relative uniformity in the legal provisions and consolidation of the administrative bodies.

In the first group of countries a policy of diversification of social security appears to have held sway unchallenged for many years, and the rapid headway it made in some of them brought into being a whole host of different social insurance schemes and bodies to operate them. In the [1960s], however, and particularly in the past few years, the pendulum in many areas has begun to swing sharply in the opposite direction. In a number of countries in the region this has taken the form of far-reaching legislative reforms based on the principle of equality of treatment for all categories of protected workers and the amalgamation of bodies performing parallel functions, which in some cases have been fused into a single entity while in others their numbers have been drastically reduced. Elsewhere this trend has not yet found practical implementation of any appreciable scale, but there is a clear tendency towards uniformity and administrative unification in respect of social security throughout Latin America.

It is the purpose of this article to begin by describing the process by which a multiplicity of schemes comes into existence, its characteristics and its effects. . . .

How Diversification Came About

The following extremely summary description of the process of diversification in social security will make it easier to understand some of its causes. The description refers in particular to Argentina [since this is a country with great disparities] in the provisions on social security and the proliferation of administrative bodies. . . .

Adapted from Alfredo Mallet, "Diversification and Standardization: Two Trends in Latin American Social Security," *International Labour Review* (January 1970), pp. 49–83, with permission of the publisher, International Labour Office, Geneva, Switzerland.

The pensions legislation enacted in the first quarter of this century benefited groups of workers in specific occupational categories. Thus entitlement to a retirement pension was conferred in 1903 upon members of the judiciary, and in 1904 upon employees of the state; in 1915 pensions were introduced for railway workers, and a fund for that purpose was set up in 1919; in 1921 came retirement pensions and a fund for the employees of public services,[1] and in 1923 similar benefits were provided for banking employees, who also had their own fund.

This by now well-established practice of setting up different schemes, each with its own fund, for different occupational categories was confirmed between 1939 and 1954, when the legislation was extended to cover almost the entire economically active population. During this period eight major schemes were set up, each with its own fund, the provisions governing which differed in various respects: for employees in journalism (1939), navigation (1939),[2] commerce and community activities (1944),[3] industry (1946), self-employed persons (1954), professional workers (1954),[4] entrepreneurs (1954) and rural workers (1954). In 1956 a special scheme was set up for workers in domestic service. There were also special schemes for members of the armed forces, the federal police and the national gendarmerie.

The result, as concerns invalidity, old-age and survivor's insurance, was that prior to the reforms introduced with a view to standardization there existed no fewer than sixteen different national schemes, each with its own administrative institution.

In these developments (unlike those in Chile and Peru) no distinction was made between manual and nonmanual workers. Self-employed persons were the exception to this rule, those performing predominantly manual work being covered by the Independent Workers' Fund and those doing nonmanual work by the Entrepreneurs' Fund. Nor was there—as in Colombia, Cuba, Ecuador and Mexico, for example—a clearly defined dividing line between schemes for workers in the public sector and those for workers in the private sector, since funds such as those for public service employees, banking employees or navigation personnel covered groups of employees working for state undertakings as well as those employed by private firms.

In 1957 two family allowances funds were set up, one for workers in industry and the other for workers in commerce; a third was set up in 1965 for stevedores and another in 1968 for employees of state undertakings.

Lastly, mention should be made of the existence of more than seventy superannuation and pension funds or social welfare institutions at the provincial or municipal level. These schemes were quite distinct from one

---

[1]This fund catered for employees of tram, telephone, gas, electricity and public motor transport, employees of private clinics, hospitals and sanatoria, and other groups.
[2]For personnel in the merchant navy, dockyards and ports, airline employees, etc.
[3]Employees in commerce, private schools, clubs and other nonprofit-making societies, workers in the beer and soft drinks industries and various other groups.
[4]Self-employed persons with a university degree or special technical, scientific or artistic qualifications.

another and many of them were very small. They provided protection for employees of provincial or municipal authorities and in some cases for members of certain professions, such as lawyers, notaries, engineers and medical practitioners.[5]

As regards branches of social security, on the one hand superannuation and pension schemes were established and on the other family allowances schemes, and there was also a maternity fund providing limited benefits. In 1915 protection in respect of industrial accidents became the responsibility of the employer, who could cover the risk with private insurance companies or employers' liability societies. . . .[6]

Differentiation Between Categories of Protected Persons

. . . The distinctions made between categories of protected persons have taken the following forms:

(a) Different schemes for workers in the public sector and workers in the private sector, as in Argentina, Brazil, Chile, Colombia, Cuba, Ecuador, Paraguay and Uruguay: additional distinctions have been made between categories of workers in the public sector in Cuba, where there used to be eleven different groups, each with its own administrative institution, and in Chile, where there are social security schemes for twenty-three different groups.

(b) Differentiation of manual workers and nonmanual workers, even within the same branch of economic activity, as in Chile and Peru; in Argentina this distinction was made only in the case of self-employed persons.

(c) Distinctions based upon occupational categories (merchant seamen, journalists, railwaymen, etc.) or upon branches of economic activity (industry, commerce, public services, etc.), as in Argentina, Brazil, Cuba and Uruguay, with a few special groups in Bolivia, Chile and Paraguay, among other countries; the proliferation of schemes deriving from this factor was quite marked in Cuba and still is in Chile.

(d) Separate schemes for self-employed persons and employees, as in Argentina and Cuba.

(e) Special schemes for certain professional workers with university degrees, as in Argentina, Chile, Cuba and Uruguay.

(f) Different schemes for certain government and local government officials and certain professional workers with university degrees according

---

[5]The categories of persons protected by the funds for professional workers with a university degree were not the same in all provinces. In Santa Fé, for instance, there were funds for lawyers and attorneys, engineers and "specialists in the art of healing," while in the province of Chaco there was a fund for the judiciary and a fund for notaries, in Tucumán a fund for notaries and another for lawyers and attorneys, etc.

[6]There was an accident fund, which did not cover this contingency but did carry out supervisory functions and provided guarantees.

to the administrative division of the country: this occurred only in Argentina, where it resulted in a whole host of small provincial and municipal funds.

The existence of different legislative provisions governing different categories of workers led to the proliferation of administrative bodies, which became particularly numerous in Argentina, Chile, Cuba and Uruguay. In some cases identical or very similar provisions are implemented by different bodies, as in the case of the funds for racehorse trainers and jockeys in Chile. In other cases, on the contrary, different provisions applicable to different categories of persons are administered by the same institution: in Chile the Public Servants' and Journalists' Fund implements social security provisions covering some ten distinct groups; in Uruguay the Fund for Rural Workers and Domestic Servants is in reality administering three different schemes. But the trend has been for each different social security scheme to have its own institution to operate it.

Another reason for the proliferation of administrative institutions is the separate legislation governing protection against different contingencies. Bodies were set up on the one hand to administer [invalidism], old-age and survivors' pensions (Argentina, Brazil, Cuba and Uruguay); in some cases sickness insurance has been handled by other institutions (Chile and Uruguay); the introduction of family allowances led in its turn to the creation of further bodies (Argentina, Colombia, to a lesser extent Chile, and Uruguay), and protection against occupational risks has been handled separately in a number of countries either by the employers themselves or by private insurance companies (Argentina, Brazil, Chile, Colombia and Cuba, *inter alia*).

Why So Many Schemes?

A knowledge of the categories of workers between whom the above distinctions have been made is helpful in deducing some of the factors that have determined this process.

1. . . . The historical background of the region helps to explain the proliferation of social security schemes, since it became a tradition to make entitlement to benefit conditional upon the exercise of a certain occupational activity (civil service, national defense) or, even more specifically, upon the performance of a certain type of job or functions; development was influenced by this tradition in some countries but not in others.

2. Political factors have played an important part. Schemes for employees of the state offering advantageous conditions in respect of pensions can be explained by the fact that in a number of countries civil servants have worked more or less hand in glove with the political regime in power, and were therefore in a position to secure better social security terms. However, since this same relationship may also imply a certain insecurity of employment, as the parties in power come and go, there has been a desire in some areas to make up for this by awarding pensions at a relatively early retirement age to public officials exposed to the risk of losing their jobs for political reasons.

The separate schemes and special provisions for members of the armed forces and the police, members of parliament and journalists are examples of cases in which considerations of a political nature may be presumed to have wielded an influence, along with other reasons which might be understandable in the case of some of these groups.

3. Strong trade-union backing enabled certain groups of workers to obtain social security schemes distinct from and superior to those for other workers who did not have such backing. Pressure of this kind was strongest where the group concerned was in an important or vulnerable sector of the social and economic complex: banking, land or sea transport, public utility services. Since in addition the groups concerned were small compared with the working population as a whole, and the wages they earned were above average, it was possible for a special scheme offering more advantageous conditions to be financially solvent, which would not have been the case for a scheme covering all workers.

4. It has been maintained that persons exercising similar occupational activities, or belonging to the same socioeconomic group, will be in a similar financial situation, have a similar attitude to health and culture and show the same preferences as to the contingencies in respect of which they wish to be protected. They should therefore be offered the same social security benefits, which should differ from those offered to other groups of workers who, by reason of their social and financial position, have a different scale of priorities and preferences.

Employees in commerce or public services, for instance, are said to be more interested in an advantageous [invalidism], old-age and survivors' pension scheme, while peasants attach more importance to a good range of sickness benefits.

Argentina, Brazil and Cuba were advocates of such a division of social security according to branches of economic activity. It should be pointed out that in some cases the homogeneity which was said to justify the existence of separate provisions and schemes did not in fact exist. One example among many was the Industrial Workers' Fund in Argentina, which covered workers of such widely differing social and financial situations as laborers in a factory and the owners of the same factory who worked in it themselves. . . .

5. The Argentinian schemes limited to a single province or municipality were an expression of the highly developed spirit of federalism in that country; this type of differentiation is not to be found in other Latin American countries with a federal structure.

6. Administrative considerations have in some cases been a contributing if not a determining factor in the setting up of separate schemes. It was relatively simple from an administrative point of view to set up a special scheme in sectors where there was sufficient job security and where employers were few in number and equipped to offer the cooperation indispensable for the operation of the scheme (affiliation, collection of contributions, and so on). It was evidently much simpler and more feasible to operate a scheme for banking employees, railwaymen or employees of public utility services than for agricultural workers or domestic servants.

7. The effect of all these factors, plus others not mentioned because they were of less importance, may well have been increased by a lack of planning in respect of social security in individual countries. In reality the very idea of economic and social development planning has come to be accepted only fairly recently in Latin American countries. It is therefore not surprising that, in the absence of planning, a succession of political, social and economic factors should have led to an uneven and disorganized expansion of social security, though the fact cannot be ignored that the undoubted progress made has in any case been extremely beneficial to the workers.

Consequences of the Plurality of Schemes

Unfairness. The variety and abundance of the legal provisions governing the various schemes resulted in substantial divergencies between the social security schemes in all the most important respects: contingencies covered, conditions of entitlement to benefit, nature and amount of benefits, manner of financing.

It may be inferred from a comparative analysis of the different schemes within each country that in the great majority of cases these divergencies were not—and are not—to the advantage of workers with a more modest financial, social or other status. In other words, far from compensating the underprivileged, they have often had precisely the opposite effect: wage earners have received less favorable treatment than white-collar workers; peasants have been offered social security far inferior in quality to that available for industrial workers; banking and railway employees and employees of large public utility undertakings have been given preferential treatment as compared with other occupational categories, even though they have a higher average income level than the categories who benefit least from social security.

So the difference in treatment is not based upon exceptional conditions of work, like the perfectly fair special provisions for the benefit of persons performing arduous or unhealthy work; nor does it have anything to do with the understandable—if debatable—lower retirement age for women, nor is it even based on the conditions peculiar to an occupation, as in the case of the armed forces or miners. An analysis of these differences and of those who benefit from them will in many cases bear out the claim that their origin lies in factors extraneous to the objectives of social security— the factors to which reference has been made above. . . .

Inadequate Redistribution of the National Income. Social security is recognized as playing an important role in the redistribution of the national income. Under a scheme where the same standards apply to all a transfer takes place from the higher to the lower income groups if—as is usually the case in Latin America—contributions are proportionate to earnings while the value of at least some benefits remains unchanged with little or no regard to the amount earned. If there are a number of separate schemes the transfer will operate only within each group as far as the contributions of the insured persons themselves are concerned.

On the other hand, experience with a multiplicity of schemes in Latin America has shown that in many cases the distinctions operate to the advantage of the highest income groups, for whom the conditions of entitlement to benefit are less strict while the amount of benefit is larger. At the same time—through the prices paid for goods and services and through the tax system—the burden of the contributions paid by the employers and by the state is transferred almost in its entirety to the shoulders of practically the whole population, with the result that all too often the lowest income groups—whose schemes are the least advantageous or who have none at all—are helping to finance the schemes of the better-off groups.[7] Thus, under the conditions described, in some countries the redistributive function has been distorted in many cases into a pattern that is socially unjust and economically undesirable.

Lack of Coordination. A worker moving from one occupational category or branch of economic activity to another covered by a different social insurance scheme was in many cases unable to secure recognition by the new institution of the period of service or contribution under the former scheme. This might cause more or less serious prejudice to the worker concerned, especially where to become eligible for a pension it was necessary to complete a relatively long qualifying period. Naturally, the more schemes there were the greater the risk of loss of acquired rights. Even before provisions were standardized and institutions streamlined, a number of countries introduced provisions guaranteeing recognition of periods of affiliation when a worker changed schemes. This was done, for example, in Argentina, Chile and Ecuador; it did away with the loss of rights, but there were still delays, administrative formalities and in some cases extra contributions to be paid, all resulting from the process of validating periods of affiliation to a different scheme. . . .

Administrative Complications. . . . Experience has shown that the cost per head of administering a social security scheme is generally in inverse proportion to the number of persons insured, and that a multiplicity of schemes results in higher costs. . . . A plurality of institutions implies the duplication of a certain structure and of basic services (directors, executives, registers of insured persons and employers, bookkeeping, statistical and actuarial

---

[7]According to a study made in Chile, the manual workers of that country were in reality bearing 21.8 percent of the total cost of social security while receiving 25.6 percent of its benefits; nonmanual workers—whose average income was substantially higher and whom the wage earners outnumbered by more then three to one—made a real contribution of 31.9 percent but received 43 percent of all the benefits; self-employed persons and entrepreneurs, among whom were people with very high and very low incomes, were really contributing 15.8 percent without receiving any benefits at all (Comisión de Estudios de la Seguridad Social, "Informe sobre la Reforma de la Seguridad Social Chilena," Superintendencia de Seguridad Social, 2 vols. (Santiago: Editorial Jurídica de Chile, 1964), pp. 830, 831, 837 and 838).

functions, etc.), with higher costs for the operation as a whole. Furthermore, institutional unification permits of a more rational utilization of the human and material resources available, and in particular of specialized staff and machinery or electronic equipment, which is important in developing countries.

A plethora of institutions creates complications for the workers, particularly when they transfer from one scheme to another and have to register themselves and their families all over again, and more especially still, as we have seen, when they have to persuade an institution to recognize periods of contribution to one or more previous schemes. It means filling in a whole series of forms, attaching documents, awaiting approval of the request for recognition of the period of service under the former scheme, communicating the decision reached to the body responsible for providing benefit, and so forth. Apart from the annoyance caused to the worker, there is considerable delay in dealing with his claim.

For the employers, diversification of social security often involves dealings with a number of different institutions, the filling in of different forms in respect of the payment of contributions (at various rates), [and] the need to bear in mind the different provisions in force for each scheme. . . .

For the state, the lack of homogeneity seriously complicates the orientation and supervision of the social security system; it is particularly difficult to plan the investment of the reserves of the various institutions in such a way as to conform with the objectives of economic and social development.

Mention might be made of other drawbacks resulting from the ultra-diversification of social security: the relatively small number of persons covered by a particular scheme decreases the likelihood of its being able to conform to actuarial predictions based on the law of large numbers; furthermore, the same plurality of institutions makes it difficult to establish the desired degree of financial solidarity between the different groups protected. Lastly, the possibility cannot be ruled out that the higher benefits available in certain occupations or branches of activity may have acted as an incentive to attract people into these occupations or activities to a degree inconsistent with the manpower planning necessary for development.

The Trend Towards Standardization
of Provisions and Institutional
Consolidation

In recent years public opinion and government circles in Latin America have tended increasingly towards the view that the division of workers into many different groups for social security purposes and the way in which this differentiation has operated have had undesirable effects, some of which have just been mentioned. In particular it has come to be realized that, contrary to the principles of justice on which social security should be based, such inequality of treatment has generally been detrimental to those categories of workers who were among the least privileged financially and socially.

For these reasons a clear trend has become apparent in the 1960s away from the diversification described above. . . .

The trend towards uniform standards and institutional consolidation in the various countries has resulted, on the one hand, in the relatively recent schemes being endowed with these two qualities. In the older schemes, for their part, where diversification flourished for so long, declarations of intent have been made and quite a few of them put into practice with a view to standardization and unification. . . .

23 Unpaid Labor in Socialist Cuba

Carmelo Mesa-Lago

. . . Cuba is a new socialist country which has relied heavily on the use of various types of unpaid labor. This experience has unusual validity because the Cuban revolution is a source of inspiration to several other developing countries.

At the end of 1966, UNESCO held in Havana its first International Seminar on Leisure Time and Recreation. In his opening address to the seminar Antonio Núñez Jiménez, chairman of the Cuban Academy of Sciences, stated:

In Cuba, since the Revolution took place, leisure time is a social value used in the national reconstruction, both in the economic and ideological fields. . . . In our effort to raise production and productivity, hundreds of thousands of persons have been mobilized to perform numerous [unpaid] tasks, such as the arduous jobs of cutting cane or picking coffee. All these tasks have been fulfilled during the leisure time of the people.[1]

Types of Unpaid Labor

Five types of unpaid labor may be distinguished in Cuba: 1) work performed by employed workers outside of regular working time; 2) work done by unemployed women; 3) work performed by students as a method of socialist education; 4) work accomplished by politico-administrative prisoners as a means of "social rehabilitation"; and 5) work included as part of the compulsory military service. Table 1 summarizes the characteristics of the various types of unpaid labor.

Unpaid labor performed by employed male and female workers is usually called "voluntary work." It is performed beyond the regular working hours, whether at the work site or any other place, in behalf of the state and commonly without pay.[2] Voluntary work may be accomplished in four different ways: as overtime hours subsequent to the regular workday; on weekends, especially on Sundays; during the annual paid-vacation time; or for a con-

[1]Antonio Núñez Jiménez, "Discurso de Apertura del Seminario Internacional de la UNESCO sobre Tiempo Libre y Recreacion," *El Mundo* (Havana: Dec. 7, 1966), p. 7.
[2]"Reglamento para la Organización de la Emulación," *Gaceta Oficial* (May 21, 1964), p. 450.

Table 23-1
Summary of the Characteristics of the Five Types of Unpaid Labor in Cuba, 1967

Typology	Employed Workers	Nonemployed Women	Performer Students	Military Recruits	Prisoners
Age bracket	18-65	—	Grammar school (g.s.): 6-12 Secondary school (s.s.): 12-16	17-45	—
Approximate number in man-years	60,000 to 70,000	5,000 to 10,000	g.s. unknown s.s. 18,000 to 23,000	84,000 to 120,000	20,000 to 75,000
Recruiter	Managements, trade unions	Federation of Cuban Women	Schools, UJC[a] students unions	Military service offices	Revolutionary courts & penitentiaries
Degrees of compulsion	Exhortations, pressures, "compromises," emulation, legislation	Exhortations, pressures	Curricular or extra-curricular duty	Forced	Forced
Length of commitment	Short term: yearly targets Long term: 1-6 months	Often, the harvest period	g.s. unknown s.s. 6 weeks	1-3 years	Depending on penalties
Place of work	Short term: work site Long term: agricultural fields	Commonly in agricultural fields	g.s. area close to school s.s. stage farms and factories	UMAP[b] camps, agricultural fields	Forced-labor camps, penitentiaries, agricultural fields

Benefits granted by the state	Short term: social security Long term: leave of absence, lodging & board, social security	Sometimes lodging & board	g.s. none s.s. lodging & board	Lodging, board, clothing, $7 per month, education	Lodging, board, clothing
Administrative direction	Secretariat of Voluntary Labor of the CTC[c]	Federation of Cuban Women	Ministry of Education	Ministry of Armed Forces	Ministry of Interior

[a] Communist Youth League.
[b] Military Units to Aid Production.
[c] Confederation of Cuban Workers.

tinuous period of several months, during leave of absence from a regular job. The last is generally known as "long-term" voluntary work: workers abandon their regular jobs from one to six months to work mainly in agriculture. Because such workers use a leave of absence, they are paid their regular (i.e., industrial) wages. Their companions who remain on the urban job site must maintain production levels by carrying out the duties of those mobilized.

Fragmentary information suggests that the number of voluntary workers (measured in man-years) rose from 15,000 in 1962 to 70,000 in 1967, and that the number continues to grow. The tasks performed by the voluntary work force are varied: planting and cutting sugar cane; picking coffee, cotton, vegetables and fruits; harvesting rice, planting trees; weeding and fertilizing fields; repairing damage caused by hurricanes; building construction; and almost any kind of industrial and service work.

With the exception of those on leave of absence, voluntary workers receive neither wages nor other kinds of pay. Long-term voluntary workers are provided with lodging and board as well as tools. Since 1963, voluntary workers suffering occupational accidents have been credited, for benefit purposes, with the time spent performing unpaid labor. Long-term voluntary workers on leave of absence are also credited with this time of service for retirement pensions.[3]

Early in the revolution, unpaid labor was donated on a spontaneous basis, but since 1962 voluntary workers have been recruited because of pressure from trade unions and the managers of state enterprises and have been organized in battalions and brigades under Communist Party guidance. The state has regulated the performance of unpaid labor by introducing several measures: criticism among voluntary workers, annual contracts binding the workers to achieve a determined number of unpaid hours of labor, management and trade union checks on the amount and quality of the labor done, weekly reports by the battalions on their own performance and that of others, inspection teams to keep discipline and discover flaws, and penalties for disciplinary violations of the state regulations.[4]

Since the Federation of Cuban Women (FMC) was formed in 1960, tens of thousands of Cuban females, particularly those doing housework, have been recruited by that organization as unpaid laborers in the cane, cotton, rice, and coffee fields. There are no accurate data on the number of women annually donating unpaid work, but a 1967 estimate, based on scattered information, of from 5,000 to 10,000 man-years seems reasonable. Women do not receive wages, and because they often perform their

[3]"Ley de Seguridad Social," Law No. 1,100 (March 27, 1963), *Gaceta Oficial* (May 24, 1963), pp. 17–23.
[4]Regulations of voluntary labor are contained in "Reglamento para la Organización de la Emulación Socialista," *Gaceta Oficial* (Feb. 7, 1963 and May 21, 1964), pp. 447–459; "Communicado Conjunto del Trabajo Voluntario," *Nuestra Industria*, Vol. 4, No. 11 (November 1964), pp. 41–43; "Declaración de Principios y Estatutos de la CTC," *El Mundo* (July 6, 1966), p. 6; and Alfredo Núñez Pascual, "Trabajo Voluntario en la Próxima Zafra," *El Mundo* (Sept. 23, 1966), p. 4.

agricultural tasks close to their homes, lodging and board facilities are reduced to a minimum.

In mid-1962, students began to perform unpaid labor during vacation time, in coffee, cotton, and rice plantations. Recruitment was mainly done through exhortations by the student unions, the Communist Youth League (UJC) and the school boards.[5] In mid-1964, the system was made compulsory by a decree of the Ministry of Education. Subject to the legislation are youngsters from six to fifteen years of age, enrolled in elementary and secondary schools, between first and ninth grades. One type of unpaid labor (titled "productive") is performed by from 150,000 to 180,000 secondary-school students on state farms and factories, on weekends and during school vacations. In the case of agricultural work, students generally remain at the work site for a period of from one to six weeks. Another type of unpaid labor (titled "socially useful") involves 1.28 million primary-school children and is aimed to suppress differences between physical and intellectual work as well as to inculcate in the children a sense of obligation to society. Toward the end of 1965, the Ministry of Education also ordered university students to participate in unpaid labor for a period of from three to six weeks a year. Students performing unpaid labor are provided food and shelter when mobilized away from their homes.[6]

Unpaid labor is used as a punishment for two classes of convicted persons: state employees and functionaries guilty of errors or transgressions committed during the performance of their functions; and political prisoners, i.e., people imprisoned for opposing the government. In both cases, forced labor has two goals: "rehabilitation" or "reeducation" of those convicted and the performance of a productive task. Political crimes are judged by the revolutionary courts while administrative faults are under the jurisdiction of the Administrative Disciplinary Commission (CODIAD). The management of labor camps is entrusted to the Ministry of the Interior.[7] According to Prime Minister Castro, in 1964–1965, there were from 15,000 to 20,000 political prisoners in Cuba, although other sources give figures ranging from 50,000 to 75,000.[8] The number of convicted state officials is unknown but is presumed to be small. Tasks to be performed by those convicted include cultivation of rice, planting trees, extraction of minerals, etc. Prisoners receive food, shelter, and clothing.

---

[5]CMQ Radio (July 23, 1962 and Aug. 21, 1964).

[6]Resolution of the Ministry of Education, *El Mundo* (May 27, 1964); Regulations of the National Education Council (Apr. 5, 1965); Resolution of the Ministry of Education (Dec. 7, 1965); and Fidel Castro, "Discurso en la Clausura del Encuentro Nacional de Monitores," *El Mundo* (Sept. 18, 1966), pp. 5–8.

[7]"Reglamento del Centro de Rehabilitación de Uvero Quemado," *Nuestra Industria*, Vol. 2, No. 3 (March 1962), p. 44; ibid., Vol. 4, No. 2 (February 1964), pp. 75–76; ibid., Vol. 4, No. 9 (September 1964), pp. 69–71; *Bohemia* (Havana), Oct. 22, 1964; and Fidel Castro, "Tercera Plenaria Nacional de la FMC en Isla de Pinos," *Obra Revolucionaria*, No. 4–5 (March 1965), pp. 12–14.

[8]Fidel Castro interview with Richard Eder, *New York Times* (July 6, 1964), p. 12; and Castro interview with Lee Lockwood, *Playboy* (January 1967), p. 74. See also *Time* (Oct. 8, 1965), p. 39.

The desire to bring a large number of "vagrants" (i.e., idle youngsters, jobless bourgeoisie, etc.) into production was allegedly a main reason for establishing compulsory military service in 1963. Included are males between the ages of sixteen and forty-five, who are obligated to serve a period of three years. Recruits are divided into two categories, i.e., those "not politically integrated" and those "free of suspicion." Those in the former group enter the so-called Military Units to Aid Production (UMAP) and are employed in agricultural work throughout their service period. Recruits free of suspicion are under a training regime which combines military instruction and productive work.[9]

The number of recruits is unknown. The Minister of the Armed Forces (FAR), charged with the administration of the military service, said in 1963 that 1.5 million persons were covered although only a selection of youngsters between seventeen and twenty-two years old would be drafted initially. The author has estimated, based on official data released in 1963, that 84,000 persons were enrolled in military service at the end of 1966.[10] In 1968, however, the Prime Minister asserted that the compulsory military system embraced practically every young man within the military age bracket.[11] Hence, the previous estimate seems conservative. Recruits receive food, shelter, and clothing, plus a monthly allowance of seven pesos ($7).[12]

When unpaid workers are totaled, it appears that by 1967 from 200,000–300,000 man-years of unpaid labor were employed in the Cuban economy. These figures may be measured against the 1967 labor force of some 2.5 million workers. Unpaid labor thus represented from 8 to 12 percent of the regular labor force. The man-year contribution from the several types of unpaid labor was as follows: 60,000–70,000 from employed workers; 5,000–10,000 from women; 18,000–23,000 from secondary school students; 84,000–120,000 from military recruits; and 20,000–75,000 from prisoners. What has been the contribution of this large unpaid labor force to the Cuban society and economy?

Significance of Unpaid Labor

There is no unanimity among Cuban leaders on whether the principal advantage of unpaid labor is ideological or whether it is economic. The so-called old communists, former members of the prerevolutionary Communist

---

[9]Fidel Castro, *Hoy* (Havana: Mar. 14, 1963); Raúl Castro, *Hoy* (Nov. 13, 1963); Law No. 1,129 (Nov. 26, 1963); and Regulations of the Ministry of Armed Forces, (Nov. 29, 1963), *Hoy* (Nov. 29, 1963).

[10]Raúl Castro announced in 1963 that in the first three years of military service, $60.5 million would be saved as the result of multiplying the annual wage of each former soldier or militiaman ($819.40) times the total number of recruits at the end of the third year. Therefore $X = 60,500,000 \div 819.40 = 84,000$ recruits.

[11]Fidel Castro, "Speech at the Commemoration of the Defeat of Yankee Imperialism at Playa Girón," *Granma* [Weekly Review (W.R.)] (Apr. 28, 1968), p. 2.

[12]Prior to 1959, the Cuban peso was at par with the U.S. dollar. After the revolution the Cuban government officially claimed the parity of the peso with the dollar, although in the black market the peso has been exchanged for $0.10 to $0.30. This paper assumes parity in the exchange; the $ stands for pesos.

Party who are committed to the Soviet line, often accept (although with serious reservations) unpaid labor as an economic tool for development purposes.[13] The new communists, those thrown up by the revolution, stress the ideological side. However, the stand of this group often is ambiguous, as two statements by the late "Che" Guevara illustrate:

Voluntary work should not be looked at for its economic importance or for its present value to the state. Ultimately, voluntary work is the element that most actively develops the workers' conscience, preparing the road to a new society.

In the history of the Ministry of Industry, only once has the whole production plan been fulfilled on schedule. This was in July 1964 when we arranged a labor mobilization to meet the goals and everyone put in voluntary work.[14]

For those who stress ideology, unpaid labor is crucial in the process of building a communist man who will be cleansed eventually of selfish tendencies. Thus, gratuitous labor must be organized systematically to permeate all stages of life. Unpaid labor begins in childhood during grammar school and continues into adolescence in secondary school. Children between six and sixteen are exposed to rural life and taught the importance of manual labor in society. Special care is taken to combine intellectual education and physical work. The transitional stage, adolescence into adulthood, occurs during military service. Youngsters between sixteen and twenty-two are trained both in warfare and useful work. By collecting idle teenagers and bringing them into the work force, compulsory military service prevents the development of a "parasitical class" incompatible with a socialist society. At any age, but especially among employed workers, unpaid labor aims to reduce differences between town and country, industry and agriculture, intellectual work and manual work. The use of unpaid female workers is the first step toward incorporating women into the labor force and toward elimination of sex discrimination.

Pathological deviations from the socialist pattern must be corrected through rehabilitation, a process in which work plays a key role. Bureaucrats committing serious administrative errors and bourgeois elements rebelling against the socialist legal system are condemned to forced labor designed to reeducate them according to communist principles.

If unpaid labor is judged according to these educational and sociological perspectives, it may be worthwhile because of its long-run effects in achieving some consensus in society.

Economic Aspects of Unpaid Labor

Despite its potential value as an ideological tool, two economic factors seem to have stimulated the initiation of the system in Cuba. The most important factor is the artificial labor shortage in agriculture caused by

[13]For example see *Hoy* (Mar. 30, 1964) and Mirta Aguirre, "Lenin: Burocratismo y Trabajo Comunista," *Cuba Socialista,* Vol. 6, No. 57 (May 1966), pp. 149–155.

[14]Ceremony during which certificates of communist work were awarded to unpaid workers, broadcast by CMQ Radio (Aug. 15, 1964).

migration to the cities of part of the rural unemployed and by the reduction of the full potential of effort and the consequent low productivity of the remaining agricultural workers, due to poor economic incentives. Optimal solutions to the artificial labor shortage include mechanizing agriculture, increasing the productivity of the employed rural labor force, or training the existing urban surplus and pointing it toward agricultural employment. But these are complex, long-term types of solutions while unpaid labor has provided an easy, expedient way to cope with the labor shortage.

Another factor influencing the utilization of unpaid labor has been the desire to reduce current inflation through wage savings—filling the labor vacuum with unpaid workers. During 1962–1967 the total wages saved through unpaid labor exceeded 300 million pesos, an annual average of more than 50 million pesos. The latter figure represents approximately 1.4 percent of the estimated annual average of the Cuban national income for this period.

Despite their economic value as manpower-supply and wage-saving devices, some kinds of unpaid labor have had negative effects on sugar production and other sectors of the economy. This is due to the low productivity of unskilled, unpaid laborers, their high operative costs, and the economic dislocation and waste caused by their utilization. Nevertheless, the total product contributed by Cuba's unpaid labor seems to be greater than its operational costs plus its alternative costs, therefore resulting in net product. This conclusion should be analyzed in more detail.

The premise is that net product always occurs when the total product resulting from the use of unpaid labor is greater than the real costs involved in its utilization. Net product may result in each of the following three cases:

1. When unpaid workers are already fully or partially employed and unpaid labor is done at the work site, net product always results from over-time, weekend work, and vacation work because there are neither operational costs involved (i.e., maintenance, transportation) nor damage inflicted on production. This is the typical case of unpaid labor done by employed workers at the job site. In this case net product is always equal to total product.

2. When unpaid workers are not already employed, net product results if the output created by them is greater than their operational costs. This is the case of military recruits, prisoners, females, and students whose output must be balanced with their transportation and maintenance expenses, plus the potential damage which they may inflict on the production process because of their lack of skills. Despite some contradictory reports, the overall trend seems to be that the use of these kinds of unpaid labor is beneficial to the Cuban economy. The best reason supporting this assumption is their continued utilization by the state.

3. When unpaid workers are already employed, either fully or partially, and unpaid labor is of a different nature than their regular job, net product results if the total output created by them, at the new place of work, is greater than their operational costs plus the potential costs induced by their absence from their original job. This is the case of unpaid workers, often

underemployed at the work site, who are recruited to perform agricultural work. Another way to approach the problem is to check whether net product generated by these workers at the unpaid job is greater than their former net product at the work site.

Alternative opportunity costs in the latter case appear to be almost negligible for two reasons: the relatively small contribution of this excess labor to the sectors from which they departed, and the extra unpaid labor required from the remaining employees at the work site to offset the deficit of labor experienced by these sectors. With regard to operational costs, the situation is not as clear, but the continuing use of long-term unpaid workers suggests that costs incurred by them are smaller than total product generated by them. In any event, the government is trying to reduce such operational costs through the following measures: selection of unpaid workers according to their previous unpaid-labor performance, organization of training courses for the heads of brigades, training of special brigades to do a given type of job, and strict regulation of unpaid labor including the imposition of output standards. Even more significant is the fact that as time passes, formal organization of unpaid labor—akin to military organization—is emerging, and the long-term types of unpaid labor are gaining in use over the short-term type. Through such a process the state seeks to eliminate the negative effects of some kinds of unpaid labor, thereby strengthening the net contribution of unpaid labor to the Cuban economy.

The . . . conclusion is that the total product created by all kinds of unpaid labor is greater than its operational and alternative costs, therefore resulting in net product. Improved organization seems to have resulted in a rising net product. Lack of data, due to Cuban secrecy on the subject, impedes quantification of this net product, but the author hopes that in the future better statistical information will permit further research.

24 Labor-Management Conflict in an Overcommitted Work Force

David Chaplin

Along with the pre-1945 concern with the problem of even being able to recruit and hold industrial workers (today seen as a problem largely for isolated rural mines and plantations) it seems to be the popular impression that most labor-management conflict was a battle of the old against the new; of a primitive or nonindustrial people trying to defend their "secure, integrated, more aesthetic" culture against "devastation" by commercialism and the horrors of factory work. I found, however, as have recent observers in many parts of the world, that the main basis for conflict today is no longer the old against the new, but what is now conventionally known as the revolution of rising expectations or an "overcommitment" to the goals of an industrial society.

One of the oldest types of industrial conflict, the Luddite riots in England, was rare in Peru and apparently absent in textiles. This conflict was the resistance by preindustrial artisans to the "degradation" of the status of their occupations and the market value of their products.[1] This confrontation was avoided in Peru by the pre-1900 elimination of organized weaver guilds by an extended period of free and cheap imports of foreign textile goods. Weaving then "degenerated" into a part-time rural woman's chore—from its old status as a full-time man's profession, well ahead of the arrival of Peruvian textile mills. I was not able to find a single case of a former full-time hand-weaver employed in a textile mill. I believe this is the result not only of what might have been their distaste for such work, but of the apparent elimination of such an occupation by the years of free trade the native product suffered prior to the establishment of the first national mills.

Another source of conflict and absenteeism more common in Peru, especially in rural and small town areas, is that of wages so low workers cannot subsist on them and so they have to regard factory work merely as a source of seasonal employment for goods which only money can buy.

In general, conflict is affected by the great social distance between management and labor. This distance is not a matter simply of subordination, since such a social relationship was traditional, but subordination to

Adapted from David Chaplin, "Observaciones sobre lo problematico en el desarrollo industrial del Peru," *Revista de Sociologia,* Universidad Nacional Mayor de San Marcos, Lima, Peru, 1966, with permission of the author. Author's original English version.
[1]Neil Smelser, *Social Change in the Industrial Revolution* (Chicago: University of Chicago Press, 1959), p. 249.

"strangers," that is, rulers without recognized authority, since most of management down to the foreman level is English, Italian or German. Such managers typically do not fulfill the traditional expectations of paternalistic responsibility but still wish to obtain the benefits of traditional subordination. Recently such conflict has also been the result of management's efforts to increase productivity by the introduction of new machines and the reorganization of production, and by efforts to reduce labor costs by avoiding the accumulation of many workers with high levels of seniority.

Thus the proper interpretation of labor-management conflict and other apparent signs of low morale is not simple. It seems that it cannot be assumed that friction per se is a sign of a recalcitrant or an antiindustrial labor force. It can as often be a symbol of, and a primary impetus for, industrial development. An examination of productivity and morale—the latter being defined as the absence of strikes or conflict and the positive expression of respect for management—revealed that they are correlated inversely in Peru. The most content workers by humanistic criteria worked in the least efficient mill (which was the one located on an isolated *hacienda*) while the most militantly organized radical union developed in the mill with one of the highest productivity rates and the highest pay scales (located in the heart of Lima). What antiindustrial conflict is to be found occurs in those mills which currently suffer from work systems frozen in an earlier era of lower wages and less commercial competition. The workers' reaction here is not unlike that of American workers fearing automation, with the added problem that there are not enough comparable alternative sources of employment in Peru. It may in fact be the case that the period of sharpest industrial conflict is yet to come. The early recruitment phase is apparently easier than it is often depicted. Later efforts to increase productivity are likely to be more painful.

We cannot conclude then that workers happily committed to their employers are fully socialized industrial workers. Their commitment is usually to a concrete organization and even to individual managers—but not likely to an abstract acceptance of industrial culture. Thus one must ask, what sort of management are they provided with as objects of commitment. All too often we find owners and managers more mercantilist than industrial in their actions and beliefs. One of the major obstacles to industrial progress in Peru is that there does not yet exist a powerful, cohesive group of industrialists, that is, men whose primary economic concern is a manufacturing operation. In many cases Peruvian textile mills are peripheral activities of men whose major interest is more apt to be commerce and real estate speculation. The lack of such an orientation is not necessarily due to ignorance or conservatism, but to the objective conditions facing manufacturing activities. These activities are among the least profitable and most risky in Peru, given recent economic and legal conditions.

Labor conflict in countries like Peru involves the government as much or perhaps more than the employers in question. In the United States most labor experts have traditionally deplored labor involvement in politics and have even underestimated the role political participation has played in the success of the U.S. labor movement. In currently developing areas, however, there seems to be no question that the politicization of labor organizations is both inevitable and in many respects necessary for labor welfare as well as national economic development.[2] In a recent study of Peruvian labor politics,[3] Payne, a political scientist, found that urban industrial labor operated successfully through political bargaining with the national government as opposed to the U.S. preference for collective bargaining with management or reliance on legal enactment. This technique, which involves threatening the security of the president of the country rather than attacking the employer directly, escapes the structural disadvantages Peruvian labor faces of an oversupplied labor market and the relatively undisciplined rank and file union members. Between 1938 and 1961, the success of this method is evidenced by the fact that the real income of the organized workers in Lima rose more than that of the unorganized. In addition, the organized *obreros* 1) realized a greater improvement than the *empleados*; and 2) achieved a real rise in their income even in the face of inflation.[4]

---

[2]Bruce H. Millen, *The Political Role of Labor in Developing Countries* (Washington, D.C.: The Brookings Institution, 1963). Miles E. Galvin, *Unionism in Latin America*, Bulletin 45 (Ithaca, N.Y.: School of Industrial and Labor Relations, Cornell University, 1962).

[3]James L. Payne, *Labor and Politics in Peru* (New Haven: Yale University Press, 1965), p. 17.

[4]Ibid., p. 19.

25 Worker Dependence in a Labor-Surplus Economy

Louis Wolf Goodman

A worker can be dependent or autonomous on the job. A worker is labeled dependent "if it is impossible for him to defend his own interests and must rely on other actors in the work situation for whatever benefits come his way."[1] This worker dependence is analytically similar to Robert Blauner's conception of the powerlessness dimension of worker alienation: "A person is powerless when he is an object controlled and manipulated by other persons or an impersonal system (such as technology), and when he cannot assert himself as a subject to change or modify this domination."[2] This essay will contrast the findings of the studies in which these two definitions were used. Since this contrast will be made in terms of questions of similar content posed in both studies, in the interest of simplicity of presentation, the label "dependence" will be used in analyzing both sets of findings.

It is important to understand the causes and consequences of worker dependence for a variety of reasons. Blauner focused on dependence because of its presumed impact on the well-being and mental health of workers. It is also important to study worker dependence because of its aggregate effect on society as a whole. Goodman dealt with the impact of dependence on the worker's ability to acquire "modern" characteristics. B. H. Millen and Karl de Schweinitz, Jr. have come to contradictory conclusions concerning the necessity of promoting autonomy among workers in order to increase national levels of social integration and political maturity.[3] Albert Hirschman and Christopher Clague have commented on the effects on worker productivity of worker dependence in capital-intensive technololgy.[4] Dependence at work, then, may affect individual well-being, individual modernism, economic productivity, social integration, and national economic productivity. This essay discusses the determinants of worker dependence. Specifically it contrasts the impacts of the nature of the individual

---

[1]From "Blue-Collar Work and Modernization," by Louis Wolf Goodman (Ph.D. dissertation, Northwestern University, 1970), p. 27.

[2]Robert Blauner, *Alienation and Freedom* (Chicago: University of Chicago Press, 1964), p. 16.

[3]See B. H. Millen, *The Political Role of Labor in Developing Countries* (Washington, D.C.: The Brookings Institute, 1963); and Karl De Schweinitz, Jr., *Industrialization and Democracy* (New York: The Free Press, 1964).

[4]See Albert O. Hirschman, *The Strategy of Economic Development* (New Haven: Yale University Press, 1958); and Christopher Clague, "The Determinants of Efficiency in Manufacturing in an Underdeveloped Country," Chapter 16 of this volume.

work situation and the nature of the larger labor market on worker attitudes which indicate relative dependence. This is possible because the studies by Blauner and by Goodman contain questions of similar content.

Each of the two independent variables is measured by a single indicator. The nature of the work situation is indicated by whether or not the worker's job could be considered "craft." Goodman drew a representative sample of the blue-collar work force of greater Santiago, Chile in 1968. In his sample a worker was judged a craftsman if he explicitly stated that his work involved the application of a skill, that he himself produced an identifiable end product, and that he was relatively free from supervision. The sample of 534 contained 121 workers identified as craftsmen and 413 noncraftsmen. Blauner's sample consisted of a study of only four industries—automobiles, chemicals, printing, and textiles. In his study, printers were classified as "craftsmen," auto workers as "assembly line" and chemical workers as "continuous process." Since there were no continuous process workers in the Santiago sample, only U.S. printers and auto workers are contrasted in this essay. Blauner's data is drawn from a 3,000 worker sample which was representative of U.S. factory workers in 1947.[5] The comparison is not perfect as some printing jobs would not be "craft" according to Goodman's definition. More important Goodman's "noncraft" category includes unskilled workers in addition to assembly-line operators. However, both of these deficiencies bias the results against the occurrence of a clear contrast. This would make one more, rather than less, confident of a result which showed a contrast between U.S. and Chilean work situations.

The nature of the labor market is indicated by the level of unemployment in the population at the time of the study. The Instituto de Economia of the University of Chile reported an overall unemployment level of 4.5 percent and a 7 percent level for blue-collar workers (obreros) in March of 1968.[6] Seventy of the 534 workers in Goodman's sample were unemployed at the date of their interview. More comparable to Blauner's sample were the rates for production workers in manufacturing. Among both craft and noncraft workers it was 9 percent. Blauner uses data collected in 1947. The overall unemployment rate for the United States in 1947 was 2.9 percent.[7] Data on industries was not published until 1959. In the printing industry it averaged 3.3 percent between 1957 and 1959 while among automobile workers it averaged 14.6 percent for the same period.[8] Thus, even before we begin to analyze levels of dependence among workers we can see that there is a difference in the meaning of craft employ-

---

[5]This sample was drawn by Elmo Roper for *Fortune* magazine. For a description see Blauner, op. cit., pp. 11–14.

[6]See *Ocupación y Desocupación: Gran Santiago* (Santiago: Universidad de Chile, March 1968), Table 18.

[7]U.S. Bureau of Labor Statistics, *Handbook of Labor Statistics* (Washington, D.C., 1948), p. 36, Table A-12.

[8]"1959 Statistical Supplement," *Monthly Labor Review* (December 1959), p. 3. Statistics were averaged because of extreme volatility of employment in the automobile industry.

ment between the United States and Chile. In the United States, a nation where there is low unemployment and where the labor market is relatively favorable for workers, employers must compete for skilled workers, thereby guaranteeing the worker job stability. In such a context a craftsman can enjoy the integrative effects of low supervision and the production of an identifiable end product. However, when unemployment rates are high and there is a surfeit of potential employees, the overriding importance of a stable job becomes the most important structural mechanism for determining both worker alienation and traits such as the ability to acquire modern characteristics.

In a developing nation like Chile the most stable jobs are not craft jobs, but jobs in rationalized firms.[9] Firms with rationalized hiring practices are less arbitrary in dismissing workers than are traditional firms. In a developed economy the relatively high quality of labor and the dearth of available replacements diminishes this difference between craft and more automated production processes. Thus it is reasonable to expect that Chilean workers who have landed positions in large, automated, unionized firms would feel more secure in their work than would workers employed in more traditional craft occupations.

Three additional comparisons of behavioral characteristics of the workers in the two samples show that differences between craft and noncraft workers are more favorable for U.S. craftsmen than they are for their Chilean counterparts. Compared with noncraft workers, Chilean craftsmen are less skilled (Table 1), more afraid to change jobs (Table 2), and less advantaged educationally (Table 3) than are U.S. workers.

Three of the measures of worker dependence used by Goodman were also used by Blauner to measure powerlessness at work. A comparison of these findings is presented in Tables 4, 5, and 6.

In Table 4 craft and noncraft workers are compared with respect to freedom of physical movement. In Chile craft workers have fewer workbreaks than do noncraft workers. In the United States it is the assembly-line workers who have less physical mobility.

Table 5 shows the proportions of workers whose jobs make them tired. In Chile, more craftsmen report tiring work; in the United States, it is the assembly-line workers who feel more exhausted.

Table 6 shows the proportions of workers who feel that their jobs are stable. In both countries greater proportions of craftsmen report feelings of job security, but this differential is far greater in the United States than it is in Chile.

Worker dependence has many additional dimensions. It would be desirable to make similar comparisons of other aspects of the immediate work situation like control over work pace, freedom from pressure, and the ability to control quantity and quality of production. Comparisons based on the larger work situation must also be made. The ability to bargain with

---

[9]See Richard Lambert, *Workers, Factories and Social Change in India* (New York: Macmillan, 1962).

Table 25-1
Skill Distributions of Workers

Chile[a]				United States[b]			
	Sk.	Md.	Unsk.		Sk.	Md.	Unsk.
Craft	40	12	48 =100%	Printing	77	15	8 =100%
Non-Craft	13	8	79	Automobiles	18	34	48

[a]Possession of special skills Coded from job description.

[b]Skill categories by length of training. Robert Blauner, *Alienation and Freedom* (Chicago: University of Chicago Press, 1964), Table 51.

Table 25-2
Proportion of Workers by Years of Service

Chile[a]				United States[b]			
	≥ 5	2-5	≤ 1		≥ 5	2-5	≤ 1
Craft	50	36	14 =100%	Printing	35	50	15 =100%
Noncraft	52	33	15	Automobiles	52	21	27

[a]"Since what date have you held this job?"

[b]"How long have you been working for your present employer?" Robert Blauner, *Alienation and Freedom* (Chicago: University of Chicago Press, 1964), Table 40

Table 25-3
Proportion of Workers by Education Completed

Chile[a]			United States[b]		
	≥ 5 yrs.	≤ 5 yrs.		HS	$\leq HS$
Craft	77	23 =100%	Printing	76	25 =100%
Noncraft	50	70	Automobiles	46	54

[a]"How many years of primary education did you complete?"
[b]Robert Blauner, *Alienation and Freedom* (Chicago: University of Chicago Press, 1964), Table 44.

one's boss, the extent to which the worker relies on his boss for nonwork services, the extent to which the worker must suffer inequities like violations of legal work rights, inordinately low pay, or health hazards, and the ease with which the worker could get an equivalent job are examples of such characteristics. This discussion is limited to the above three comparisons because of lacks in the data of one or both of the studies.

In summarizing the comparison of these two sets of findings it would

Table 25-4
Proportion of Workers Free to Take Half-Hour Break

Chile[a]		United States[b]	
Craft	78	Printing	81
Noncraft	85	Automobiles	60

[a]"Do you have any breaks besides your lunch break?"

[b]"Is yours the kind of job on which someone would have to take your place if you had to leave your work for a half an hour or so, or could you let your work go for half an hour and catch up on it later?" Robert Blauner, *Alienation and Freedom* (Chicago: University of Chicago Press, 1964), Table 36.

Table 25-5
Proportion of Workers Whose Jobs Make Them Too Tired

Chile[a]		United States[b]	
Craft	45	Printing	12
Noncraft	32	Automobiles	34

[a]"Is your work very tiring?"

[b]"Does (your job) leave you too tired at the end of the day or not?" Robert Blauner, *Alienation and Freedom* (Chicago: University of Chicago Press, 1964), Table 34.

Table 25-6
Proportion of Workers Who Feel Jobs Are Steady

Chile[a]		United States[b]	
Craft	74	Printing	92
Noncraft	68	Automobiles	73

[a]"Is your job stable?"

[b]"Do you think you can have your present job as long as you want it, except for temporary layoffs – or do you think that there is a good chance that the job won't last as long as you want it to?" Robert Blauner, *Alienation and Freedom* (Chicago: University of Chicago Press, 1964), Table 31.

appear that type of work (craft or noncraft) has opposite effects on determining levels of worker dependence in Chile and in the United States.

However, in coming to a conclusion it is not appropriate to search for a single explanation for worker dependence as is implied by the above paragraph. Rather, one should specify under which conditions certain variables become relevant and others assume lesser roles. The situations represented by the two studies under consideration provide an opportunity to do just that. In Blauner's study of workers in a labor market where workers are a relatively scarce commodity, structural conditions of work— like closeness of supervision, producing an identifiable end product, and other attributes of craft employment—operate to diminish worker dependence and encourage worker autonomy. However, in a labor market where the supply of workers exceeds demand, such factors cannot compensate for powerful effects of the constant possibility of losing one's job. Hence, in situations of full employment, conditions of work are more important for determining worker autonomy-dependence; in situations of widespread unemployment or underemployment, vulnerability in the labor market is more important. This is not to say that only one set of variables operates in each situation. Both conditions of work and vulnerability in the labor market have important effects in both situations, but they have different orders of importance in the two situations.

Managers

26

Management, Entrepreneurship, and Development Needs

Albert Lauterbach

In Latin America as elsewhere the development process is affected both by the managers who show much entrepreneurship and those who do not; those who have much objective opportunity to show entrepreneurial initiative as owner-managers, senior partners, or uncontested heads of corporations, as well as those who face strong restraining influences from stockholders, family links, or a division of responsibilities within management. Presence of entrepreneurial initiative within the framework of managerial attitudes represents a highly significant trait of the latter but cannot be taken for granted in Latin America.[1]

There is no convincing evidence indicating that entrepreneurship, given certain conditions of technological, financial, and political organization, can or will develop *anywhere*. Initial accumulation of wealth may lead to dissipation through luxury consumption, to hoarding, or to usury just as easily as to productive or commercial initiative in the entrepreneurial sense. The prevailing value system in a community may either encourage or discourage innovation and individual initiative, or it may confine such opportunities to a socioeconomic and cultural elite to the exclusion of all the other groups, especially those of a tribal character. An Indian of the South American *altiplano,* for instance, has little hope ever to become an entrepreneur in the Western sense even within his own community, let alone the Peruvian or Ecuadorian economy as a whole.

An additional reservation suggests itself concerning the relationship between entrepreneurship and private ownership. In Western Europe and North America, the two concepts have been closely associated historically, although it was often the state which actually provided many of the conditions, incentives, and rewards of private entrepreneurship. Generally, it was assumed there that the entrepreneur was either identical with the private owner of a firm, or at least, was his direct representative. In contemporary Latin America such assumptions would be only partly true and sometimes not at all. The major initiative for economic innovation often comes from

Reprinted from Albert Lauterbach, *Enterprise in Latin America: Business Attitudes in a Developing Economy.* Copyright © 1966 by Cornell University. Used by permission of Cornell University Press.
[1]Compare Heinz Hartmann, "Managers and Entrepreneurs: A Useful Distinction," *Administrative Science Quarterly* (March 1959); see also David McLelland, *The Achieving Society* (Princeton, N.J.: D. Van Nostrand Company, Inc., 1961), Chs. 6–7; W. P. Strassmann, "The Industrialist," in *Continuity and Change in Latin America,* ed. John J. Johnson (Stanford: Stanford University Press, 1964).

a government planning agency, and the planning officials and politicians assume much of the real risk that is involved in such initiative.

What then is the outlook for entrepreneurship in Latin America? Much has been written on ways to arouse an entrepreneurial spirit in areas of the world which somehow have never caught on in the past to a great drive for material progress through profit-minded, competitive, innovating, risk-taking enterprise.[2] To what extent is this a realistic way to regard the future outlook for the enterprise manager and the pattern of economic development in Latin America?

Of the elements just mentioned, only profit-mindedness is present there on any widespread scale, and even this concept requires substantial qualifications, as will be shown presently. To make much money promptly is undoubtedly a popular endeavor among enterprise managers and many other people, but this seldom means a drive for profit maximization through systematic productive effort or long-range planning. The necessity of an "industrial attitude" is frequently stressed but not easily adopted by those many who at heart are still merchants. Such attitudinal change is expected by the intellectual fringe to come from improving education, a hope which in the light of modern psychology appears to be only partly justified.

Entrepreneurship is not readily compatible with the expectation of a small market for any given product or enterprise, which we found to persist in large parts of Latin America. The typical attitude toward customers still assumes that the latter are quite limited in numbers and will remain so for the foreseeable future. This is especially true of countries with a "dual economy."

. . . Many enterprise managers have assumed traditionally that the majority of the population will never understand what modern industrial products are for, and will never have the cash to buy them. The new urban proletariat, the dwellers of shantytowns on the fringe of the larger cities, are not yet considered very seriously insofar as marketing possibilities are concerned.

Enterprise managers, therefore, tend to believe that high prices and profits are indispensable in dealing with that minority of the population that *is* able and interested to buy their goods. Aggregate demand is admittedly influenced by population growth but on the whole is judged to be so imperfectly elastic in the direction of expansion, at least, that price reductions and low profit per unit are considered ineffective, even dangerous, as they reduce the capital accumulation of enterprises and, with it, their ability to survive and expand. It is clear that such attitudes do not help the process of economic development.

For the same reason any large expenditure for advertising or any other

---

[2]Bert F. Hoselitz, "Entrepreneurship and Economic Growth," in *Sociological Aspects of Economic Growth* (New York: Free Press of Glencoe, 1960). Bendix' interesting discussion, based on industrial history of England, the United States, and Russia, of a "change from entrepreneurial to managerial ideologies" seems to have very limited applications to Latin America thus far. Reinhard Bendix, *Work and Authority in Industry* (New York: John Wiley & Sons, 1956), esp. Chs. 1 and 4.

drive for constant expansion of markets tends to be interpreted as a waste of effort and money. In fact, it might even make the consumers suspicious and might generally run afoul of unwritten codes of proper business behavior. This is also true of any ardent or "excessive" competition. . . . Very often lip service is paid to the abstract principle of competition which is presented as an incentive for greater efficiency. When practiced in a specific field of business, however, competition is usually criticized as wasteful or inappropriate for a small economy, if not outright immoral. Admiration for the competitive results of North American or European industry is accompanied by polite regret that this lofty principle is unfortunately inapplicable to the poor country in question. The head of an important public finance institution in Northeast Brazil maintained, therefore, that private enterprise in that area had to be taught how to compete, especially through industrial production, and that his organization considered *generating* private entrepreneurship to be one of its decisive tasks.

The agrarian and family basis of enterprise management explains in part the traditional expectation of small markets, although a good many managers are willing to expand production if and when there has been *previous* evidence of expanding demand. An association of profit with market size often does not exist, or the profit urge itself assumes forms rather different from those in North America or Western Europe.

Even in advanced economies the role of the "profit motive" in guiding management or in stimulating economic development has often been overrated. There has also been insufficient clarity concerning the possible meanings of profit, especially the difference between short-range and long-range considerations and between making a profit (even a high one) and maximizing profit.[3]

The prevailing attitude toward profit in Latin America remains affected by the desire to get rich quick and then perhaps to retire early and to live happily—that is, idly—ever after. Here again things are beginning to change in certain areas which are past the initial stages of economic development. But at this point the extreme short-range view still predominates, especially in smaller firms, even when expansion is aimed at in a general way. . . . A variety of reasons were offered in the interviews to explain the impossibility of long-range considerations in Latin America even when investment intentions exist in a general way. Inflation or, at least, inflationary experiences and dangers were often mentioned. Next to inflation, political instability—meaning anything from frequent change of ministers and development plans to social revolution—was cited frequently, one must make profit promptly while one's friends are still in the government. Others emphasized more permanent or structural reasons such as the national character, chronic economic stagnation, or the dependence of the country's chief export product on fluctuating world markets, and, perhaps, also on the vagaries of the climate.

---

[3]See James K. Dent, "Organizational Correlates of the Goals of Business Management," *Journal of Personal Psychology* 12 (Autumn 1959).

Still others felt discouraged here again by the smallness and vulnerability of the domestic market, or the extreme difficulty in obtaining credit and capital for the enterprise and the high and often discriminatory rates of interest. As a result they saw a need for immediate huge profits as the only possible source of investment. In other words, management was deemed to operate in an inadequate and constantly changing environment. A leading Chilean manager felt that the financial uncertainty during the mid-fifties had its favorable side: If enterprise managers had foreseen a mere fraction of the financial headaches they were going to encounter, they would not have started any new projects. It was only the uncertainty or ignorance concerning the future which made them stick their neck out in the short run, at least. A Brazilian manager commented, "You can *perhaps* plan here for twenty years ahead, but not for one!"

Undoubtedly there is some truth in the reasons given for the short-range approach, in a degree that varies according to the developmental stage and economic condition of the country. Yet there is also a good deal of rationalization in such explanations of the prevailing concentration on the short-range view, which clearly impedes a developmental orientation of management. The reasons given are mostly valid to some extent but not quite as valid or permanent as they are claimed to be, and not always a convincing excuse for waste, high prices, or failure to look for new customers. The example of certain companies shows that it is not impossible to overcome the objective difficulties listed through systematic action. Some of the managers who accepted these difficulties with resignation seemed quite content to have found a justification for living and managing their business on a day-to-day basis thus being spared the strain of long-range planning.

Profit expectations are influenced in Latin America in an incomparably greater degree than in advanced economies by nonmarket factors such as family status, political pull or instability, civil strife, social unrest, or the outlook for peace or war in the world. Uncertainty, far from meaning merely the objective impossibility of knowing or evaluating fully a competitive market situation or the trend of consumer preferences, involves the extreme difficulty of sizing up the effect of the weather on the next harvest in the absence of protection against floods, erosion, and plant diseases; the fluctuations of the world market for the major export product of the country; the probability of another clique or junta taking over the government by force, or the possibility that latent popular unrest may lead to riots and violence.

Similarly, risk refers in these countries not only to incompletely defined hazards in putting a new product on the market, for instance, but to the possibility that the total investment and assets of a firm or an individual, and perhaps his life, may be lost as a result of the possible fluctuations mentioned; a possibility, therefore, which it may be wiser to *avoid*. Confidence, under these conditions, means not merely an affirmative evaluation of the market prospects for specific kinds of goods or service, or even of the prospects of prosperity in a strictly economic sense, but an overall picture of promising factors in the political, international, social, and economic outlook for the nation and area concerned. This is why there often is little public confidence in "paper," including not only money but company and government bonds.

The parameters of profit expectation, therefore, differ considerably here from those in more advanced economies. On the one hand, any rational drive for profit maximization would look like an impossible proposition since so many noneconomic as well as economic influences cannot be sized up or evaluated, let alone calculated with some degree of exactness. On the other hand, very high profit is considered indispensable precisely because of the great dangers involved in business activity and also because of the virtual impossibility of financing the growth of enterprises in any other way. The predominant aim, therefore, is very high profit without much concern for its maximization, and also the desire to achieve this profit quickly, without much thought to the more distant future and without any great predilection for systematic effort as the basis of profit.

For similar reasons, high productivity is more frequently admired than enforced, although this lag is beginning to shrink in a number of countries. Productivity is still thought of quite often as a luxury which only rich countries with a big market can afford—not as the basis of their wealth.

Such attitudes are enhanced by the frequent inadequacy of social overhead facilities in Latin American countries. When public arrangements and services such as water and power supply, transportation, housing, repair and market facilities cannot be counted on in a sufficient degree, the motivation for quick high profit (or, at least, the possibility of its public justification) increases. So does the objective need for resourcefulness of the management in providing some of these facilities on its own as the next best thing that can be done; but this does not necessarily mean that management is always aware of this need and ready to meet it. Why spend money and effort on the maintenance of equipment if future conditions are quite uncertain and risky in any case?

27 The Development of Latin American Private Enterprise

Frank Brandenburg

On Profits

The true level of profits in Latin American business is cloaked in myth and haphazard bookkeeping procedures. The native entrepreneur says that he anticipates a higher rate of return than that generally prevailing in Europe and the United States because he feels his risk is much greater and the capital markets in which he operates much weaker. In Colombia, Mexico, and Venezuela, large industrialists uniformly say they expect a rate of return above 15 percent; medium industrialists, above 25 percent; and small industrialists, above 35 percent. Small, medium, and large industrialists in the inflated economies of Argentina and Chile persistently mention the need for returns above 30 percent. In the hyperinflated economy of Brazil, profit expectation now exceeds 60 percent.

But profit expectation may be far from reality. What does a profit of 60 percent mean in a country such as Brazil, experiencing an annual inflation in excess of 50 percent? If profits were exceptionally attractive in real terms, would Latin American businessmen who regularly engage in capital flights resort to this practice to the extent that they do? We hear of the big fortunes accumulated in Latin America, but nobody has undertaken a serious assessment of the number of business failures or of the level of profits of a nation's total industrial plant. Of 113 securities registered on the Bogotá Stock Exchange on December 13, 1962, only 95 paid a dividend during the preceding year. This means that 16 percent paid no dividend. Business failures probably are more common in Latin America than they are in the United States.

Just as U.S. investors are discovering that net after-tax profits are higher from European and even from domestic ventures than from Latin American investment, thousands of small and medium-size Latin American industrialists are learning that they have been operating for years believing that profits are much higher than they actually are. Confronted by growing competition, labor union demands, and regulations of and taxes on business, native industrialists are finding that presumed high profits result partly from inadequate provisions for amortization, depreciation, and reserves. They are experiencing the additional impediments to higher profits raised by the

Adapted from Frank Brandenburg, *The Development of Latin American Private Enterprise* (Washington, D.C.: National Planning Association, 1964), pp. 36–47, with permission of the publisher.

relative nonliquidity of their investment, the absence of active stock ex-
changes and strong capital markets, and the consequent difficulty in converting their investment to marketable securities. Devaluation and inflation
can catch them off guard. Their raw material supply is frequently subject
to sudden tariff changes. Small industrialists, in particular, lack the strong,
continuous ties with established financial institutions that are enjoyed by
large industrialists.

On Efficiency and Competition

Until recently, competition rarely transcended the bounds of gentlemen's
agreements made among a few families in each of the several branches of
industry. Private industries tended to be family owned, with each family
concerned about protecting its particular investments against encroachments
by outsiders. Professional business administrators who were not members
of the family were also regarded as outsiders. Placing confidence in managers outside closed family circles was looked upon as a retreat from a
desirable way of life and a danger to traditional patterns. In such circumstances, inefficiency and low risk were commonplace.

In the most populous Latin American nations, there are a growing
number of socially progressive entrepreneurs who have established or who
operate relatively efficient, low-cost industries. Their modern technical,
managerial, and merchandising achievements are increasingly exerting
pressure on traditional business practices. Family management, with or
without competence, is still prevalent in all sizes of industrial enterprise.
But competition from new quarters is no longer easy to meet through cir-
cuitous political devices. Improvements in product and plant efficiency are
the outcome.

The average Latin American industrialist still tends to embrace notions
antithetical to competition, his exhortations in defense of private enterprise
notwithstanding. His usual expression of distaste for monopolies, cartels,
and trusts requires examination. He readily reveals an antipathy for foreign
subsidiaries, which he may charge with monopolistic practices regardless of
the facts; yet monopolies and oligopolies dominated by domestic business
interests are evident. At the top level of Mexican industry, for example, a
group of professional bureaucrats and politicians manages formerly foreign-
owned monopolies along with other state enterprises. Beside them is a
group of nine giant private financial-commercial-industrial complexes exercising monopolies and oligopolies over much of the nonpublic sector of
big industry.[1] Ricardo Lagos, in the latest edition of his study on the theory
and reality of economic concentration in Chile, records that "eleven financial groups, or really three (Sud American, Chile, and Edwards) because they are so intertwined with the other groups, dominate 70.6 percent

[1]Frank R. Brandenburg, "A Contribution to the Theory of Entrepreneurship in the
Developing Areas: The Case of Mexico," *Inter-American Economic Affairs* 16
(Winter 1962): pp. 3–23.

of all Chilean capital invested in business corporations."[2] Tomás Fillol, in his prize-winning study done at M.I.T., reports similar patterning in Argentina.[3] Monopolistic practices also characterize industrial activities in other nations of Latin America. Of course, monopoly is difficult to avoid as long as existing markets fail to expand appreciably.

Lack of competition at the top has by no means eliminated the rigors of stiff competition for tens of thousands of small and medium industrialists, and for some large industrialists in Argentina, Brazil, and Mexico. The attitudes of this group on profit expectations are shaped and reshaped by growing competition, excess installed capacity, and cost differentials. Lush public works contracts in Argentina, Mexico, and Venezuela, which gave birth to thousands of small and medium industries, are less freely available now. Nor is another impetus on the scale of Brasília immediately in the Brazilian offing. Many tax concessions favoring new industries in Argentina, Chile, and Mexico have expired, reducing profit margins. At the same time, the evolution of an industrial way of life, with its demand for quality control, exerts increasing pressure on small and medium industrialists to produce higher quality goods. This is certainly the case in Buenos Aires and Córdoba, Mexico City and Monterrey, and Belo Horizonte and São Paulo. In fact, small and medium industrialists interviewed in Argentina, Brazil, Chile, and Mexico saw the twin specters of Castroism and government intervention as less immediate threats than extinction through local competition. Colombian and Venezuelan industrialists, in contrast, tended to subordinate the dangers of excessive competition to those of Castroism and potential government control.

On Inflation and Growth

The belief that inflation is an indispensable, readily available, and indefinitely applicable tool for increasing capital formation is held to varying degrees by native industrialists everywhere in Latin America. It is most pronounced among Argentine, Brazilian, and Chilean industrialists, and least pronounced among Mexicans. Mexicans anticipate less inflation than Colombians and Venezuelans, and the latter expect decidedly less than Argentines, Brazilians, and Chileans. Awareness of the real causes of inflation is universally low among industrialists, as could be expected. While more sophisticated perspectives on economic development are discovered among large industrialists, willingness to support political reforms leading to the changes in social structure necessary for sustained economic growth —as contrasted with continued reliance on the inflation-devaluation cycle— is rare among Brazilian industrialists and infrequent among big Argentine and Chilean industrialists. The conviction among big industrialists that

---

[2]Ricardo Lagos, La concentración del poder economico. Su teoría. Realidad chilena (Santiago: Editorial del Pacífico, 1962), p. 165.
[3]Tomás Roberto Fillol, *Social Factors in Economic Development: The Argentine Case* (Cambridge, Mass.: M.I.T. Press, 1961).

expansionist monetary policies must be avoided is most noteworthy in Mexico, Peru, and Venezuela.

Argentine, Brazilian, and Chilean industrialists appear insufficiently concerned with the ways excessive inflation distorts patterns of investment and hinders real growth to reshape their inflation-mindedness voluntarily. Specialists on the ABC countries differ on whether expansive monetary policies have been a deterrent to industrial investment in these countries. Some specialists contend that the industrialist in the ABC countries borrows as much as he can and invests as fast as possible because he can repay in depreciated currency, or if his funds are in plant investment, their value will increase with inflation. They further argue that budgetary and balance-of-payments assistance from foreign governments and international agencies has tended to retard the internal solution of basic problems. If the attitudes of private industrialists in the ABC countries are taken into account in an anatomy of local industrial growth, the traditional assumption that inflation is a deterrent to investment requires some refinement. The differences between structuralist and monetarist schools of thought on inflation in Latin America lead to one conclusion: there is no stock explanation for the causes of inflation and its effects on growth.

On Markets

The market orientation of Latin American industrialists varies, with notable exceptions, according to the size of plant, degree of competition, and nature of the product manufactured. Small and medium industries are normally more locally and regionally oriented than large industries, but there are significant exceptions. Small and medium plants enjoying product monopolies, such as makers of high-quality nipples for baby bottles or of select automobile parts and accessories, sell nationally while large producers of cement, beer, some heavy chemicals, and brick and clay products cannot compete nationally. Markets for goods in the latter group are, as elsewhere, more circumscribed by transportation costs than markets of big enterprises in such "rural industries" as processing and packing of fruits and vegetables. Native manufacturers of end-use consumer goods, who account for the bulk of small and medium industrial output, incline more toward local markets than do manufacturers of capital goods, industrial raw materials, or industrial intermediates. However, large consumer goods manufacturers also sell in national markets. Many Argentine, Brazilian, and Mexican industrialists in the metallurgical, chemical, machinery, electronic, and transportation equipment fields produce capital goods as well as industrial intermediates, selling some products locally and others nationally. The paucity of reliable industrial surveys precludes estimation of the number of enterprises simultaneously manufacturing end-use consumer goods, industrial intermediates, and producer goods, to say nothing of the ratio of each to total manufactures. . . . Industrialists beset by excess capacity for existing domestic markets and businessmen highly concerned about market growth frequently hold back support of measures aimed at industrial decentralization. The larger Argentine, Brazilian, and Mexican manufacturers, in particular, question the wisdom of industrial decentralization. They contend that setting up a series of new industrial plants manufacturing the same or similar products will virtually prohibit progressive lowering of unit costs in existing industries. Both old and new plants, they say, will suffer from lack of adequate markets. Existing plants will face weighty problems of excess capacity and new plants will remain high-cost, low-output operations.

The issue also spills over into the potential export of industrial goods. Larger domestic sales within a Latin American country normally represent the *sine qua non* for reducing costs to a level that will permit exports of manufactured goods to compete in world markets. Exceptions are found in the fishmeal industry of Peru, which accounts for substantial sales in world markets without large sales at home, and in select industrial exports of other nations of the region. Rapidly expanding consumer durable sales in Brazil, whose internal market can grow into one of the world's largest, may assist Brazilian industrialists in pushing unit costs down to competitive levels. It is going to be difficult, however, for Latin America to drop unit costs sufficiently to permit much industrial export to world markets.

On Labor Relations

In much literature about the region, the Latin American industrialist appears as a paternalistic, authoritarian mogul, who expects government to guarantee him a docile, obedient labor force. But in fact, entrepreneurial practices are adapted to advanced labor laws and privileges. The private industrialist may prefer lower wages to higher wages; a conciliatory labor force to obstinate strikers; merit, skill, and modernization to job security; unilateral managerial decision-making to collective bargaining; and lower costs to higher costs. But he must often obtain the sanction of the government, union leaders, or both, if he expects to increase his efficiency under existing legislation on minimum wages, maximum hours, social and job security, union organization, and collective bargaining.

The key to labor policy rests in the hands of government. When industry-wide circumvention of labor legislation passes unchallenged, the fact may usually be taken as evidence that it coincides with the government's labor and development policies. When organized labor persists in exceeding the boundaries of collective bargaining or otherwise enjoys favored treatment, it is almost certainly because the government sanctions such action. Governments lead; most businessmen and trade unionists follow. Both labor and private industrialists are subject to the mixed blessings of labor movements inextricably tied to politico-governmental machinery.

The cost structure of Latin American industry is automatically determined by certain basic labor rights and welfare legislation. These became well established in Brazil and Mexico in the 1930s, in Argentina in the 1940s and early 1950s, in Chile in the late 1930s, and in Colombia in the

1950s. They have proven difficult to alter. Severance payments, indemnities, and sometimes the requirement of prior court consent make it difficult and expensive to discharge employees. In most Latin American nations, even bankruptcy does not discharge an industrialist's liabilities to his workers, since employees may exercise prior rights in enjoining the liquidation and distribution of physical assets. Labor legislation is advanced even by U.S. standards, and presently enforced social welfare laws are decidedly more comprehensive and liberal than those of Western Europe and of virtually every country in Africa and Asia.

Latin American industrialists protest the constant pressure by industrial labor to extend the scope of social welfare measures. They believe too large a share of industrial output is already put aside for social security and other welfare benefits. Such "savings" are unconvertible into new private investment. Businessmen say they cannot finance extensive welfare measures and simultaneously provide new industrial investment to the extent required for accelerating the growth of national income and employment.

A considerable number of medium and large industrialists believe that the true interests of workers are advanced faster under a company union than through national or regional trade union affiliation. They feel that a closed shop subjects an industrial plant to the vicissitudes of predatory unionists and politics. They point for substantiation to the rarely matched privileges enjoyed in the company unions of the Garza Sada-G. Sada industrial complex in Monterrey, of the Ruiz Galindo industries in Mexico City, of Eugenio Mendoza industries in Venezuela, of the Bangu textile mills and Ypiranga paint factories in Brazil, and of the subsidiaries of several foreign corporations.

Perhaps the most serious shortcoming in the attitude of many Latin American businessmen on collective bargaining is their apparent inability to relate labor-management relations to real national economic growth. Pay increases, immediately accompanied by expansionist monetary policies, accomplish dubious advances in real income and output. A healthy private sector, . . . requires greater consideration of the concept of the national interest by both management and labor than is the case today virtually everywhere in Latin America.

28 Risk, Diversification, and Profits

Edgardo Jurgensen

The purpose of this article is to show how the variability in profits among Latin American business firms is directly related to the extent of diversification in these companies, and that this diversification is itself largely determined by the managers' attitudes towards risk. This may be seen schematically as:

Risk Aversion   Diversification   Profit-Certainty

It is expected that managers who are less willing to take high risks would tend to diversify the operations of their firms in order to reduce the year-to-year profit variability. Another way of stating this proposition is that firms that have their "eggs in different baskets" are managed and/or owned by rather risk-avoiding persons, whereas companies that cover a narrower range of business operations are directed by more risk-aggressive managers.[1]

The research was carried out in Chile in 1971, six months after a Marxist government had been freely and democratically elected. The leftist political parties had announced sweeping structural changes that triggered a wide-ranging feeling of uncertainty, particularly in the private sector. During the time of this research the government was fully engaged in nationalizing several foreign interests, buying out private banks, expropriating large underproductive land holdings, and taking over the management of some private business firms. The impact of these changes on the profit expectations of the Chilean managers was largely a matter of speculation.

One hundred and five top executives and/or owners were interviewed in seventy firms, selected at random, and belonging to eleven industries. The interviews established measures for the three key variables, risk-orientation of the managers, and diversification and profit of the company, to answer some of the following questions: How risk-averse or how risk-aggressive are Chilean managers? What kind of firms tend to have risk-aggressive managers? Do attitudes toward risk vary by industry? What are the profit and risk characteristics of the different firms and industries? How do the profit expectations of the Chilean managers in 1971 compare to the historical performance of the companies?

---

[1]This research is based on correlation analysis. Methodologically, correlation analysis demonstrates statistical degrees of association, not cause and effect; for that you need theory. An alternative hypothesis to the one stated above would be that diversified firms seek risk-averse managers.

Managerial Attitudes Towards Risk

On the basis of the interviews and questionnaire items, managers were classified into five categories, as shown in Table 1.[2]

Table 28-1
Attitude Toward Risk

	Percentage	*N*
Extreme risk-aversion	17%	18
Moderate risk-aversion	13	14
Neutral	50	52
Moderate risk-seeking	12	13
Extreme risk-aggressive	8	8
Total	100%	105

It can be seen that the attitudes cover a wide range but that, on the average, the Chilean manager is a risk-averter. More specifically, half of the sample had neutral feelings; according to our classification 30 percent were risk averse, more than half of this group extremely so; and 20 percent were positively disposed toward risk, with a few extreme risk lovers.

By industry, managers in chemicals, cosmetics, and plastics were the most risk-averse; those in textiles, shoes, and lumber were the most risk-aggressive; and those in radio and TV, printing and publishing, canning, garments, and household appliances were closest to the average.

When managers in industries are grouped by the average size of firm, as measured by total assets, a clear pattern emerges: those in small firms are the most risk-averse, those in medium-sized firms had the largest group of risk-aggressive managers, and those in large companies held the largest number of risk-neutral managers.

Market Diversification in Firms

Three measures were used to study the degree of market diversification by company: past, present, and desired degree. The first two were based on standard industrial classifications of product groupings and the third was according to the executives' preferences. The average diversification per industry was highly concentrated around three markets, though patterns varied between one and eight markets. The number of markets were de-

---

[2]Risk aversion was measured by exposing each respondent to a series of alternatives. A manager was asked, for example, to choose between an absolute certainty of 8 percent profits or a 50-50 chance of 5 or 15 percent profits. On the basis of his choice, the amounts were then varied several times until he could no longer indicate a preference for one alternative over the other.

fined in terms of the respondent's perceptions. One shoe manufacturer, for example, identified three distinct markets: men's, women's, and children's shoes; but another manufacturer considered all consumer durables (e.g., toasters and refrigerators) to constitute one market. A general trend towards a higher degree of diversification was revealed by a comparison between the historical and the current levels. The desired diversifications indicate some preference in keeping with this trend but, on the whole, the preferred degrees of diversification are close to the current positions. This would indicate a general conformity with the market structures, in spite of the environmental developments occurring at that time.

Profit Variability

The dependent variable in our study, profit variability, was measured by the standard deviation of the average real return on equity. For Chilean firms during the period 1965–1970 this was 8.9 percent, ranging from 0.5 percent return for the lumber industry to the 18 percent experienced by the radio and TV industry. Twelve percent of the individual firms studied recorded a negative average rate of return during this period, while 30 percent of the firms had profits higher than 12 percent on equity. Contrasting this historical information with the profit expectations of the Chilean executives for the period 1971 to 1975, it is significant to observe that on the average they foresee a yearly return on their net investments of 5.6 percent. Thus, we could infer that the economic and political circumstances, as interpreted and evaluated individually by each manager, negatively affected their profit expectations, making them anticipate a reduction of 37 percent (5.6 percent compared to 8.9 percent) when compared to the historical performance of the firms. An additional insight is given by the fact that managers in 15 percent of the companies expected to be unable to make profits and only 11 percent expected to make profits higher than 12 percent a year in real terms.

It is necessary to relate the above analysis on profits with the degree of certainty each manager attaches to his average return expectation, in other words, with the subjective chances he attributes to his profit forecast. The relevant question in this context is: regarding the profits of their firms, do managers perceive a wider range of possible outcomes when compared to the historical ranges of the returns of firms? For this purpose a standard statistical processing technique was used on both the historical and the expected data on profits to define and identify nine different categories of uncertainty.

The results indicate that 16 percent of the firms had experienced very stable rates of return (i.e., nonfluctuating) in the past, while 20 percent of the companies had had very unstable rates of return. The information gathered in relation to the *expected* profits, however, reverses this pattern. In fact, 25 percent of the top executives expect very stable returns or a very narrow range of possible profits, and only 11 percent of them anticipate erratic profits or a wide range of possible rates of return on equity. By industry, only two of the eleven studied expected to achieve their indicated average profits with more uncertainty than their past experiences indicated.

Thus we can say that while the sample of managers expect a decrease in the firm's profits by 37 percent, they at the same time anticipate a reduction in risk by 31 percent. In other words, the Chilean executives' profit projections are such that they see it difficult to obtain extremely high returns, but they also see a small chance of making extreme losses. We see that both dimensions, the expected average return and the certainty or the risk implicit in such expectations, are necessary to evaluate properly the managers' profitability prospects.

Risk, Diversification, and Profits

Now that the characteristics of the variables used in this study have been presented, we are in a position to analyze the results obtained in relation to our initially stated behavioral model. The relationship between the three basic variables were measured separately for the firms within each industry as well as for the aggregate of firms in the sample.

At the industry level, it was found that the managers' attitudes towards risk and the degree of diversification of the firms were closely associated in the case of five industries: shoes, lumber, cosmetics, garments, and household appliances. The absence of a positive relation between attitudes towards risk and diversification in the six other industries requires further examination. The degree of diversification of the firms of three other industries, textiles, chemicals, and plastics, is better explained by their historical growth rates in sales than by the attitudes towards risk of their top executives. In fact, strong evidence was found to support the argument that the degree of diversification in these cases is the result of the growth experienced by the firms. Those firms with higher growth rates were more diversified than the companies that had not grown as fast as the other firms in these industries during the period under study. A conceivable explanation for this result could be that in the Latin American countries with small internal markets, stable market shares, and limited opportunities to export, the firms are forced to direct their growth potential to new small internal markets. Several tests of association were performed for the other three industries (radio and TV, printing and publishing, and canning), but no significant explanation was found to account adequately for the degree of diversification of their member firms.

On the other hand, and still at the industry level, we found eight industries in which the degree of diversification of the firms was significantly related $(+)$ to the stability experienced in their returns. In other words, the more diversified a firm relative to the other firms in its industry the more stable have been its returns and, similarly, the least diversified firms within each industry had experienced the most unstable returns.

In the case of two industries, cosmetics and household appliances, a stronger relationship was found by using the market share as a determining variable of the variability in returns of the companies. This result suggests that the larger firms within these two industries are in a position to fix their profits at a certain level by using price and cost controlling mechanisms to which they have access. We were unable to find a satisfactory determining element of the variability of returns for firms in the chemical industry.

At the aggregate level, that is when all firms were considered at the same time for the purpose of testing our behavioral model, a new and surprising element appeared to explain both the attitudes towards risk of the executives and the historical variability in profits of the firms. As can be seen in Figure 1, the size of the firms measured by the level of their assets is associated with the risk preferences of the managers, the historical diversification of firms, and the variability of the returns of the different companies.

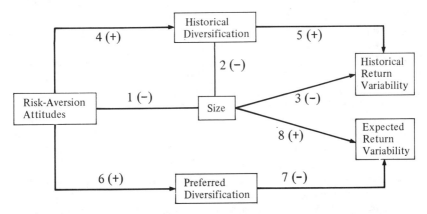

Figure 28-1. The diagram depicts the *actual* relationships of the variables, as distinct from the hypothesized relationship, when the firms are undifferentiated by industry. (Inverse relationship indicated by (–); positive relationship by (+).)

In fact, large firms seem to have fewer risk-adverse managers (1), a lower degree of diversification (2), and, unexpectedly from the point of view of our model, they have had more stable rates of return (3). The actual positive relationship between risk-averse attitudes and the degree of diversification (4) was consistent with our predictions, but the relationship between the latter and the variability of profits (5) was opposite to our expectations: undifferentiated by industry, the more highly diversified firms had less certainty of profits.

There are two possible and nonconflicting explanations to the contradictory results of the within-industry measurements as compared to the aggregate-level measurements. The first one is that the concept of diversification as measured in this study (that is, product diversity within a single industry) loses its meaning and relevancy when firms of different industries are compared. The second is that, given the institution of price-setting based on a cost-plus criterion and in which the large firms have a more influential role in the negotiation process, these larger firms can settle on prices that imply more stable profits.

The bottom part of the diagram is helpful in isolating the past from the expected data. The expectational variable indicates that risk aversion is positively related to the preferred degree of diversification (6) and that the latter is negatively related to the expected relative variability in returns (7): that is, risk-aversity leads to a strategy of diversification in order to increase the certainty of profits. The most interesting discovery of the analysis made along this dimension is that the expected risk of firms is directly related to their degree of diversification, the least diversified firms being the most vulnerable ones, and, that size ceases to be the controlling element of the variability in returns. If there is any degree of association between size and the variability in returns, it is one that suggests the opposite from what has been historically true, i.e., the executives of the larger firms perceive a more uncertain future regarding the profits of their firms than the executives of smaller enterprises (8).

On the basis of the evidence provided by the behavior of these Chilean firms, we may conclude that stable profits are due more to size than to a policy of diversification. This, to some extent, corroborates Davis's hypothesis (see pages 275–287 in this volume) that success in business in Chile is due more to one's power than to strictly business criteria such as policies of diversification to insure profits. The actual practice of the Chilean executives, however, is in sharp contrast with their expectations. Managers were able to forecast the profits of more diversified and of smaller firms with more certainty than they could for less diversified and larger companies. Political exposure due to large size is a two-edged sword of larger actual profits together with greater perceived risks. Chilean managers' actual projections hardly sustain their commentary that the firms are at the edge of survival.

29 Market Size and Foreign Trade in Mexico

Harry K. Wright

A significant problem facing businessmen in Mexico and an impediment to the continued industrialization of the country is the limited size of the market for domestic manufactures. One possible solution would be to increase the domestic market at a faster pace than is now occurring. While the total population of the country is approaching 50 million, a large percentage of its people are outside the market for many modern-day products. Not only is at least 40 percent of the population classified as rural, most of whom are ejidal and small subsistence farmers, but there are large numbers of urban poor, and even the average industrial worker probably does not earn enough to enable him to buy very much more than the essentials of life. The government's efforts at tax reform and the increased benefits to labor under the profit-sharing law and the 1969 labor law are helpful but perhaps seem timid when measured against the scope of the problem. However, any aggressive move by the government toward effecting a significant redistribution of wealth in order to raise living standards and increase the domestic market would undoubtedly be taken by the private sector as antibusiness and would not be easy under a political system in which consensus is considered highly desirable and in which every effort is made not to offend any source of power in the country.

The other possible line of attack on the problem is to develop an export market for Mexican manufactured products. The foreign market for Mexico's traditional exports of fibers, food, and minerals is not flexible enough to fulfill the country's requirements of foreign exchange earnings, and it is universally agreed that Mexico must increase its exports of manufactures if it is to sustain its economic growth. The government has made real efforts to create an export consciousness on the part of Mexican businessmen, and its efforts have had some effect. The real obstacle to the creation of an export market for Mexican manufactures is the high cost of production. This is the result of several factors. The limited size of the domestic market restricts production and in many cases the market is divided among too many producers. In the automobile industry, for example, there are numerous producers when one manufacturer could satisfy the country's needs and still have excess capacity. The cost of domestically produced raw materials is high, again because of the limited market and short production. Further-

Adapted from Harry K. Wright, *Foreign Enterprise in Mexico* (Chapel Hill: University of North Carolina Press, 1971), pp. 358–362, with permission of the publisher.

more, the high cost of utilities, transportation, port handling charges, and similar overhead expenses adds to the burden.

The government is fully cognizant that the country's products must be competitive in international markets, and its earlier attitude that the Mexican consumer had to pay the price of industrialization by bearing the high cost of production has changed. Various measures have been taken to force domestic producers to reduce their production costs. For one thing, increased domestic competition has been permitted. Before 1965 the number of producers in a particular line of production was often strictly limited, apparently on the theory that the domestic market could not support more than a few producers. The administration of President Díaz Ordaz has reversed this policy and has permitted the entry of new producers in fields that were formerly closed to them. This has, of course, further divided the market and compounded the problems of many companies. Furthermore, one of the conditions consistently imposed on the approval of new manufacturing programs by the Ministry of Industry and Commerce is that the manufacturer's products may not be sold at more than 25 percent above the foreign cost of the products.

High production costs have also been attacked by restricting somewhat the tariff protection granted to new manufacturers and by permitting greater competition of imports. Tariff protection is no longer being granted for an indefinite period but is limited to a specified term, usually three to seven years. Thus, a decision on the future role of protectionism is being postponed to the next presidential administration, and presumably protection will not be automatically renewed but will be re-examined in the light of conditions at that time. Furthermore, import licenses for products for which there is a domestically produced substitute are no longer automatically denied in all cases. The policy announced in 1965 that prices, quality, and delivery terms would be taken into account has at least given importers a basis on which to make a case for imports. Of course, there has been no across-the-board policy to permit foreign imports to compete with domestic goods, but in some cases where the quality and price of a domestic product are at substantial variance from international standards, the licensing of imports of foreign goods has been used as a pressure tactic to force domestic producers to improve the quality and reduce the cost of their production. At the same time, there has gradually developed a trend to define "substitutability" with greater precision. Formerly, there were many complaints that there was no real understanding within the import-licensing apparatus of what was substitutable and what was not, and a product produced in Mexico was often considered to be a substitute for all similar products, without much regard for whether or not it actually fulfilled the same requirements. More recently, more careful consideration is being given to importers' arguments that domestically produced goods are not substitutes for the products they seek to import.

Also significant in the effort to reduce costs and increase exports has been the decision to permit imports of raw materials and component parts, even if they are produced domestically, when the end product is to be exported and the use of domestic components would make the product noncompetitive internationally.

The practical result of these policies is that there has been some degree of liberalization of foreign trade, at the same time that foreign investment has been subjected to greater limitations. Although it will be many years before Mexico is able to export substantial quantities of manufactured products, there are probably a number of existing producers that could develop an export capability by cutting their production costs. Some observers think that exports of manufactures can be increased to 25 or 30 percent of total exports within the next five to ten years. And it may not be too optimistic to predict that, as the volume of exports increases, the process of trade liberalization will continue and that at some time in the future Mexico will have a liberal trade policy.

The lawyer observing the Mexican regulatory system is struck by the fact that the restrictions on the conduct of enterprises in Mexico are not often reflected or even suggested in the legislation. While Mexican private law—the law governing relations between private persons—has been notably stable, sufficiently detailed, and readily ascertainable, the same cannot be said of its public law. The laws governing relations between private persons and the state have seen frequent and substantial changes, which have tended to give to the executive branch of the federal government, first, increasingly greater powers of intervention in the economic life of the country and, secondly, ever greater discretion in the exercise of those powers. Furthermore, powers of control under existing legislation have sometimes been exercised to achieve goals for which the powers were not intended. This has permitted the government to formulate and enforce policies with only the vaguest of statutory guidelines or no guidelines at all. The result is that, more and more, relations between private persons and the state are governed by a policy system rather than a statutory system. Consider, for example, the broad discretionary powers of governmental agencies over the life of a corporation. The Ministry of Foreign Relations, theoretically at least, controls its very birth and parentage through its power to grant or deny a permit to incorporate and its authority to limit foreign ownership of the company. The Ministry of Internal Affairs has almost unlimited freedom to refuse or permit the entry of foreign technicians and managerial personnel to operate it. The Ministry of Industry and Commerce may, as it sees fit, grant or deny licenses for the import of its plant equipment and raw materials or afford it protection or not against competing imports. So pervasive is its power over imports that the Ministry of Industry and Commerce has been able, through it, to assume the authority to restrict new foreign investments, force industrial integration, and impose price controls on industry, despite the fact that there is no general law on foreign investment and only a handful of statutory restrictions on its entry, no mention of integration is found in the statutes, and the price-control law is aimed at basic consumer goods and not at the great majority of manufactured products.

This system has, of course, afforded the government great flexibility to shape its policies to meet changing needs and circumstances, but the absence of statutory standards also has meant that there is less predictability in everyday dealings with the government and greater opportunity for favoritism and discrimination in the government's treatment of private investors. Nevertheless, it must be said in all fairness that the government has not frequently abused these powers and that, on the whole, its policies have proved to be constructive. The restrictions on the entry of foreign investment and the Mexicanization policy have stimulated the growth of domestic savings and investment. Without limitations on the entry of foreign employees, the training of skilled Mexican workers would not have progressed as it has and most technical personnel would probably still be foreigners.

There is no doubt that Mexico deserves the reputation it has as a highly attractive country for foreign investment. Its long history of political and monetary stability and its record of economic growth are achievements envied by many other developing nations. Foreign enterprises that are sympathetic to Mexico's problems, goals, and aspirations and possess an understanding of the limits within which foreign participation in the country's economy is acceptable have an opportunity to contribute to and benefit from her further development.

30 The Latin American Entrepreneur: Style, Scale, and Rationality

Peter Evans

The contemporary Latin American businessman finds increasingly that his competition is the international firm rather than his fellow countrymen. It is a competition which he appears to have a poor chance of winning. Despite his uncertain future, understanding of managerial behavior in Latin America would be incomplete without examination of the indigenous entrepreneur. Brazil provides a particularly good setting, not only because it has the largest market and one of the most highly industrialized economies in Latin America, but also because it has the largest amount of American investment in manufacturing.

In the 1950s and 1960s it became increasingly clear that the private entrepreneur in Brazil was becoming relegated to a marginal role in all but traditional industries.[1] Thirty-two of the top fifty private industrial corporations (by assets) were foreign-owned.[2] Foreign ownership was particularly prevalent in the faster growing industries, reaching almost 90 percent in the case of drugs and automobiles.

The rise of the international firm has been seen by foreigners and many Latin Americans as caused by its superior technical and economic efficiency which, in turn, is rooted in a highly rational and sophisticated mode of organization. The converse of this idea is that locally owned businesses are inefficiently organized and managed. Their inefficiency is commonly attributed to the outlook of the Latin American entrepreneur. He is viewed as a small-time feudal patriarch, whose failure to stand up to the foreign competition arises largely from his despotic, old-fashioned style of management.

The impulse of the foreign observer to emphasize the archaic, paternalistic management style of the Latin American businessman is reinforced by a survey of the sociological literature. Analyses of European management styles, such as the one developed by Crozier and popularized by Servan-

This article is based on research done in connection with the author's doctoral dissertation: "Denationalization and Development: A Study of Industrialization in Brazil" (Harvard University, 1971).

[1]For discussion of the rise of foreign firms in Brazil, see E. N. Baklanoff, "Foreign Private Investment and Industrialization in Brazil," in *New Perspectives on Brazil,* ed. E. N. Baklanoff (Nashville: Vanderbilt University Press, 1966). See also Eduardo Galeano, "Denationalization and Brazilian Industry," *Monthly Review* 21 (December 1969): pp. 11–30.

[2]"Os 500 Maiores Sociedades Anonimas do Brazil," *O Dirigente Industrial* 11 (October 1969): pp. 33–52. See also *Banas Informa* (July 28, 1969), p. 12.

Schreiber, vindicate the general line of reasoning.[3] Analyses of Latin American culture provide further support by stressing the central role of paternalism.[4] Direct empirical confirmation is supplied by both North American visitors and Latin Americans themselves.

Among the foreigners, Alfred Lauterbach reports family membership to be an attribute of importance in the selection of management, and a frequency of "paternalistic feelings" toward personnel.[5] A study of Brazilian entrepreneurs by F. H. Cardoso is one of the most extensive surveys of managerial styles. Cardoso says that "the excess of direct, personal control restricts the limits of efficiency" in the Brazilian firms.[6] He goes on to explain that family control makes it difficult to delegate authority to outsiders, that "loyalty" and "trustworthiness" are the qualities most looked for in subordinates and that family is often more interested in the maintenance of its control than in the growth of the firm.[7] According to Cardoso, excessive fears over loss of control lead the entrepreneur to eschew both technological innovation, which might lead to his displacement by "experts," and other forms of expansion which might spread his operations out geographically or force him to bring in outside capital. He concludes that the rationalization and planning which characterize subsidiaries constitute their most important competitive advantage over locally owned firms.[8]

Viewing the competitive disadvantages of the local businessman as arising from a cultural style which is economically irrational fits in well with more general theories relating underdevelopment to traditional attitudes. The post-World War II successes of the multinational firm become additional evidence that the traditionalism of the Latin American industrial elite was responsible for Latin America's failure to industrialize autonomously. Furthermore, this perspective suggests that an important positive by-product of the intrusion of the international firm may be the inculcation of exogenous cultural styles which are more economically fecund.

Cultural explanations for the demise of the Latin American entrepreneur are attractive. They provide a general, all-embracing explanation which seems to integrate a large number of disparate empirical observations. Before accepting such a theory, however, some serious attention should be paid to its assumptions and the variables which it ignores. First, the contrast

[3]Michael Crozier, *The Bureaucratic Phenomenon* (Chicago: University of Chicago Press, 1964), chapter 8; Jean Jacques Servan-Schreiber, *The American Challenge* (New York: Atheneum, 1968), p. 10.
[4]The classic statement for Brazil is the work of Gilberto Freye. See, for example, *The Masters and the Slaves,* trans. Samuel Putnam (New York: Alfred A. Knopf, 1964). For a more recent, more empirical treatment, see Marvin Harris, *Town and Country in Brazil* (New York: Columbia University Press, 1956); or Harry Hutchinson, *Village and Plantation Life in Northeast Brazil* (Seattle: University of Washington Press, 1957).
[5]Alfred Lauterbach, *Enterprise in Latin America* (Ithaca: Cornell University Press, 1966).
[6]Fernando Henrique Cardoso, *O Empresário e Desenvolvimento Industrial no Brasil* (São Paulo: Difusão Europeia do Livro, 1964).
[7]Ibid., p. 101.
[8]Ibid., p. 120.

between Latin American and North American managerial styles is usually based on a comparison between observations of small, owner-operated firms and an ideal-typical abstraction of how a giant industrial corporation in the United States is operated. Even when the comparison is an empirical one (as in the case of Cardoso's study), very little allowance is made for the effects of scale differences on administrative procedure. Second, the emphasis on the traditional paternalistic conservatism of the Latin American entrepreneur jibes so neatly with earlier description of Latin American landowners and politicians . . . that one can't help but wonder whether the power of a pre-existing stereotype is responsible for orderliness of current observations.

Data sufficiently systematic and representative to prove or disprove the cultural explanation is lacking, but observations of a less systematic or representative nature can be used to illustrate some of the reasons for doubting the primacy of the cultural explanation. Interviews among pharmaceutical and chemical firms in Brazil form one set of such observations. They were conducted among both locally owned firms and subsidiaries of international firms and were focused mainly on the pharmaceutical industry. The firms covered represent a majority of the top 40 sellers in Brazil and account for 60 percent of the sales of the top 40. All of the locally owned firms in the top 40 were interviewed.

A quick look at Brazilian pharmaceutical firms confirms the idea that they are closely held and that shared ownership often parallels kinship ties. Of the roughly 20 local firms for which it was possible to estimate the distribution of ownership,[9] two-thirds had equity concentrated in the hands of a single individual or family. In the remaining one-third, those holding significant amounts of equity were a group of less than half a dozen persons. Family ownership also seems, at first glance, to be associated with inability to compete. Of the seven firms in the sample that were old enough to have been in the hands of the same family for more than one generation, the majority had sold out to foreign companies. Up to a point the data is quite consistent with depictions leading to a cultural explanation. Further examination produces some anomalies.

In the first place it appears, at least on the basis of the pharmaceutical industry, that it is a mistake to consider acquisition by a foreign company as a sign of management failure by the old owners. If anything it is recognition of their success. Foreign firms would rather start a subsidiary from scratch than take over a "weak sister"; almost without exception acquired firms have been leaders in the industry.

The second anomaly from the point of view of a culturally based theory is that the old family owner-managers were retained in top management positions by the acquiring international firms.[10] Since the scions of former owning families should be most imbued with whatever maladaptive cultural

---

[9]This includes two local firms which have since become subsidiaries.

[10]Of the four cases in which a firm had been in the hands of the same family for at least two generations, and was acquired by an international firm, the family retained top management positions in three. Some equity participation was also maintained. In the fourth case, the transaction was still not completed at the time of the field work.

traits characterize Latin American entrepreneurs, this would seem a curious choice for a modern multinational firm to make if the cultural explanation is a correct one.

The skeptic might still argue that the retention of former owners isn't really evidence of competence. The international firm may be retaining them, despite their bad attitudes, because they promote good relations with the surrounding local business community. Such a skeptic would be disappointed by the opinions of international corporate managements in the United States. Asked whether Latin Americans employed in their Brazilian subsidiaries tended to be resistant to change and innovation, corporate executives responded with incredulity or indignation. The idea that their Latin American managers were less sophisticated or "modern" than North Americans of equivalent status was considered either as an aspersion on their corporate hiring practices or a sign of the interviewer's naïveté.[11]

Whenever men who have been socialized in an owner-entrepreneur tradition appear able, with no apparent strain, to assimilate the managerial modes of the modern international firm, cultural explanations must seem undermined. Nonetheless, there does seem to be a distinctive managerial style prevading locally owned Brazilian firms and characterizations of this style as paternalistic, centralized and authoritarian do not appear unjustified. Indications of this style appear frequently in interviews in locally owned firms. Asked about the planning process, a manager may typically say that there is no reason for it since the owner-founder-president makes all the decisions himself. Chief executives speak of their firms' activities in personal terms. ("*I* bought some land on the other side of town and will build a new plant there." "*I* have increased the sales of the company two and a half times since taking over from my brother," etc.) Even where a small group of associates run a company together, impersonal, bureaucratic procedures have little place in the management of the firm.

If a culturally based explanation for the distinctive style found in locally owned firms is abandoned, however, what alternative explanations might be offered? Scale effects are an obvious candidate. Taking the pharmaceutical industry in Brazil as an example, one finds that the size distributions of subsidiaries and locally owned firms are almost nonoverlapping; that is, most of even the smaller subsidiaries are bigger than the biggest locally owned firms. If the size of the entire international corporation rather than the scale of the subsidiary itself is used as a standard of comparison, then the very biggest locally owned firms are no more than 4 or 5 percent of the scale of their international competitors.

Keeping in mind massive differences in scale, differences in managerial style began to make more sense. Take one cornerstone of efficient, imper-

---

[11]Positive assessments of the capabilities of local managerial personnel are not limited to their superiors. John C. Shearer, author of one of the few empirical studies on the subject, characterizes Brazilian managers as no less competent than their American counterparts and advocates their increased use by subsidiaries. See John C. Shearer, *High-Level Manpower in Overseas Subsidiaries* (Research Report 98; Princeton: Industrial Relations Section, Princeton University, 1960).

sonal bureaucratic administration—the formal planning process. For an international firm, planning is essential if the corporate management is to know what its subunits are doing. For the small locally owned firm its benefits may be minimal. The president of a locally owned firm dealing in basic chemicals could not help being skeptical of the potential returns to planning:

For one of our products there are only two customers in Brazil and only one competitor. If the competitor succeeds in getting the customers we must switch to producing another product. How can you do long range planning under such circumstances? What we need is the ability to change course rapidly.

While this case is extreme, the general point is valid: the increased unpredictability associated with small scale diminishes the returns to planning. Lacking the volume to cushion it against fluctuations in its economic environment or the power to control such fluctuations, the small firm must be ready to respond rapidly to external variation. The ability to alter plans quickly and decisively may be more valuable than attempts at systematic projection. Quick and decisive action requires centralized controls.

Other kinds of deviation from ideal-typical prescription of modern management also appear less irrational in view of the exigencies of small-scale operation. Even if authority were distributed very evenly among all managerial personnel, there are a few locally owned pharmaceutical firms in which a group of more than a half-dozen men would be implicated. Bureaucratization in such circumstances is hard to envision. Stressing familial or personal loyalty instead of loyalty to the firm as an institution, or adherence to impersonal norms, may also be a rational strategy in a firm of small scale. If the firm as an institution is a fragile entity which may or may not continue to produce income in future years and roles are of necessity diffuse, reliance on family or personal ties may be the best strategy for creating a cohesive, solidary organization.

Reconsideration of the "Brazilian" or "Latin American" mode of management suggests then that it may in fact be more accurately characterized as a "small-scale" managerial style. If the nature of the style is conceived as arising more from organizational and economic exigencies than from cultural tradition, then its divergence from the management patterns found in corporations of larger scale bears no necessary implication of irrationality. The scale explanation seems at least as plausible as a cultural one, but before it is accepted, even as a working hypothesis, the plausibility of some of its implications should be considered.

First, a scale-based explanation would suggest that the behavior of independent entrepreneurs operating on a small scale in the United States should diverge from ideal-typical corporate patterns in ways which roughly parallel the divergence observed in Latin American firms. While no systematic data can be brought to bear on this question, a survey of the literature on smaller-scale operations in the United States certainly gives the impression that this is the case. Discussion of "indulgent" personalistic ties to employees, strong fears regarding loss of control, and the importance of support from close kinsmen sound familiar after reading descriptions of Latin American operations.[12]

A second implication of a scale-based explanation is that "Latin American" management patterns should not necessarily be associated with traditionalism or conservatism in other areas such as technological change or the introduction of new products. In looking at this issue, reference to pharmaceutical firms—half subsidiaries, half locally owned—showed no

Relative to locally owned firms the international company has an indisputable technological advantage. In evaluating the behavior of the local entrepreneur, however, the issue is whether he shows a conservative bias against the exploration of technological change or whether he is willing to innovate to the degree that his means allow. Looking at the reported history of product innovations developed within Brazil by about thirty pharmaceutical firms—half subsidiaries, half locally-owned—showed no evidence of conservative bias on the part of the local entrepreneur. In fact, when technological activities within Brazil are in question, the local entrepreneur appears more aggressive than subsidiary managements. When the relative size of firms was taken into account the effects of ownership are quite striking. Among firms with sales over $2.5 million a year, all locally owned firms did local product development. Only one-third of the subsidiaries could make a similar claim. A survey conducted by the *Instituto de Estudos para o Desenvolvimento Social e Econômico* with the support of the *Instituto Roberto Simonsen* and the *Federação des Indústrias do estado do São Paulo* indicates that this association between local ownership and a greater propensity to do research holds outside the confines of the pharmaceutical industry.[13]

In their estimation of the sophistication of the Brazilian market as well as their willingness to undertake local technological work, locally owned firms often seemed less "traditional" than foreign subsidiaries. A small locally owned pharmaceutical firm, rather than an American or European firm, was the first to make an antismoking pill in Brazil, which is especially surprising considering that the formula for the drug was largely derived from a popular American product. Likewise, it was a locally owned firm that was first to successfully introduce an artificial sweetener in the Brazilian

---

[12]Alvin Gouldner describes how a paternalistic "indulgency" relation gives way to bureaucratic norms with the advent of a manager responsive to corporate headquarters in an American plant. See *Patterns of Industrial Bureaucracy* (New York: The Free Press, 1954). The Lynds' *Middletown* also describes the paternalistic style of local entrepreneurs in the United States. Collins and Moore illustrate the fears of control loss and consequent desire for family control of equity in *The Organization Makers* (New York: Appleton-Century-Crofts, 1970). They also contrast the style of the entrepreneur with that of the executive in the large corporation. Other studies, such as John Bunzel's *The American Small Businessman* (New York: Alfred A. Knopf, 1962) point in the same direction.

[13]Instituto de Estudos Para o Desenvolvimento, *A Pesquisa Technólogica na Industria Paulista* (São Paulo, 1967); for a discussion of the results see Vincent Chiaverini, "Pesquisa Technologica na Industria," in Instituto Roberto Simonsen, *Pesquisa Technológica na Universidade e na Industria Brasileiras* (São Paulo, 1968), pp. 22–23.

market. A local firm was the first to introduce in Brazil plastic containers, lighter and less subject to breakage than glass ones, for handling intravenous feedings. Innovations produced by locally owned firms, like those initiated by subsidiaries, are not likely to be fundamental contributions to medical science, but at the very least they indicate a progressive attitude toward technological change.

As would be expected the larger Brazilian firms are the most technologically active. A good example of this activeness is a firm we will call *Laboratórios Dynamico* (all company names in this paper are pseudonyms). In addition to the usual *conselho scientifico* (council of scientific consultants), *Dynamico* has a department of chemical research and a department of pharmacological research. It also does its own biological and clinical testing. The directors say that they always conduct clinical tests on new substances even if they have been tested abroad, since it has been their experience that their own tests often produce results at variance with previous findings; an experience which they point out is not too different from that of the Federal Drug Administration. The directors also set up an affiliated company to produce needed chemical raw materials so that they would not be so dependent on outside sources of supply. The commercial success of these policies can be seen in the fact that *Dynamico* has not lost ground relative to affiliates of foreign firms, but has managed to grow faster than several subsidiaries.

A firm we will call *Laboratórios Familial* is another example. In 1961 *Familial* reported to the Commission of Inquiry of the Pharmaceutical Industry that their research had permitted the launching of 50 new pharmaceutical and dietetic formulas, and that a project on a barium preparation for radiography of the bronchial tubes had resulted in findings sufficient in originality to be published in an American research periodical. From 1964 to 1968 *Familial* has tested about 120 compounds a year and developed a total of about 30 new products. While this doesn't compare with the 2–4 thousand substances tested by a major American firm it is impressive in view of the fact that *Familial*'s sales amount to only 2 or 3 percent of a major American firm.

Relative to his resources, the local entrepreneur is more willing to risk undertaking local product innovation than is the foreign subsidiary. The international firm chooses to centralize product innovation, despite lack of firm evidence that there are significant economies of scale to be gained by such centralization.[14] The reasoning of the international firm is entirely understandable. Anxiety over the difficulty of controlling R&D facilities at a distance, the tendency to try to avoid the uncertainty of products tailored only for particular local markets, and the more interest-laden desire to maintain proprietary control over new technology combine to provide good reasons for the corporate management to feel that dispersing research and development might be problematical. Understandable or not, however, the effect of such reasoning is conservative as far as the technological develop-

---

[14]For an econometric analysis of economies of scale in pharmaceutical research and development see William S. Commanor, "The Economics of Research and Development in the Pharmaceutical Industry" (Ph.D. dissertation, Harvard University, 1963).

ment of industry in Brazil is concerned, indeed, it is more conservative than the local entrepreneurs' brand of rationality. In sum, this brief examination of a sample of the technological behavior of Latin American enterprises should help undermine the view that the Latin American businessman is trapped by his culture into running his business in an irrational and ineffective way. Not only do the patterns of authority and ownership observed in Latin American businesses appear to make sense in terms of the exigencies of running a small firm in an uncertain environment, but, in addition, these patterns of ownership and authority appear to bear no necessary relation to traditionalism or to excessively conservative decision-making in the area of technological innovation.[15]

Having argued that the management patterns observed in locally owned firms are rational and in some cases technologically progressive, it might seem natural to suggest that the Latin American businessman has a good chance of regaining a dominant position in local industries. Such a prognostication is unjustified. In the perspective that has just been developed, the prospects of the Latin American businessman appear essentially similar to those of the small businessman in the United States. Successful development of his enterprise is likely to be followed by its absorption into some larger corporate entity. The major difference is that in the case of the Latin American the larger corporation will probably be a foreign one.

Ceasing to attribute the problems of the Latin American businessman to ingrained cultural predilections does not change prognostications for his survival. The likelihood remains that as an entrepreneur he will be a marginal participant operating in the shadow of larger foreign-owned firms. The main effect of interpreting his behavior more positively is to raise doubts about the effects of his demise. As long as he was considered a kind of feudal lord in business-dress, his replacement by the international firm could be interpreted as a step toward a more modern and efficient capitalist economy. If, on the other hand, he has been behaving as a rational entrepreneur, the progressive effects of his demise are much more doubtful.

---

[15]It must, of course, be kept in mind that interindustry variation has not been considered. For example, the behavior of local entrepreneurs in the cotton textile industry, with its long history of excessive tariff protection and statutory restrictions on production, is likely to be different from that of local entrepreneurs in pharmaceuticals and chemicals. See Stanley J. Stein, "The Brazilian Cotton Textile Industry," in *Economic Growth: Brazil, India and Japan,* ed. Simon Kuznets, W. Moore, and J. J. Spengler (Durham, N.C.: Duke University Press, 1955).

Part Three

Power and Politics in the Industrial Setting

Introduction to Part Three

The typical conception of Latin American politics is one of instability, strongman rule, conflict between elitist control and mass movements, sporadic violence, and a very slow pace of change in the shaping of modern political institutions. As one moves past these stereotypes and grapples with the complexity of Latin American politics, one fact stands out for the politics of the Latin American industrial setting: the state is at the apex of power in a triangular relationship with management and labor. The base of the triangle, management-labor relations, is the least critical element and more important are the relations of each of these two groups directly with the state. The state, here, may be an individual dictator, a ruling junta, or a political party, but in all cases the two industrial groups constantly look up and not to one another for the source and balance of power.

The political problems confronted by workers therefore involve issues of government regulation, the role of the working class vote in national politics, and the ability of unions to voice labor's interest on the national scene even more than within local plants. Managers, on the other hand, are more concerned with their relative weakness within the local private sector, competition from the foreign private sector, and their struggles with the public-sector bureaucrats and technocrats. The selections in this part of the book examine these concerns in greater detail. It may also be noted that, although they focus on Latin America, the issues discussed below are often quite salient to developing areas in general as well as to politics and industrial relations systems in some industrialized nations in Europe.

Worker Politics

The first selection in Part III includes an example of a Latin American collective bargaining agreement. It gives concrete examples of the kinds of solutions workers and managers may find for problems of wages, inflation, absenteeism, work hours, work conditions, and fringe benefits. It is atypical, however, in that most workers are not sufficiently organized to hammer out such agreements, and typical union-management relations are still heavily mediated by state controls. The Goodman article describes some of the effects of these legal controls and speculates on their intent.

The International Labour Office article shows that the evolution of state-worker-manager relations can be characterized by three stages. First, there was a situation of absolute paternalism in which workers were entirely dependent on owner-managers for every aspect of their well-being. As managers began to develop large-scale enterprises, and labor began to unionize, Latin American governments promulgated various bodies of labor laws. These were designed to smooth bargaining by installing the state as the ultimate arbiter of labor and management affairs. However, according to the Strassmann piece, the typical managerial attitude towards labor is still dominated by such paternalism, and when the paternalism of managers declines, the role of the state, not of labor, has been strengthened. The final stage occurs when collective bargaining directly between management and labor replaces statutory regulation of working conditions. In contemporary Latin America one can find examples of all three of these styles of labor-management relations. However, the dominant mode is strong state control with absolute paternalism only present in rural areas and in artisan industry. Examples of full reliance on collective bargaining are rare, but increasing in incidence.

Wendell C. Gordon's article traces the history of the Latin American labor movement and outlines the nature of its current organization. Gordon's article along with the Landsberger, Barrera, Toro discussion of union leader attitudes balance the gloomier picture presented by Goodman. Gordon describes unions as coherent and purposive. Landsberger reports that union leaders are somewhat satisfied with labor-management relations and are primarily concerned with economic rather than political issues. It should be remembered, however, that unionized workers represent only the most privileged 15 percent of the Latin American work force, and that Landesberger's leaders represent some of the strongest unions among these few.

Apart from organizing through unions, workers can exercise political power through the ballot box. Yet, it is not always clear that workers vote for political parties which purport to recognize working-class interests. For this reason it has been suggested that Latin American politics should be called the Politics of Conformity.[1] Individuals, according to this interpretation, aspire to attitudes of the social class they would prefer to be a member of, rather than those of their own social class, and their voting behavior reflects this shift.

Zeitlin and Petras, however, analyze data from the 1958 and 1964 Chilean presidential elections and conclude that, by and large, Chilean workers do vote in terms of their class interests. During the last two decades voting regulations have been changed so that youth and illiteracy do not rule out a worker from voting. If Petras and Zeitlin's findings can be generalized beyond the Chilean case, the working-class vote will assume increased importance in future Latin American elections.

Managerial Power

Throughout this volume we have concentrated on managers as those who run enterprises in the private sector. When considering the political dimension of the managerial role, however, it is necessary to turn to an examination of managers in the public sector as well. Here, we are largely in the realm of the economic technicians working for the government. The power of these *técnicos* does not lie in their ability to shape public policy directly, but rather in their position to select the technical alternatives that are to be presented to the heads of government. Despite the circulation of leaders at the top these bureaucratic men in the middle main-

[1]See Claudio Veliz, ed., *The Politics of Conformity in Latin America* (New York: Oxford University Press, 1967).

tain their importance on the basis of their technical knowledge and not on their use of force.

The selection by Raymond Vernon analyzes this group of *técnicos* in one of their strongest enclaves, the Mexican government. This group of managers is oriented towards the definition and implementation of government policies of industrialization. Their ideological position calls for a reduced reliance on economic growth through the export of raw materials, a reduced dependence on imports of manufactured goods, and a strategy of industrialization through the formation and use of domestic capital markets.

This ideological conception calls for a regulated private economy in which the managers from the public sector have significant controls on investment and the direction of business activity in the private sector of the economy. Politically, this group of *técnico* managers presents a much more coherent and cohesive platform than do the majority of managerial bodies in the private sectors of each Latin American republic. It is this lack of unity and solidarity, according to Jose Luis Imaz, which results in the weakness of managers from the private sector to act as a significant power factor in the Argentine political scene. Unlike other organized groups, such as the military and the landed oligarchy, says Imaz, the industrialists follow a more traditional economic model where each one watches out for his own interest, or those of his family, thus inhibiting the development of a strong voice among the industrialists. Imaz also suggests that wealth is sought as a means to status, not to power, and that industrial managers adopt the values and

ideology of the traditional rural sector.

The Davis selection on Chile examines a corollary of this organizational incapacity on the part of the private sector. What we have, in effect, is a case study of W. I. Thomas' classical sociological theorem of the self-fulfilling prophecy. Chilean private enterprise has been in terrible shape for many years, long before Allende and the left came to power. The ideological belief of Chilean businessmen, that capitalism is struggling for survival in their country, therefore may be seen as cause as well as effect of this increasing probability. Businessmen exist in such a politicized environment that survival replaced profit-making as the predominant orientation, and the means became an end in themselves. Under such circumstances, the external environment has far more relevance for the success of an enterprise than do any internal efficiencies of organization. Taken together, the Vernon, Imaz, and Davis selections underscore the importance of political forces of the state, which are external to the use of power within industrial organizations, for the manager.

The last article in this volume turns to the internal use of power, how managers control and direct the activities of workers and employees. Examining the use of authority in Mexican enterprise, Davis emphasizes the centralization of decision-making and its effect upon subordinates' unwillingness to accept responsibility and their tendency to bypass intermediate levels in order to deal directly with *the* boss.

These managerial methods of wielding power are closely related to another Latin American characteristic and type of leader, the *caudillo*. The leadership of the *caudillo,* the strongman, is personal and not based on any organization, political party, institution, constitution, or ideology. He rules because he is able to rule, not because he has been born or elected to the position. Under such circumstances, maintaining himself in office supersedes other issues such as the formulation and implementation of policies for economic development. Moreover, since power is not institutionalized, it must be held totally and cannot be shared with other branches of government or with lesser functionaries. Thus power is centralized as well as personalized; and often it is not institutionalized into an effective organizational structure.

These historical factors are intimately related to the nature and use of power among Latin American managers today. It can be seen in the treatment of managerial tendencies towards paternalism by several authors in this volume; in the centralization of authority and an unwillingness to delegate decision-making power downward; and in the frequent absence of articulated policy, planning, and effective organization. Despite the problems caused by historical and cultural attitudes towards power, however, management-labor problems internal to industrial organizations are superseded in importance by the bases of power that are tied to external circumstances in the national political arena.

31 Latin American Collective Bargaining Agreement: An Illustration

James O. Morris

Collective bargaining in Latin America is generally both far less extensive and far less sophisticated than it is in the United States—even if we include within the term "collective agreement" the numerous bargains arrived at in Latin America through some kind of government machinery, as well as the very few which result from direct negotiation between the parties. There may be relatively more workers in Mexico and Argentina covered by industry-wide agreements than there are in the United States, but, even if so, this may reflect more the practice of government extension of contract terms agreed upon locally than actual industry-wide bargaining patterns.

The Latin American countries can be divided into three groups in terms of the development of collective bargaining: 1) an advanced group best exemplified by Mexico and Argentina; 2) a much larger middle group where bargaining is spotty and unbalanced, being advanced in some of the larger undertakings, existing in simpler form in some of the smaller firms, and absent elsewhere; and 3) a large third group where bargaining is virtually unknown. Brazil falls in the middle group, and the contract which follows, signed by employees and management of the Volta Redonda steel works, is one of the leading agreements of that country in the bargaining experience and professionalization it reflects.

It is essentially a crisis-type wage agreement, designed to recover the mountainous real-income losses of an inflation-ridden country. Inflation seems to operate as both cause and effect in helping to explain the relative weakness of the institution of bargaining in underdeveloped areas. It takes so much effort to stand still that little is left for progress. The agreement has few, if any, of the work rules (seniority provisions, promotion, transfer, layoff, dismissal, and grievance procedures) so common to North American agreements. These differences do not, however, always or necessarily reflect a lower level of development. For example, most grievances are handled in Brazil by local conciliation boards. To emphasize the overshadowing importance of "inflation bargaining" in Brazil, it can be noted that in four years after this was signed, the *cruzeiro* slid more than 600 percent relative to the dollar, indicating that roughly the same percentage increase in the internal cost of living had taken place.

Frequently in Latin America, the government will suggest a percentage wage and salary increase due to inflation and the private parties then adjust

Reprinted from the *Industrial and Labor Relations Review,* Vol. 17, No. 3 (April 1964). Copyright © 1964 by Cornell University. All rights reserved.

accordingly. This may be what happened in Brazil in 1959—the government may have suggested a 44 percent increase against which the steel company, with the consent of its workers, offset a 10 percent increase it had already granted. The contract also establishes a shift differential, overtime rates, and premium pay for particular jobs (probably the really hot and/or dangerous ones, although, curiously, the applicability of the provision is not defined).

The family allowance feature of the contract is common in Latin America and, apparently unlike the Volta Redonda case, is usually only one of a maze of special nonwage income sources which can, in the aggregate, be more important to some workers than wage income itself. The nonwage income content of the agreement can be explained in a variety of ways, the validity of which varies from country to country. For one thing, there is simply a cultural difference which in Latin America prescribes that a family allowance be given as a matter of justice to the married worker. For another, the employer usually does not pay social security taxes on nonwage income, and he therefore encourages demands in this area. Finally, the generally low economic level of existence requires that a worker receive special consideration during the crises and important events of his lifetime—weddings, births, deaths, and so forth.

Attention should be called to the several provisions which outline a biweekly premium system for regular attendance. Tardiness is evidently a serious problem and its existence may point to a larger difficulty of commitment to the industrial labor force. A word also about the ten-year premium. This has evidently been bargained as a complement to the "ten-year" law which makes discharge both difficult and costly after an employee has completed ten years of satisfactory service.

Other interesting or noteworthy provisions of the contract are Clauses 4, 5, and 9 and the final paragraph. Clauses 4 and 5 point to a difference in the treatment of blue- and white-collar workers, the latter enjoying a virtual noontime siesta (two hours) while the former are allowed the more common lunch period (forty-five minutes). Clause 9 suggests an advanced personnel section evidently interested in experimental questions, such as, for instance, how vacations affect work attitudes. The final paragraph is important because it indicates that in Brazil the government reserves the right to bring about changes in collective contracts. Less obvious, but equally true, is the implication of this paragraph that in Brazil a properly executed collective agreement has the force of law and its enforcement devolves upon the Ministry of Labor, Industry, and Commerce.

Volta Redonda Steel Works—1959
Collective Agreement Entered Into by the
Metal, Mechanical and Electrical
Industries Workers' Union of Barra Mansa
and the National Steel Company

The parties to this Agreement are, on one side, the Metal, Mechanical and Electrical Industries Workers' Union of Barra Mansa, with headquarters in

Volta Redonda, State of Rio de Janeiro, as the representative of the respective professional status of its members and represented by its President, Mr. Othon Reis Fernandes; and on the other side, the National Steel Company (CSN), with headquarters in this capital, represented by its Vice-President and Acting President, Mr. Joao Kubitschek de Figueiredo, and by its Secretary and Director, Dr. Paulo Monteiro Mendes, in accordance with the following clauses:

Clause 1: All employees of the Company, unless expressly excluded under this Agreement, will receive a 44% wage increase over the salary scale in effect as of October 1, 1958, and there will be deducted from this amount, as compensation, the 10% increase granted by the Company on April 1, 1959.

1. This increase will also apply to bonuses paid to employees holding committee-appointed jobs (confidential technical jobs, confidential jobs and confidential officers), as well as to bonuses paid for the use of stenography and foreign languages.

2. In compliance with the provisions of this clause, all salary scales in effect as of November 30, 1959, will be changed, beginning December 1, 1959 in accordance with the attached table.

Clause 2: The family allowance will be increased to Cr$ 480.00[1] for each properly registered dependent.

Clause 3: The premium payment for specific jobs, dealt with in the fifth clause of the previous Agreement, effective as of October 1, 1958, which is now Cr$ 570.00 will be increased to Cr$ 816.00 to be paid in strict accordance with the eligibility standards and conditions expressly set forth.

Clause 4: Office personnel working in Volta Redonda, whose present office hours are from 7:30 a.m. to 5:45 p.m., with two hours for lunch and rest, will work from 7:45 a.m. to 5:15 p.m., with two hours for lunch and rest, from Monday through Friday. Saturday working hours will be from 7:45 a.m. to 11:30 a.m.

Clause 5: Pending changes in the shift working hours which, during an 8-hour working day, would allow for the main meals to be eaten at the employee's home, 45 minutes without interruption will be allowed, on each shift, for meals and rest, applicable to all personnel working on shifts of 8 consecutive hours, exclusive of emergencies which may arise during this period. To this effect, the Company will make up lists which will be posted at the time-clocks for the information of those concerned.

1. When, because of work demands, it is not possible for an employee to take 45 minutes for rest and meals, the Company will pay overtime for this period. In case it should become permanently impossible for him to take this time off, the CSN will list the places and personnel working thus, during the time involved, in order to determine the corresponding overtime pay.

2. Meal and rest hours should be set between the 2nd and 5th hours of each shift, and during the course of a week each employee should have the same hour set aside for rest and meals, except when his shift is changed.

Clause 6: Employees will work either in day or night work, at the Company's discretion, and night work will be subject to a 20% bonus and will be rotated. Hours of work are those performed between 10 p.m. and 5 a.m., and will always be computed on the basis of 52 minutes and 30 seconds.

Clause 7: Working hours will be lengthened in cases of real necessity, or when the employee's replacement does not arrive, in which case the employee will continue working until his replacement arrives. Overtime will be paid at the following rates, over and above standard rates:

---

[1]The average exchange rate in 1959 was 190 *cruzeiros* to the $1.00 U.S.—J.M.

20%—for the first two hours
30%—for the next two hours, and
50%—for the remaining hours.

The Company will provide adequate meals for operational personnel, in cases of overtime work in excess of 3 hours.

Clause 8: The Company will set up a Committee, with the participation of the Union, to study the possibility of standardizing daytime working hours in the Plant and Field. This study should be finished within 90 days.

Clause 9: The Company will not require of its employees, upon their return to work after vacations, any psycho-technical examination.

Clause 10: All employees receiving wage differentials for temporary assignment to particular jobs at a higher wage rate, for more than one consecutive year, will be placed permanently in the higher wage category.

1. This clause will apply to employees who, during the period of the previous Agreement of October 1, 1958, fulfilled these requirements, even though, for any reason, they may have ceased to receive such wage differential.

2. In cases of provisional or probationary assignment to a particular job at a higher wage rate, the Company will continue vacation pay on the basis of the salary in effect, plus the corresponding wage differential when, at the beginning of such vacation, the employee has been receiving said wage differential for more than 6 consecutive months.

Clause 11: For purposes of the payment of the bi-weekly premium provided for in Art. 142 of the Company's Personnel Regulations, every 5 late arrivals, if not made up, will equal one absence.

1. Late arrival is defined as the employee's arrival for work up to 3 hours after the normal starting time.

2. When an employee's normal working period is less than 3 hours, absence from work during the entire period will be considered a half absence, for each working period, on days when he works two periods; or one absence if his normal working period corresponds to that period, because of individual or group schedules.

3. The provisions of this clause revoke the present system of converting late arrivals and absences into tenths of absences; however, this system will remain effective for other purposes in connection with the bi-weekly premium.

Clause 12: An employee who is twice ineligible for the bi-weekly premium only because of a doctor's excuse or leave for health treatment, during the period in question—may, by means of a written statement signed during working hours, request that the computation of the time prior to his last absence on a doctor's excuse or for health treatment be canceled, in which case, on the date immediately following that absence, a new period will begin for purposes of eligibility for the double bi-weekly premium.

1. An employee who makes use of this provision may not, under any circumstances, reconsider his choice previously made in writing, and may only receive the premium, single or double, at the end of the new period corresponding to his expressed choice.

2. An employee who receives payment of the simple bi-weekly bonus on an ex-officio basis through the Personnel Dept., will be considered to have renounced his rights to the option mentioned in this clause.

Clause 13: The Company will re-write paragraph a) of Art. 252 of its Personnel Regulations, dealing with exemption from penalties, as follows:

"a) *Effective exercise* during the period indicated below, for each type of penalty, beginning as of the date of imposition of the most recent penalty:

I. 6 months for each warning;
II. 1 year for each reprimand;
III. 2 years for each suspension, plus one month for each day of the duration of this penalty;
IV. 5 years, according to the number and degree of penalties."

Clause 14: In cases of determining eligibility for the ten-year premium, the Company will examine the possibility of granting ex-officio exemption from penalties to those employees who have not yet achieved this, provided they fulfill the other requirements set forth in the previous clause.

Clause 15: The Company will study the benefits to be granted to its employees who have completed 20 years of active service, it being already established that one of these benefits will be an extra 20 working days of vacation.

1. The CSN will determine such eligibility ex-officio once a year, on a date chosen by it.

2. This benefit will be granted once only, and the employee may take his extra 20 working days of vacation at any time after they have been added to any normal vacation period for which he is eligible; the Company reserves the right to determine the date for commencing such vacation, according to law.

3. At the option of the employee, these extra days of vacation may be paid in cash.

Clause 16: The Child Care Center will give free attention to maternity cases and to babies, for employees up to class 40 on the attached table, as well as to their respective dependents.

Clause 17: The amount of monthly deductions for hospital care will not be in excess of 10% of an employee's wages, not including the family allowance.

Clause 18: The following are not included under this Agreement:
a) teachers and students of the Pandia Calogeras Technical School;
b) crews of the Department of Navigation.

Clause 19: The benefits and duties derived from this Agreement include workers in the Rio de Janeiro, São Paulo, Rio Grande do Sul, Belo Horizonte and Pernambucco offices, with the exception of those excluded under the eighteenth clause.

Clause 20: All other provisions mentioned in previous agreements which do not appear expressly here, whether changed or not, are revoked and declared void as of January 1, 1960, except those which already constitute acquired rights, which will remain in force as established.

Clause 21: This Agreement will be in force from January 1, 1960, to December 31, 1960; except for the first, second and third clauses, which will go into effect December 1, 1959, and remain in force until December 31, 1960.

This Trade Union Agreement will only be valid following ratification by the General Membership Meeting of the Union and by the Minister of Labor, Industry and Commerce, according to law.

Rio de Janeiro.

Workers

32

Labor Legislation and Collective Bargaining in the Americas

International Labour Office

The Role of Legislation

... In Canada and the United States the greater reliance placed on collective bargaining as distinguished from statutory regulation of working conditions is in part a reflection of the pragmatic approach characterizing Anglo-American legal concepts, which are based on common-law principles and on a traditional preference for contract and custom rather than statutory provisions. On the other hand labor law in Latin America follows the Roman tradition, i.e. it consists of written law established by nonjudicial bodies.

While people in Canada and in the United States usually speak of "labor relations" or "labor-management relations," thus emphasizing the wider nature of the relationship between men at work, people in Latin America usually think in terms of *derecho del trabajo* or *derecho social* (labor law), thus stressing the legal aspects of a relationship which, in their view, is primarily a set of legal rights and obligations. These two approaches should be borne in mind but the distinction should not be overestimated.

The legal approach of the Latin American countries finds its typical expression in the tendency to codify all conceivable matters relating to labor and social questions into one comprehensive statute book. Rather voluminous labor codes exist in Bolivia, Brazil, Chile, Colombia, Costa Rica, the Dominican Republic, Ecuador, Guatemala, Honduras, Mexico, Nicaragua, Panama and Venezuela. In Argentina, Paraguay, Peru and El Salvador, codification is at present either envisaged or under discussion. This concept of codification is largely foreign to the Canadian and the United States systems.

The desire for legal perfection which is so strong in Latin America sometimes leads to a situation where the law is in advance of the real economic and social situation. . . . On the other hand it should not be overlooked that the function of the written law in some of the Latin American countries is sometimes more educational than normative in character. This concept of the role of legislation is somewhat alien to national traditions in Canada and in the United States.

Determination of Wages and Working Conditions. Statutory determination of minimum wages and working conditions finds its genesis in the responsi-

Adapted from *International Labour Review* (October 1961), pp. 269–291, with permission of the publisher, International Labour Office, Geneva, Switzerland.

217

bility of the state to protect the worker, as the economically weaker party in the employment relationship.

Legislative minimum-wage-fixing systems exist in all but a very few of the countries of the American region. They assume particular importance in a number of Latin American countries in view of the low level of wages resulting in part from the relatively low degree of economic development and the concomitant fact that collective bargaining has not yet achieved an effective role in regulating wages and other conditions of work. In this connection it is interesting to note that legislative minimum-wage-fixing may have a special significance in respect of the interrelationship between legislation and collective bargaining in that the form such wage-fixing may take (i.e., bipartite or tripartite discussions) is often a precursor of collective bargaining and, indeed, can itself constitute a rudimentary form of collective bargaining.

The fixing of minimum wages directly by legislation in which the minimum wage is expressed in the form of a specified amount of money is to be found in its largest sense in the United States, where a minimum wage is fixed on a nation-wide basis by the Fair Labor Standards Act, as amended. However, direct, overall legislative minimum-wage-fixing is comparatively rare in the American region. . . .

By far the most prevalent form of legislative wage-fixing in the American region arises out of enactments providing for the determination of minimum wages through the medium of special bipartite or tripartite boards. . . . These boards may be set up on a regional or occupational basis, or both, or they may be part of a tiered system at two or more levels. Their functions may be merely advisory in nature or they may have the power to make decisions or occupy a status somewhere between these two. . . . Virtually all provide for equal representation of employers and workers.

In reviewing systems of minimum-wage-fixing it should be recognized, as mentioned above, that such systems are of differing importance in various countries. For instance minimum-wage-fixing is of crucial importance in the less developed areas of Latin America, where, in effect, the minimum-wage scales are frequently the wage rates actually paid. On the other hand in the United States, in Canada, and in some areas of Latin America, a well-developed economy including a strong trade union movement and effective collective bargaining have served to create a relatively high general wage level. Hence for these countries and areas minimum-wage-fixing is less of importance, at least in respect of the relative number of workers upon whom the minima have a direct effect.

In addition to wages, legislation in the region deals . . . with virtually all other conditions of work. While a maximum of normal hours of work is fixed by legislation in almost all the countries of South and Central America, in the United States and in several provinces of Canada, the situation is somewhat different with regard to annual leave with pay. Such leave is recognized in the legislation of all countries in Latin America and in Canada. In the United States, on the other hand, there is no general legislation in this field, but in practice workers who are not covered by collective agreements are usually entitled to an annual paid vacation on the basis of established custom.

Statutory provisions on weekly rest periods and public holidays form an integral part of the legislation of most Latin American countries but are less common in Canada and the United States. . . . In the United States legislation is silent in this field, but employees not covered by collective agreement standards are still not unprotected, as the statutory maximum of 40 hours a week plus the relatively high overtime pay (usually time-and-a-half) together with local Sunday regulations constitute an effective curb on excessive work on weekends or public holidays.

Another area in which legislation is rather abundant in the whole region is that of protection of workers' health. The prohibition of child labor, special measures to protect employed young persons and women and the installation and maintenance of safety and health facilities of various kinds in undertakings form the subject matter of quite extensive statutory provisions in most of the Latin American countries.

There are quite a number of other conditions and benefits which are provided for by legislation in Latin American countries but on which there is less legislative regulation in the United States and Canada. These include, for instance, the payment of various forms of cash bonuses, long service and severance allowances, transport and housing facilities for workers, authorized absences from work with or without pay under specified circumstances (e.g., family events, civic functions), breaks and rest periods, funeral expenses, supply of work clothes, probationary periods and, in particular, special conditions for specified occupational groups of workers such as commercial employees, domestic servants, seafarers, agricultural workers, apprentices, etc. Furthermore, the law often specifies in great detail the matters to be contained in works rules.

These few examples show that legislation plays a far greater part in the determination of working conditions in South and Central America than in Canada and the United States. This is partly due to the low degree of development of collective bargaining in many of the Latin American countries, which obliges the State to intervene in the interest of the otherwise unprotected workers; but it is also an expression of the Roman law traditions of Latin America, under which legislation (as in many countries in Europe) regulates in great detail the individual contract of employment and the mutual rights and obligations of employers and workers arising out of it.

Settlement of Disputes. . . . In Latin American countries a distinction is sometimes made between collective and individual disputes and sometimes between economic and legal disputes. An economic dispute (or a dispute over interests) arises where the two parties cannot agree on the terms of a collective agreement. A legal dispute (or a dispute over rights) arises where the parties cannot agree on the interpretation or application of a collective agreement which has already been concluded or on the interpretation or application of provisions contained in laws, regulations or individual contracts of employment. The classification of controversies into economic and legal disputes has been adopted in the following discussion . . . because this distinction corresponds, at least in its general concept, to the distinction between industrial disputes [economic disputes] and grievances as recognized in [legal disputes in] Canada and the United States.

Economic Disputes. The legislation of all countries in the American region makes provision, in one way or another, for the prevention and settlement of economic disputes, and in all of them the law recognizes the basic right to strike. The differences between the various national systems are thus less ones of principle than of degree and are reflected in the extent of the limitations imposed on the exercise of the right to strike and in the extent of possible government intervention in the prevention and settlement of disputes.

The great majority of the countries leave it to the parties themselves to settle their economic disputes, in the belief that they are the best judges of their own interest; public settlement is usually invoked only where the parties cannot agree. To help the parties to reach an amicable settlement the legislation of all the countries concerned provides for the establishment of conciliation machinery.

While conciliation is voluntary in the United States, where employers and trade unions are free to decide whether they wish to avail themselves of the assistance offered by the Federal Mediation and Conciliation Service or by similar institutions established at the state level, it is compulsory in Canada and in the great majority of the Latin American countries. In the latter countries legislation usually provides that no strike or lockout can be lawfully declared before the conciliation proceedings have been exhausted. In the majority of them the legislation also provides for voluntary arbitration machinery which may intervene if conciliation efforts fail.

Another way in which governments intervene in disputes, and one that is a common feature of almost all the countries of the region, is the restriction or interdiction of certain types of strikes, usually those involving services and economic activities the interruption of which would be particularly harmful to the national welfare. . . . Moreover, a number of Latin American countries provide in their legislation that before a strike is declared it must have been approved by a specified majority of the workers concerned, in a secret ballot; this is aimed at preventing strikes which might be decided upon hastily and without due deliberation. . . .

Most of the American countries, while recognizing the right to strike as a principle, have nevertheless thought it necessary to enact legislation that limits and restricts complete freedom in the exercise of this right.

A similar effect is achieved in certain countries by the statutory provision of compulsory settlement of economic disputes. . . . [In Brazil] the labor court which is competent to settle all types of labor disputes, may, if conciliation efforts fail, settle economic disputes by issuing a binding award. . . .

Compulsory arbitration as the final step in the procedure is, for instance, provided for in the law of Ecuador and of Peru. Other countries where strikes are restricted or prohibited in public services or essential activities usually also have a system of compulsory arbitration for them. In Argentina the legislation permits compulsory arbitration in certain activities and cases, but it does not seem to be applied very often in practice. . . . In Mexico arbitration is not compulsory for the workers but only for the employers. . . .

Quite apart from the formalized settlement procedures prescribed in great detail by legislation, it is constant practice in many of the countries concerned for the Ministry of Labor or the Minister himself to intervene in industrial disputes. While this intervention is limited in some countries to appeals or to conciliation proposals addressed to the parties in major disputes only, there are others where it is more frequent and goes much further. In some Latin American countries intervention in labor disputes seems to be an essential part of the day-to-day activities of the Minister of Labor. Sometimes it is even the head of the government who intervenes. This frequent and direct intervention in concrete disputes often brings a political element into the case, with possible repercussions on the status and position of the Minister and even on the general stability of the government itself.

Legal Disputes. . . . The situation is more complicated with regard to legal disputes. Here a clear distinction is justified and necessary between Canada and the United States on the one hand and the Latin American countries on the other. While in the first two countries legal disputes are settled through procedures established by mutual agreement between employers and trade unions and embodied in their collective agreements, Latin American countries have created statutory machinery which is more or less connected with or integrated in their general judicial system. . . .

In the United States the formulation of grievance procedures, usually providing for arbitration as the final step, depends entirely upon the voluntary agreement of the parties and legislation plays a part only inasmuch as it states that final adjustment by a method agreed upon by the parties is declared to be the desirable method for the settlement of grievances arising out of the application or interpretation of an existing collective agreement. . . .

In Latin America most countries have established a system of settlement of legal disputes which is based on legislation and administered by judicial bodies. Whether these bodies are called labor courts as is the case in Argentina, Bolivia, Brazil, Chile, Colombia, Costa Rica, the Dominican Republic, Ecuador, El Salvador, Guatemala, Nicaragua, Panama and Venezuela, or conciliation or arbitration boards, as in Mexico, or whether in the absence of special labor courts it is the ordinary courts that are competent for the final settlement of such disputes as in Cuba, Haiti and Uruguay, the principle that the solution of legal conflicts is entrusted to statutory bodies remains constant. In many countries of the region complaints arising out of the employment relationship, if not settled within the undertaking, are in the first place brought before the labor inspector or another administrative authority, but there is usually the possibility of recourse to the courts against the decision of this authority.

. . . The legislation usually includes very detailed prescriptions for procedure (which is often modelled after the general court procedure in ordinary civil cases, but is usually less formal). In addition, the principle is usually set out that during the preliminary hearings an effort at conciliation must be made by the judge or court and that only when this fails can a judgment be rendered. This judgment, like that of any ordinary court, is binding on the parties, subject only to such rights of appeal as may be prescribed.

The difference underlying the grievance procedure in the United States and in Canada and the labor court procedure in Latin America lies in the fact that while the former method has the character of a private conciliation and arbitration machinery, the latter is based on the idea that legal labor disputes are not distinguishable on juridical grounds from other civil legal disputes and must therefore be settled by judicial bodies forming part of the general judicial system of the country. This is yet another reflection of the basically different approaches to labor-management relations in the two parts of the American region.

It should, however, be added that there is a trend in Latin America, at least in those countries where collective bargaining has acquired an important role in industrial relations, to have legal differences arising out of collective agreements resolved by the parties themselves. This evolution is sometimes also recognized and encouraged by legislation. . . .

Promotion of Collective Bargaining. Apart from its effects on the determination of wages and working conditions and the settlement of labor disputes, legislation can, and in fact often does, have a very strong influence in promoting collective bargaining by the establishment of an appropriate legal framework. In almost every country of the American Continent there are legal prescriptions which, although showing great variety, directly aim at this goal.

In the first place, all the countries of the region have legal provisions granting a greater or smaller degree of freedom of association and regulating—sometimes in great detail—the status, constitution and dissolution of employers' and workers' organizations. There is also a wealth of legal prescriptions for the protection of the worker's right to organize vis-à-vis his employer. . . .

Furthermore, there are often statutory provisions concerning the determination of the bargaining partners. While the right of individual employers or their associations to conclude valid collective agreements usually does not give rise to difficulties, the determination of the bargaining agent for the workers constitutes a more complicated legislative problem in various countries of the region. The questions involved are closely connected with the level at which bargaining takes place. . . . In Latin America, in accordance with civil law traditions, trade unions usually must be recognized by the state and registered before they can contract obligations and, in general, exercise their rights. A registered union may normally conclude a collective agreement without any requirement of majority representation. This does not seem to constitute a problem in those countries and economic branches where bargaining takes place at the industry level. In respect of plant-level bargaining, a multiplicity of unions does not, at least in theory, hamper collective bargaining in the many countries where the law explicitly or implicitly allows separate agreements to be negotiated within one plant. Moreover, even in those Latin American countries where the law permits only one collective agreement to be concluded in a given undertaking, it usually contents itself with very general principles with respect to the representative union, without providing for a procedure for its determination.

In many countries of the region there are also legal prescriptions dealing with the process of collective bargaining itself. Inspired by section 43 of the Mexican Labor Code, which provides that "every employer of persons who belong to a trade union must conclude a collective agreement with such trade union if requested to do so," many other Latin American countries, including Bolivia, Costa Rica, Ecuador, El Salvador, Guatemala and Venezuela, have introduced in their legislation the legal obligation of the employer to conclude a collective agreement. Under the law of Canada and the United States it is only the refusal of an employer to bargain in good faith that would constitute an unfair labor practice and would make him liable to sanctions. However, the employer is not compelled to reach agreement. . . .

Finally, the tendency to define in great detail the legal effects of collective agreements and to give them legal force almost as great as that enjoyed by statutory provisions is a characteristic feature of Latin American legislation. . . .

The existence, in most Latin American countries, of a rather abundant legislation on collective agreements, their contents, legal effects, etc., should not overshadow the fact that, except in a few countries, collective bargaining is much less developed than in Canada and in the United States. . . .

The Role of Collective Bargaining

The role played by collective bargaining in fixing wages and working conditions and settling labor disputes varies immensely between different parts of the American region. Whereas it is the normal way of regulating employer-employee relationships in certain countries, it is hardly known in others. . . .

The Latin American countries where collective bargaining has reached the highest level of development are Argentina, Mexico, Cuba and Venezuela. . . . In the other countries of Latin America collective bargaining seems to play a less important part in industrial relations and is in several cases restricted to some of the more important undertakings. . . .

With regard to the question of whether agreements should be negotiated at the plant level or on an industry-wide basis, concepts and practices vary widely between the countries of the region. . . . In the [Latin American] countries with the longest bargaining tradition there is a definite trend towards larger bargaining units which go beyond the individual undertakings. Agreements frequently cover all undertakings of the industrial or occupational sector concerned within a certain town (often the capital), region or province or in the entire country. The degree to which industry-wide bargaining is possible depends, of course, on the nature of economic activities, the strength and organizational structure of trade unions and employers' associations and a number of other factors. In Argentina, for instance, only 27 percent of the agreements in force in February 1956 were plant agreements, whereas one-third were industry-wide national agreements, one-third were industry-wide agreements concluded for the capital and province of Buenos Aires and the rest covered other areas. . . .

In most of the other Latin American countries, where collective bargaining is still in its embryonic stages, the agreement concluded for a particular undertaking is the usual form. However, the reason for this seems to be not so much the conviction that plant-level bargaining is preferable to industry-wide bargaining as the fact that insufficient economic development as well as the limited size and importance of trade unions and employers' associations restricts bargaining possibilities to the few existing major undertakings. . . .

From the Latin American point of view there are, however, special considerations favoring larger bargaining areas. The efforts deployed by governments for economic reasons to have wages and working conditions as uniform as possible within given industries and sectors of the economy; the widely accepted principle that unorganized workers should be entitled to the benefits stipulated by collective agreements; and the general attitude in the countries concerned towards legislation—all these have contributed to the development of concepts under which collective agreements often approach the status of statutory enactments.

This development is particularly apparent in those Latin American countries where collective bargaining has acquired a certain maturity. In Mexico, Argentina and Venezuela legislation provides for the extension of collective agreements, i.e., bringing under the coverage of their terms all employers and workers in the same industry or branch of industry in the region or in other regions although they are unrelated to the signatory parties. . . .

Determination of Wages and Working Conditions. The determination of wages and working conditions is, of course, the *raison d'être* of collective bargaining and is the central theme of collective agreements. In this context the term "working conditions" embraces the various benefits, duties and obligations arising out of the employment relationship. . . .

It might be assumed that inasmuch as there is a greater degree of legislative regulation of wages and conditions of work in Latin America than in Canada and the United States, collective agreements in Latin American

countries would not be as ample in their coverage of working conditions
.... However, the range of subjects covered in agreements in those countries
of Latin America where collective bargaining has developed to a substantial
extent, as well as in collective agreements in certain major industries or
undertakings in other countries, is quite broad, and agreements frequently
deal with matters seldom treated in agreements north of the Rio Grande.

Mexican and Argentine collective agreements normally contain numerous
and extensive provisions, often supplementing and improving on statutory
norms. Wages are fully treated and fairly detailed provisions are prevalent
regarding rates, incentive systems, piecework and job classifications. Also
quite common are provisions dealing with hours of work, overtime, filling
of vacancies, transfers, promotions, paid annual leave and holidays, special
paid and unpaid leave, and industrial safety and health. Dismissal procedures are not usually included in collective agreements in Mexico and
Argentina, although they are to be found in some agreements. Seniority
provisions also occur, but apparently to a greater extent in Mexico than in
Argentina. . . .

In most other countries of Latin America collective agreements appear
to be less elaborate. They are usually concluded for a single undertaking,
often deal only with wages and even treat this subject in a very limited
fashion. However, agreements for larger undertakings, although relatively
rare, are sometimes quite complete. . . .

Settlement of Disputes and Regulation of Labor-Management Relations.
Quite apart from the disputes-settlement machinery established by law
there is a growing tendency for collective agreements in the American
region to provide for procedures for the efficient and fair settlement of
disputes and sometimes also for joint bodies designed to reduce friction
and promote cooperation in the relations between the parties.

. . . Provisions of collective agreements which deal with the adjustment
of controversies usually relate to differences that may arise out of the application or interpretation of the collective agreement concerned or to grievances in general. . . . It is likely that with the growth and expansion of
collective agreements the parties will devote increasing attention to the
negotiation of clauses providing for the settlement of grievances by voluntary procedures before submitting them to outside authorities or to the labor
court.

The peace function of collective bargaining is, however, not only expressed in terms of the contractual stipulation of procedures which are to
be followed in the settlement of disputes and grievances. It is also reflected
in agreed solutions to labor-management relations problems in a wider
sense. Many of the major collective agreements concluded in the various
parts of the American region contain a great variety of provisions regulating
labor-management relations. For instance clauses are often found in which
the contracting parties recognize each other as representatives of the interests of management and workers respectively. Collective agreements often
spell out in great detail the rights and obligations of the workers' representa-

tives in the plant, and facilitate their work by granting them increased job security and by permitting them to exercise their functions during working hours with full pay. Union security clauses or check-off provisions are other examples. Furthermore, collective agreements in the American region often provide for the establishment of works rules and regulate order and discipline in great detail. There are, in fact, innumerable ways in which they may regulate the many facets of the relationship between management and labor in an effort to reduce tensions to a minimum and to find smooth and efficient solutions to any problems that may arise.

Problems of Collective Bargaining
in Latin America

Collective bargaining, already highly developed and generally accepted in Canada, the United States, Mexico, Argentina, Cuba, Venezuela and a few other countries of the American region, is acquiring increasing practical importance in most of the remaining countries. The existence of comprehensive collective agreements side by side with equally comprehensive labor legislation in a number of Latin American countries indicates that both collective bargaining and legal enactment are by no means mutually exclusive but can be, and in fact often are, complementary. While there are no indications in Latin America of an intention to lessen the volume of legislative prescriptions in the labor field, efforts are being made in many countries to promote collective bargaining as a result of a growing awareness of its advantages, and a number of governments have made it their declared policy to facilitate and promote the practice. However, progress has been slow in some parts of Latin America . . . .

The evolution of collective agreements, like that of sound labor-management relations in general, is, of course, dependent on certain prerequisites of a more general character, many of which are not yet apparent in a number of Latin American countries. These prerequisites include a certain degree of industrialization; the organization of undertakings as production units of a certain size; a certain stability of the work force; a certain level of literacy and basic education; a political structure of the community and a general economic development which are favorable to collective bargaining; the existence of a basic legislative framework setting out clearly the mutual rights and obligations of labor and management; and a willingness on the part of both parties to accept collective bargaining.

In addition to the absence of these prerequisites in many Latin American countries, there are two other major practical obstacles which have impeded the development of collective bargaining, namely the weakness of the trade union movement and certain obstacles arising out of legislation regulating labor-management relations.

The Weakness of the Trade Union Movement. One of the main prerequisites for the success of collective bargaining is undoubtedly the existence of strong, stable, independent and responsible trade unions. This condition is far from being fulfilled in many Latin American countries. The weakness of Latin American trade unions is primarily due to a predominantly agrarian economic environment . . . . The widespread illiteracy in certain parts of the region, the great poverty of large sections of the population and the high degree of instability of the labor force in certain areas resulting from seasonal migrations are other hindrances to trade union expansion. Industrialization schemes launched during recent years have already brought about an appreciable change in the economies of, for example, Argentina, Brazil, Chile, Mexico, Uruguay and other countries where manufacturing industries are developing at an increasing pace—a development which has its parallel in the growth of the respective trade union movements; but, in general, industrialization is still in its initial and experimental stages in Latin America, as is, at least in several countries, the trade union movement.

Another factor which has so far inhibited a full-fledged spread of trade unionism in several Latin American countries is the various legislative and administrative measures which have tended to curtail freedom of association. Sometimes the law even denies to certain categories of workers (e.g., agricultural workers or public officials) the right to form trade unions; sometimes legislation imposes obligations on the unions applying for registration that actually imply a measure of government control; and sometimes the activities, the administration and the financial affairs of trade unions are placed under government supervision.

. . . The history of the labor movement in Latin America is characterized by continuous rivalries and conflicts between groups holding different political or ideological beliefs, which in turn have led to a close alliance between trade unions and other organizations and institutions, primarily political parties, and to the concentration of their activities on political issues such as nationalism and agrarian reform, to the detriment of their effectiveness in collective dealings with employers. A contributory factor to this situation is the role played by politicians and other "outsiders" in the labor movement. . . .

Another element which is retarding the growth of efficient trade unions in many Latin American countries is their financial weakness and unstable membership. Furthermore the trade unions often do not have enough members and officials sufficiently qualified to deal with the economic and social problems confronting them and sufficiently experienced in the strategy and tactics of direct negotiations with employers. Finally, trade union officials often do not have enough authority over their fellow workers in persuading them to abide by the standards that have been negotiated and agreed upon. Here lies one of the main tasks of workers' education.

Legislative Obstacles. While the weakness of the trade unions is certainly the major handicap to the growth of collective bargaining in many Latin American countries, its development may, at least in several countries, also be curbed as a consequence of government action. The state undoubtedly has the obligation to protect through legislation workers who are unable to protect themselves in the absence of strong associations. But legislative action—especially in a cultural environment which is favorable to legalistic perfection—may develop in a way which narrows the area of free collective bargaining to an extent where negotiations between labor and management are not only not stimulated but also lose a large measure of their usefulness and practical significance. This situation constitutes a real problem in some of the Latin American countries. If legislative provisions fixing working conditions are implemented in practice and if they not only contain minimum standards but rather constitute the most favorable conditions which can reasonably be expected under a given economic situation, rendering improvements by negotiations impossible, then a collective agreement can add nothing to the statutory provisions. A combination of legislation and collective bargaining as it is practiced in many, and attempted in other, Latin American countries can only work if the legislative enactments constitute merely a minimum on which improvements are possible, or take the form of general principles and standards which must be adjusted to practical needs or specific situations, or are limited to those questions on which legal action is indispensable. Further, legislation on conditions of work can be a useful means of promoting collective bargaining if it suggests expressly that the details with regard to certain standards should be filled in by collective agreements or that certain conditions apply only insofar as the parties have not agreed on other solutions. . . .

An area in which these problems are particularly apparent is the determination of wages. As has been pointed out above, virtually all the countries of the region have, in one way or another, established statutory wage-fixing machinery. In view of the insufficient development of collective agreements in the majority of Latin American countries, the statutory minimum wage fixed by this machinery plays a very significant part for large sectors of the working population. On the other hand, the determination of statutory minimum wages may also impede the growth of collective bargaining, particularly in cases where the wages are fixed directly by governments, without bringing labor and management into the picture, or where the statutory minimum wage is actually also the maximum wage or where the whole concept underlying the wage-fixing system is oriented towards statutory machinery under government control rather than towards independent collective bargaining. . . .

In the legislation of certain Latin American countries the subject-matters which *must* be contained in a collective agreement are enumerated. If applied in practice, such a provision would prevent the conclusion of separate agreements dealing only with special matters such as wages, hours of work, holidays, etc., and would thus limit the freedom of the parties to select for themselves the bargaining issues. Where, however, legislation enumerates the possible contents of a collective agreement as examples for the guidance of the parties, its effect may be to promote and facilitate the conclusion of agreements. . . .

It is apparent that, in spite of the difficulties facing it in some countries, collective bargaining has in recent years shown a steady development in Latin America, and that its continued growth is probable. Moreover its rate of growth will undoubtedly be accelerated with its increasing recognition by governments, employers, and workers and with the reduction of the various obstacles peculiar to Latin America which are still inhibiting its effective practice in some parts of the region.

33 Legal Controls on Union Activity in Latin America

Louis Wolf Goodman

Labor rights are guaranteed in the laws of most Latin American nations. An unusually complete list of these rights appears in Article 14 of the Argentine Constitution:

Labor in its several forms shall enjoy the protection of the law, which shall insure to workers: Dignified and equitable working conditions; a limited working day; paid days of rest and vacations; fair remuneration; a flexible minimum essential wage [*salario minimo vital movil*]; equal pay for equal work; a share in the earnings of enterprises, with control of production and collaboration in management; protection against arbitrary discharge; stability of public employment; free and democratic organization of labor unions, recognized by simple inscription in a special register.

Trade unions [*gremios*] are hereby guaranteed: The right to conclude collective labor agreements; the right to resort to conciliation and arbitration; the right to strike. Union representatives shall enjoy the guarantees necessary for carrying out their union tasks and those relating to the stability of their employment.

The State shall grant the benefits of social security, which shall be complete and irrenounceable. In particular, the State shall establish: Compulsory social security, which shall be under national or provincial entities with financial and economic autonomy, administered by the interested parties with participation of the State (but with no overlapping of contributions); flexible retirement pay and pensions; full protection of the family; protection of family welfare [*bien de familia*]; economic compensation to families, and access to decent housing.[1]

Such guarantees should make it easy for Latin American labor unions to pursue the interests of their members. However the interests of other members of Latin American society are also included in legislation which affects Latin American workers. Politicians feel the necessity to exercise some control over labor lest it utilize its mass base and become dominant in national politics. Employers share this feeling because they fear that inordinate union strength would curtail their freedom to manage their own enterprises. Finally anti-Marxist intellectuals, simultaneously believing Marx's prediction of a revolution of the proletariat and searching for a means to prevent such an occurrence, have had a hand in divising legislation which severely restricted union activity.[2]

---

[1]Translation from *Constitution of the Republic of Argentina 1853* (Washington, D.C.: The Pan-American Union, 1963).

[2]For an excellent discussion of the role of anti-Marxist intellectuals in the drafting

Labor law in Latin American nations almost invariably contains both a carrot and a stick for organized labor. The carrot takes the form of statements like the above section of the Argentine Constitution and other statutes governing work conditions. The stick has two forms, one blatant and one more subtle. Laws which regulate the organization and procedures of labor unions structure union activities in obvious ways. Other legislation such as social welfare laws and laws governing work conditions operate more subtly.

Two principles seem to be implicit in the design of bodies of Latin American labor law: 1) divide the working class so that its more volatile elements are isolated; 2) rigidly regulate union activities so that organization for revolutionary social change is impossible. The working class of a given nation can be divided through the use of up to four mechanisms. 1) Making it difficult to form a union. The bureaucratic conditions which must be fulfilled are time consuming, expensive, and often arbitrary. The establishment of a union must be a carefully planned operation. The fact that only 15 percent of Latin America's work force is organized is an indicator that workers must be relatively secure and very determined if they hope to found a union.[3] The first division in the Latin American work force separates the organized workers from the unorganized. 2) The second division separates blue-collar workers (*obreros*) from white-collar workers (*empleados*). Drafters of labor laws legally distinguished blue-collar from white-collar workers because the two groups had distinct interests. They then made this a self-fulfilling prophecy by creating systems of wage payment, work-condition regulation, and welfare benefits which were widely divergent for the two groups. Given the scarcity of resources in developing nations these two groups have rarely paused to pursue common interests, but have been in active competition to preserve and expand their separate rights. 3) The third mechanism for dividing the working class are statutes which fragment the categories of *empleado* and *obrero*. In some countries this is achieved by prohibiting unions from national organization on industrial or craft lines and restricting them to single workplaces. In other countries further fragmentation can be achieved by enforcing geographic or type-of-industry divisions. Another divisive force is the common prohibition against public and private employees joining the same union. 4) Finally, the fact that none of these distinctions is "hard and fast" further divides the work force. When workers organize or change places of employment they discard one set of interests and adopt a new one. More dramatic is the situation in Chile where overnight a category of workers can be reclassified *obrero* or *empleado* by the Chilean Congress and suddenly be governed by different laws and benefit from different elaborate welfare systems.

This complex fractionalization of the work force is especially effective given the low standards of living and constant monetary inflation which plague most Latin American countries, and the fact that the government is

of the Chilean Labor Code see Victor Valdes S., "Las Relaciones del Trabajo en la Industria del Cobre," (Santiago: INSORA, 1967), pp. 11–55 (mimeo).
[3] *Statistical Abstract of Latin America, 1969* (UCLA), p. 106.

the final arbiter for the wage and welfare demands of most workers. These conditions cause organized workers to compete against unorganized, *empleado* against *obrero,* and factory A against factory B in a war of all against all to extract the best conditions from the government. Thus worker energies are often expended, not making demands on employers, but in competing against other workers for scarce resources doled out by the state.

The second principle implicit to labor law involves the regulation of union activities. This includes legal definition of the functions of unions, control of practices of internal union organization, and the regulation of labor-management relations. By defining the functions of unions, governments can extend and retract union authority to participate in politics, negotiate collective contracts, call strikes, form confederations, organize schools, social security funds, cooperative societies, and so on.

Government control of internal union organization extends to countless details of membership, elections, leadership, and finances. Often a workplace cannot be unionized unless it employs a minimum number of workers; similarly, a worker often cannot join a union unless a specified number of his work-mates agree to form one, and then all workers are required to be members. Leaders often must meet citizenship and work seniority requirements and must rotate year by year. The development of a professional cadre of union leaders is further inhibited by limitations on union activity during work-time. Elections are also closely regulated, with the right to vote often dependent on meeting seniority requirements.

Union finances are also subject to complicated controls. Dues are often collected through an automatic check-off, but its transfer to union coffers may be uncertain. Funds are sometimes not even under the direct control of union officers but, as in pre-Allende Chile, must be deposited in the Government Bank and invested by a government official and the manager of the firm. Expenditures must be carefully requested and justified. Chilean Union leaders cannot write checks for more than 2 *escudoes* (14¢ in 1971) without permission of the Ministry of Labor.

Labor-management relations can also be circumscribed by the government. The right to strike may be suspended—as in Argentina from 1966 to 1967. In Peru a national formula for profit-sharing was dictated by the government in 1969. Countries truncate the process of collective bargaining at different stages and impose compulsory arbitration. In Cuba trade unions have disappeared, having became an arm of the government charged with raising worker productivity through the organization of campaigns of socialist competition.

It can be seen that the basic rights of workers are considerably weakened by the overt controls put on unions by complex sets of laws. However, there is an additional more subtle means of undermining union strength which must be discussed. Latin American nations have promulgated a body of welfare legislation which is in advance of what their economies could support if fully enforced. It has been asserted that one result of this legislation has been the slowing down of economic development as "social security expenditures represent consumption rather than investment . . . at the bottom of the developmental ladder."[4]

The intention of these laws was to soften the blows of the "stick" side of the labor laws by guaranteeing work conditions such as minimum wages, work hours, and child labor and by insuring workers against risks such as sickness, work accidents, unemployment, maternity, old age, and death.[5] However, another consequence of this legislation was the pre-structuring of the legal context within which labor unions could operate.

The existence of these laws effectively subverted the logical basis for the organization of unions in Latin America. Since the laws were already on the books there was no apparent need to organize workers on welfare issues. The real situation, of course, was far different from one in which benefits had been clearly defined and fought for by an organized work force. Traditional Latin paternalism was merely transformed into welfare state paternalism with the government acting as "patron." Benefits were sometimes awarded in an arbitrary fashion with the government retaining the power to decide when and to whom they should be given. Provisions such as the Chilean practice of reclassifying job categories can easily lend themselves to the co-option of powerful worker groups and the alienation of others.

Thus the legal defense against unions is formidable. This condition is compounded by the Latin cultural tolerance of paternalism, the widespread hostility of employers to trade-unionism, the opposition of governments and parties to competing institutions, the limited availability of effective union leadership, and the weak bargaining position of individual workers. It is therefore no surprise that unions rarely take the lead in battles to transform economic, political, and social structures in Latin America, and concentrate their energies on keeping worker wages ahead of galloping inflation.

[4]Walter Galenson, "Social Security and Economic Development," *Industrial and Labor Relations Review* 21 (July 1968): p. 559.
[5]For a discussion of social security legislation in Latin America see Alfredo Mallet, "Trends in Latin American Social Security," Chapter 22 of this book.

34 The Latin American Labor Movement

Wendell C. Gordon

The traditional device by which working people have attempted to use self-help measures to raise their level of living has been the labor union.[1]

Development of Movement

Latin American labor was treated roughly before 1910. (There was legal slavery in Brazil until 1888.) As a reaction to such treatment, militant underground unions, frequently anarcho-syndicalist in philosophy, were being formed by the late 19th century. The Flores Magón brothers were active in such activities in Mexico. Strikes were called at the Cananea mines in Sonora in 1906 and at the Río Blanco textile mill near Orizaba in 1907. Díaz supported the employers and put the strikers down with military force and bloodshed. This was a rather common type of procedure in other Latin American countries in those days.

Generally during the 19th century, legal codes in Latin America prohibited the worker from signing a contract with his employer. In colonial times, such provisions had protected the worker from signing an agreement he did not understand. But the provision later retarded the rise of the labor union movement, which has been predicated on the signing of collective contracts between employers and labor unions.

Even the mere formation of a labor union was quite generally illegal until well into the 20th century. But, by 1910, the labor movement had gained headway in spite of these difficulties. Mutual unions, encouraged by the Catholic Church, had been established in several countries, and more militant, underground unions were fairly common.

In Mexico in the 1910–20 decade, legislation favorable to labor union organization was adopted. And the legality of labor organizations was subsequently affirmed in most of the Latin American countries.

Adapted from Wendell C. Gordon, *The Political Economy of Latin America* (New York: Columbia University Press, 1965), pp. 109–119, with permission of the publisher.

[1]Among the more significant books on the Latin American labor movement are: Robert Alexander, *Labor Relations in Argentina, Brazil, and Chile* (New York: McGraw-Hill, 1962); . . . Moisés Poblete Troncoso and Ben G. Burnett, *Rise of the Latin American Labor Movement* (New Haven: College and University Press, 1960).

* * *

In Latin America . . . the relation between the government and unions is fundamentally different from the United States situation. In the United States the unions have operated in substantial independence of government interference in such matters as the selection of officers. In Latin America, once the government has decided to deal with unions at all, it has proceeded to influence their internal organization and to use them for political ends. In consequence, unions have alternately been the fair-haired instruments of government or been vigorously suppressed (if the government found the latter procedure expedient).

Current Organization

International Organizations. . . . In the post-World War II period, Latin American national unions have belonged to three different international organizations.

(1) One has been the International Confederation of Free Trade Unions with headquarters in Brussels. This is the international organization with which the AFL-CIO of the United States has been affiliated. The Latin American regional organization which is affiliated with the ICFTU is the Organización Regional Interamericana de Trabajo (ORIT). Individuals are not members of the ORIT itself; rather, they are members of national unions recognizing some degree of affiliation (sometimes rather nebulous) with the ORIT. The General Secretary of the ORIT in 1963 was Arturo Jáurégui Hurtado.

(2) A second international organization, with headquarters also in Brussels, has been the World Federation of Trade Unions. It has been, more or less, Communist or Russian dominated or influenced. During much of the postwar period the regional organization in Latin America affiliated with the WFTU was the Confederación de Trabajadores de América Latina (CTAL). But efforts seem to be in progress on the part of the WFTU to substitute a new regional affiliate for the CTAL.

(3) A third regional organization is the Confederación Latinoamericana de Sindicalistas Cristianos (CLASC). It was founded at a 1954 conference in Santiago, Chile. This regional organization is affiliated with the Confédération Internationale des Syndicats Chrétiens, which dates back to a 1920 conference at The Hague. Ideologically, it adheres to the principles of the papal bulls Rerum Novarum (1891) and Quadragesimo Anno (1931).

National Organizations. The national labor organizations in Latin America have been involved in internal conflicts which have been partly ideological in nature, partly struggles for power. On the ideological side there have, of course, been involved the conflicts among 1) the Marxists (currently divided between the Stalinist-Chinese and the Russian-oriented wings); 2) the pragmatic unionists (oriented toward the methods used by the AFL-CIO in the United States and emphasizing material gains in wages, hours, and fringe benefits rather than emphasizing political action); and 3) the Catholic-oriented.

But frequently more important than the ideological struggle has been the struggle of personalities. The Latin American worker has been more attracted by the personality of some contestant for leadership than by his ideology. And the personal ties, *personalismo* in the relations between leaders and followers, can become extremely strong. There is personalismo involved not only in the relations of the union members to the leaders of the union, there is also personalismo involved in the relationship of the union to the various political leaders on the national scene. . . .

. . . In Latin American countries there may be at least three organizations operating at the national level: 1) a Communist-oriented group of unions; 2) a group of unions officially recognized by the government; and 3) a group oriented to the Catholic position. But it is just as likely that there exists only one real national union and the three groups are struggling for power within the single "official" union. Of course, in each country, there are special local variations on these relations.

In general, the officially recognized union organization obtains certain perquisites. Its leaders will be the official channel by which the government consults with the labor movements; also, they will be part of the government-management-labor triumvirate that is institutionalized in many American countries as a major political force. It is important to the union to have these channels of communication.

Occasionally, dynamic individuals, such as Lombardo Toledano in Mexico, gain control of the labor movement, dominate it for a time, and have sufficient prestige so that the government must treat them with respect. More often, however, the labor unions have been junior partners in the government-management-labor triumvirates. They have gotten some fairly attractive crumbs only when the government, on the basis of political considerations, desired to be pro-labor. The labor movement has not generally been strong enough to demand significant concessions as a matter of right.

It is a result of these circumstances that it is not possible accurately to identify specific national unions in terms of their affiliation with the major international unions and then count heads and say how much of the Latin American labor movement is associated with the ICFTU, how much with the WFTU, and how much with the Confédération Internationale des Syndicats Chrétiens.

Hierarchy. The basic organization in the union hierarchy is the *sindicato,* the organization at the level of the individual plant. The sindicatos are generally organized either functionally or geographically into *federaciones.* The federaciones will then be organized into a *confederación nacional* of the federaciones (or sindicatos) in a particular industry. There will also be a national confederación of the industrial confederaciones, including much, if not all, of the labor union movement of the country.

This is much too simplified a description. The organization is complicated by the occasional existence of competing hierarchies affiliated with the ORIT or the CTAL or the CLASC. In Brazil there are two hierarchies of organizations, one of which grew out of the efforts of the Vargas regime in the 1930s to form a corporate state; the other grew up out of other efforts to form a national labor union movement. All in all, the structure is not uniform from country to country, but the variations are not especially geared to the craft-union, industrial-union distinction that has been important in the history of the labor movement in the United States.

The laws of many of the Latin American countries provide for the obligatory existence of the sindicato-federación-confederación structure mentioned above. And those laws establish the legal rights and duties of the unions. Much of the struggle among Marxists, Catholics, and others, then, takes place within a framework involving such a hierarchy of legally recognized unions. And for tactical reasons, it is desirable for the competing groups to be in the officially recognized organization—more perquisites being obtained that way. But there also exists the possibility of a nonconformist hierarchy in addition. Which international organization the national confederación affiliates with constitutes a running battle in most of the Latin American countries, except perhaps currently in Cuba. And delegations from the officially recognized confederaciónes may attend the international conferences of first one and then another of the international organizations.

Membership Size

It is probably worthwhile to try to say something about the membership size of the Latin American labor movement, in spite of the statistical difficulties involved. It has been estimated that there are about 12.5 million organized union members in Latin America.[2] About 2.5 million of these are in Argentina, 2.5 million in Brazil, 2 million in Mexico, 1.5 million in Cuba, and 1.5 million in Venezuela. These five countries thus account for about 80 percent of the labor union movement of Latin America in terms of numbers. A well-informed observer, Robert Alexander, has, however, estimated the Mexican, Venezuelan, Cuban, and Brazilian figures to be substantially smaller than those given above and has indicated a belief that total, genuine membership in the Latin American labor movement is nearer to 6.5 million.[3] The organized labor movement in the United States, an area with slightly less population than Latin America, has about 18 million members. In spite of its smaller membership, the Latin American union membership probably represents as high a percentage of the industrial labor force as is the case in the United States.

Procedures

Collective Bargaining. In the United States, collective bargaining is the approved means for working out disputes between employers and workers.

---

[2]*Statistical Abstract of Latin America, 1962* (UCLA), p. 4.
[3]Mildred Adams, ed., *Latin America: Evolution or Explosion?* (New York: Dodd, Mead, 1963), p. 180.

And in what is considered the standard working of the process, the government is not involved as a third party. By contrast, in Latin America labor disputes are much less likely to be settled by direct negotiations between employers and workers discussing the issue of wages and working conditions. In Latin America, it is much more likely to be the case that the government dictates the terms of settlement in a process that frequently does not involve the employers and workers as effective participants in the bargaining process.

Strikes. In the pre-1910 Mexico of Porfirio Díaz, the government was quite ready to take the employer's side and suppress strikes, with force if necessary, and the same was generally true throughout Latin America. Things began to change in Mexico with the Revolution of 1910, and they began to change over much of the rest of Latin America at about the same time. . . . The right to strike as a technique for gaining ends is now quite generally admitted in Latin America, but the strike is more likely to be successful if the government backs it than in the contrary case.

In fact, Latin American strikes are rather likely to have a political motive, to be intended to influence elections or political trends. One-day general strikes as gestures indicating how labor feels about public issues are rather common occurrences. And the completeness of the shutdown involved is frequently taken, especially by foreign newspaper correspondents, as a gauge of how the political winds are blowing. Be that as it may, such activities may have very little to do with wages and working conditions.

Mediation and Arbitration. In Latin America neither collective bargaining nor strikes have served as effective devices for dealing with labor's pragmatic problems: wages and working conditions. Most Latin American countries now have provision for conciliation, mediation, or arbitration under various circumstances, which are generally laboriously spelled out in the laws. And such procedures have been used in a rather orderly way in such countries as Mexico, Venezuela, and Brazil. In other countries, the procedures may be used more or less at the whim of the executive branch.

*   *   *

Discharge. Increasingly, the Latin American laws protect the worker from arbitrary discharge. Notice before discharge and additional pay at the time of discharge are now generally required. A common provision is that three months' pay must be given at the time of discharge—even if the company is laying off all labor and planning to go out of business.

Ostensibly, the worker is better protected now than formerly against arbitrary action by his employer. However, over much of Latin America this protection is sporadic and unreliable. It is not easy for the individual worker, especially away from the capital city, to press his claim for such protection against an employer who has political connections.

Right to a Job. Latin American labor laws have covered basic theoretical issues which have been avoided in United States legislation. An example of this has been the inclusion in some of the laws of the provision that the individual worker has a right to a job. The Brazilian law, for example, has such a provision. But for such provisions to have much meaning, someone must have an obligation to give him, not only a job, but also a reasonably good job.

Problems

Revolutionary Action versus Pragmatic Action. Are Latin American labor unions in the future likely to be a force working toward gradual improvement in the welfare of the workers or are they likely to be a force tending to precipitate revolutionary change? The United States press rather tends to give the impression that the Latin American unions are Communist-infiltrated agents of the devil working for revolutionary change and the establishment of Communist regimes in Latin America.

Celso Furtado, in speculating about the future role of unions, has hazarded the guess that the rural landless, for example, in Brazil the Peasant Leagues of Francisco Julião, are more likely to be the instruments of violent change than are the labor unions in manufacturing. According to Furtado, it is already obvious to the urban labor unions that they have much to gain in terms of real standard of living by a policy of gradualism. They can see possibilities for significant improvement in their own welfare as employers yield on wage, hour, and fringe benefit demands. They are not likely to forfeit these possibilities for the cause of violent revolution. On the other hand, the rural landless are confronted with a rigid, resistant class structure, bitterly fighting even minor changes. To them the only alternative seems to be cataclysmic disruption of the system. This is the reason the Northeast of Brazil is such a powder keg.[4]

Still, in many parts of Latin America, the labor unions in mining and manufacturing seem to have considerable propensity for serving as direct-action political instruments. Riots in Bogotá in January, 1963, were a reminder of this possibility. And the behavior of the Federación Sindical de Trabajádores Mineros de Bolivia (FSTMB), led by Juan Lechín Oquendo, continues to indicate potential in the same direction.

Whether in the future the labor unions of Latin America are going to be essentially pragmatic or essentially political and revolutionary is one of the really important questions in the Latin American field. The assumption by the United States press that Latin American unions are essentially committed to Communism does not help with intelligent discussion of such an issue. . . .

---

[4]Celso Furtado, "Brazil: What Kind of Revolution?" *Foreign Affairs* 41 (April 1963): esp. p. 533.

35 The Chilean Labor Union Leader: Attitudes Toward Labor Relations

Henry A. Landsberger, Manuel Barrera, and Abel Toro

Our study was confined to *sindicatos industriales* [plant-based unions] which are the backbone of Chilean blue-collar unionism.

By law, each union elects annually an executive committee of five. The committee members elect a president, secretary, and treasurer from among themselves. The first two are, in Chile, as elsewhere, the two most powerful individuals. This study was confined to the position of president, in order to avoid introducing another variable and because the union would expect the president rather than the secretary to be interviewed.

. . . The study was limited to Chile's three major industrial centers: Santiago, the capital; Valparaiso, the chief port; and Concepción, center of an area containing Chile's coal resources, steel-mill, a substantial part of its textile industry, and important navy yards.

In Valparaiso and Concepción, an attempt was made to interview the presidents of all locals. Forty-seven presidents in the first city, and 34 in the second were actually interviewed. They constituted well over 90 percent of the possible total. In Santiago, in the case of locals with more than five-hundred members, an attempt was likewise made to interview all presidents. Eighteen of a possible 21 were obtained (85 percent). A sample of approximately 50 percent of locals with fewer than five-hundred members was selected (stratified by industry, with slight overweighting of industries with few unions). All but three of a possible 134 were obtained (98 percent), making a total of 150 for Santiago as a whole, and a grand total of 231 for the entire study.

The study, then, can be regarded as highly representative of presidents of blue-collar locals in Chile's major industrial centers. Interviews lasting between an hour and a half and three hours and a half were conducted by the two Chilean authors and by university students. Questions were fixed, answers either predetermined or open, and later coded.

Labor-Management Relations

The authors of this article expected to find the picture of company-union relationships one of unrelieved gloom. Both general principles and empirical evidence had led us to the same conclusion. General principles lead us to

Reprinted from the *Industrial and Labor Relations Review,* Vol. 17, No. 3 (April 1964). Copyright © 1964 by Cornell University. All rights reserved.

expect that a country relatively little-industrialized would have a weak and persecuted union movement. (And Chile, while urbanized, is of course not solidly industrialized, since it suffers from overdeveloped tertiary industries like other Latin American countries.) Its work force, if not its union officers, is unskilled and hence should be easily coercible. It can be replaced by any employer who wishes to rid himself of obstreperous elements by substituting from among the many unemployed only too willing to accept jobs in the small, but relatively well-paid industrial sector, even at the price of docility. These deductions from principle were reinforced by empirical evidence in the form of well-known instances of companies fighting the union as such, and by a good deal of opinion that this was typical rather than exceptional.

The evidence of this study indicates a more complex picture. It has led us to conclude that different facets of the labor-management relationship need to be kept separate, because what may be true of one is not necessarily equally true of another. In particular, management attitudes toward the union as an institution need to be analyzed separately from management's willingness to satisfy basic worker demands on wages.

Acceptance of the Union as an Institution. . . . We asked these union presidents what policy, in their opinion, management pursued in relation to the union, giving our respondents five alternatives from which to choose. These ranged from "tries, in so far as possible, to eliminate it because they think it undesirable" to "cooperates as much as possible with the union." The answers . . . are weighted toward the positive rather than toward the negative end of the scale. As many presidents said that management was trying to cooperate all it could [17 percent][1] as said that management was trying to eliminate the union [18 percent]. Fewer companies were following a policy of "containment" (27 percent) than were helping the union, albeit within limits (31 percent). Even more surprising was the distribution to a broadly phrased question: "In your opinion, how are relations between management and unions?" Twenty-five percent described them as "very good," only 3 percent as "very bad," 48 percent as "more good than bad," and only 23 percent as "more bad than good." Even the personal treatment of union officials was highly positive—58 percent described it as courteous and friendly, only 9 percent as discourteous and arbitrary, the remainder as courteous but cold.

In our view, the interpretation of these, to us, highly unexpected findings of the relative scarcity of negative relationships is likely to be a combination of the following. In the first place, since the study was by nature confined to establishments which *had* unions, those companies whose antiunion policy was effective enough to have prevented the creation of a union altogether were automatically excluded from our survey. In short, our population is, by its nature, biased. Second, and in our opinion more important, Chilean management, once it has been obliged to accept a union by law, probably

---

[1]All figures in brackets were extracted from a table originally in this article but not presented here.—Eds.

learns to live with it in the same way as management has learned to live with it in the United States.

The generally positive results which we have cited above should, however, be put into their context first, by citing such comparable United States figures as there are. The only study known to us of union leaders' evaluation of management's attitudes toward the union is that of Stagner, Chalmers, and Derber.[2]

To the United States question most similar to the one presented ("Has the management tried to undermine the union position through direct dealings with the workers, or has it been careful to safeguard the union position in such contacts?") only 9 percent of the Illinois establishments had a clearly negative score ("occasionally tries to weaken the union" or "frequently tries to weaken the union"). This may be compared to the two negative . . . items in [Chile] which come to 52 percent—very substantially more than the Illinois figure.

Results are, however, by no means uniformly far apart. As the equivalent to our broad question, "What do you think about union-management relations?" we might take the Illinois question: "In general, how do you personally feel about your union's relations with the company?" In Illinois, 78 percent were moderately satisfied or better. . . . In the Chilean study, 73 percent replied "more good than bad" or "very good." . . . We conclude that, while relations in Illinois are better than they are in Chile (as is only to be expected), the real surprise is that the quality of Chilean relationships is as frequently within hailing distance of the United States, as they are.

The Satisfaction of Worker Needs. A more substantial modification of the impression that Chilean labor-management relations are surprisingly good occurs if management's attitude toward workers, rather than toward the union as an institution, is measured. The conclusion is clear that, in the union president's eyes at least, management is predominantly uninterested in the well-being of its workers, and that it pays low wages despite the fact that the plant is efficiently run, is making a good profit, and could easily pay more. Asking about interest in worker welfare results in a large majority choosing the negative alternatives. A comparison with a similar question asked by Stagner, Chalmers, and Derber also shows a very wide gap. Table 1 presents the results of the two almost identical questions put in the two countries. While in the United States, 68 percent of the respondents regard management as "pretty much" interested or better (plus some at least of those located toward "slightly"), in Chile only 37 percent, or approximately half of the United States percentage, feel that management is interested. The contrast is perhaps even stronger at the negative end of the scale, where only 2 percent of the United States respondents (representatives of

[2]Ross Stagner, W. E. Chalmers, and Milton Derber, "Guttman-Type Scales for Union and Management Attitudes Toward Each Other," *Journal of Applied Psychology* 42 (October 1958): pp. 293–300. Data very kindly tabulated and provided by Professor Stagner.

Table 35-1

Company Interest in Worker-Welfare. Illinois: "Are the management officials interested in the welfare of workers?" Chile: "Do you think your employers are really interested in the welfare of the workers?"

Illinois		Chile	
Very much so	12%	14%	All the time interested.
Midpoint	15		
Pretty much	41	23	Often show interest.
Mid point	17		
Slightly	10	42	Show interest only sometimes.
Midpoint	2		
Very little	2	20	Never show interest.
	100% (41)	100% (231)	

one establishment) felt that management is "very little" interested, while 20 percent of the Chileans felt that management was "never" interested.

How deep this feeling goes is further illustrated by the profound discontent shown with wages paid by the companies. Only 8 percent of the respondents described them as good, against 53 percent who described them as low, the other 39 percent calling them "acceptable." It is highlighted, in addition, by their pessimistic expectations of management for the future. About half the respondents were asked to what extent they thought the workers would benefit from any favorable change in the fortunes of the company—since it is so frequently said that the fate of worker and company was bound together. . . . Only one-third of the respondents felt that the workers would be allowed to share fully or at least substantially in any benefits. Sixteen percent thought the workers would not be affected, and 50 percent that the effect would be minimal.

Union Demands and Their Satisfaction. This section will deal with the nature of union goals in general, with the demands which the union is interested in making on management, and with the success which the union feels it has had, and will have, in satisfying these demands.

Our first concern was to establish what basic union goals (not necessarily *collective bargaining* goals) were in a society where the researcher might well have contradictory expectations. The phenomenon of "rising expectations" and the notoriously low income of blue-collar workers in a society with low and unequally distributed national income would lead one to expect a high emphasis on "more"—more pay. The heavy Marxist influence would lead one to expect emphasis on the union as a tool to foster the political consciousness of the working class. The lesser, but definitely notable Catholic influence would lead one to expect an emphasis on education. Moreover, the reputedly strong paternalistic tradition in Chile is claimed by many to lead to innumerable demands for benefits in kind rather than straight increases in pay.

To clarify which of these contradictory suppositions was, in fact, the correct one, we asked a series of questions about the president's long-range goals for the union, as well as past union demands on the employer, and demands planned for the immediate future. In each instance, we also asked whether the demands had been, or would be, won and on what the union officer based his optimism or pessimism.

First, as regards long-range basic union goals, Table 2 indicates unambiguously that economic betterment is far ahead of any other area of concern for the union president, and that political education is not in the picture, not even as a second and third choice. The two goals which do have strong secondary importance are education, on the one hand, and a series of steps designed to strengthen the union externally and internally, on the other.

To clarify, in the case of those who had chosen the first alternative, "economic improvement," whether they thought primarily in terms of straight wage increases, fringes, or paternalistic benefits in kind, respondents were asked to elaborate. It was apparent that 75 percent of those asked thought in terms of straight wage increases. Most of the remainder had one particular fringe benefit in mind: severance pay. This is indicative of the high expectation of unemployment, and a frame of mind which is inclined to mitigate its effects rather than try to prevent it.

When asked to judge whether they had in the past, and were likely in the future, to win the demands they were making, considerable optimism was shown. Optimism about the future seemed to be greater than warranted by past experience although that, too, was by no means uniformly negative. As regards "last year's" most important demand, 29 percent felt they had won it completely, and another 27 percent that they had obtained a "good deal." Only 14 percent thought they had obtained absolutely nothing. As to the future, there was even more optimism. Only 9 percent felt they would not be able to obtain anything related to their most important demand, while 45 percent felt they would surely win it.

It is the explanation given by the presidents, however, both for their optimism and for their pessimism that is of special interest, since it shows their great dependence on the employer's good will and their feeling that, in negotiations at least, such good will will be found, however much they may have previously complained of general lack of interest in worker welfare.

. . . Union presidents who had stated that they thought their most important demands in the coming negotiations could be partly or wholly won were asked to state why they thought so. . . . More than a third attributed their likely success to the company's favorable attitude; another 9 percent attributed it to the company's good economic situation. Similar, but in each instance lower percentages, attributed their future success to the union's strength [31 percent] and good economic position [5 percent].

Just as the company is seen as the single most important source of hope, so also is it seen as the single most important source of such difficulties as exist between the union and management [45 percent]. The question here,

Table 35–2
Long-Range Union Goals. "Thinking of the next three to five years, which of the following goals do you think should the union try to reach?

	1st Choice	2nd Choice	3rd Choice	Total
	62%	9%	5%	76%
1. Obtain economic benefits such as salaries, severance pay, pensions, etc.				
2. More weight and respect for the union in the industry; more influence in the administration of the company	5	12	9	26
3. The unification and strengthening of the union movement in Chile	10	19	14	43
4. Improve the education and spiritual development of workers	8	23	15	46
5. Make workers fully politically conscious	1	4	5	10
6. Develop more union spirit, participation, and more solidarity among the workers	6	15	15	36
7. Establish a full program of social activities	0	1	7	8
8. See that the influence of the union as a worker's organization, is felt in, and benefits the community, by taking an interest in schools and education, protect and create green zones, etc.	6	11	19	36
9. Obtain better physical conditions at work (lighting, temperature, space, etc.)	1	6	11	18
	100% (230)	100% (230)	100% (230)	

. . . was an open one, answers being coded later. Apart from the importance of the employer, the following are of great interest to note in these spontaneous replies. First, the small percentage of replies specifying as the major obstacle to better relations the company's attitude toward the union as such [7 percent]. Second, it is of interest to note the *relatively* high incidence of replies admitting that workers, or union officials, or both had at least some responsibility in keeping relations from being better: a total of 19 percent, which, given the nature of the admission, we regard as high. Third, it is noteworthy that 17 percent of the presidents felt they could give no reasons for difficulties because there were none. Finally, the very small percentage who felt that the legal framework of labor relations was the cause of difficulty is of interest [2 percent] an assessment which the authors do not necessarily share.

36

The Working-Class Vote in Chile: Christian Democracy versus Marxism

Maurice Zeitlin and James Petras

Chile is the only country in Latin America (Cuba excepted) in which the organized working class is politically and socially significant *and* is led by Marxian socialists and communists. The socialist movement has had a political base in the working class for many decades, especially among miners, and in the fifties based on growing working-class support, it began to become a serious contender for political power. Between 1952 and 1956, the working-class movement became increasingly unified; on the trade union level, a central labor organization, *Central Unica de Trabajadores* (CUT) was formed; and in the political arena a broad electoral bloc emerged uniting the major parties of the left, the socialists and communists, and several splinter parties, in a coalition called the Popular Action Front (*Frente de Accion Popular*—FRAP). While the organized strength of the labor movement declined under the quasi-caudillo Ibañez regime, 1952–1958, working-class militancy and combativeness rose. The number of strikes, the number of workers affected and of man-days lost were all far higher during this period than the preceding post-war years.[1] From FRAP's formation in 1956 to the present, its electoral strength has risen rapidly. In the presidential elections of 1958, the FRAP candidate, Dr. Salvador Allende, received 29 percent of the vote; by 1964's presidential elections, he received 39 percent. If not for the low women's vote for the FRAP candidate, in 1958, Chile would have been the first country in Latin America in which a Marxian socialist government gained power—and the first such government in the world established as the result of an electoral victory in a capitalist political democracy. FRAP lost by a margin of 35,000 votes out of 1.3 million cast.

This ascent of the Marxian political parties has been paralleled by the rise of the Christian Democratic Party—a party which transformed itself in the space of a few decades from just one more splinter party of the right with corporatist ideas into a developmentalist reform party at the head of a mass movement whose major leader, Eduardo Frei, was elected President

Adapted from the *British Journal of Sociology* (March 1970), pp. 16–29, with permission of the publisher.
[1]The median annual number of strikes rose from 121 in the period 1947–1950 to 208 in 1952–1958; the median annual number of workers affected [rose] from 45,000 to 105,000, and of man-days lost from 1.2 million to 1.5 million. Merwin Bohan and Morton Pomeranz, *Investment in Chile* (Washington, D.C.: U.S. Department of Commerce, 1960), p. 23; *Estadistica Chilena: Sinopsis, 1958,* Servicio Nacional de Estadistica y Censos.

in 1964. The traditional parties of the right, as well as the centrist Radical Party, faced by the rapid rise of the Marxian left, fell behind and strongly supported Frei in 1964.

The ideology of Christian Democracy in Chile is an amalgam of vaguely defined nationalist, corporatist and populist ideas. It competes with the socialists ideologically in its appeal to popular sentiments for social reform, while maintaining firm bonds with the business community and foreign capital, and friendly relations with the United States government. The Christian Democrats regard themselves explicitly as an "alternative" to the Marxian parties, speak in a populist, even revolutionary, idiom, and call for a "revolution in liberty." There are obvious strains and tensions within the movement, but its ideological focus is on national integration, mobilization of social energies and development. The dominant wing of the party emphasizes reforms within the framework of capitalism which, with explicit coordination and planning by the government, will promote industrial development. Its more radical and militant activists talk about building a "communitarian society" through "antiimperialism" and a "noncapitalist path of development."[2]

On a theoretical level, it would be an exaggeration to ask whether Christian Democracy can serve as a functionally equivalent ideology of working-class protest since it does not explicitly refer to the working class as a bearer of its vision nor identify it as its agency of historic change, as Marxism does. Yet Christian Democracy, with its rhetoric of "mass participation" in reconstructing Chilean society and its emphasis on the "dignity" of the poor, undoubtedly has an appeal to the working class. It combines the appeals of nationalism and populism with a muted corporatism calling for the cooperation of all classes in the attainment of "national goals." This might be of special importance to workers only recently removed from the social control of the landowners, and in a society which still tends to be permeated by traditional, even seignorial and paternalistic relationships and values. Such an ideology, representing as it does some sort of a synthesis of elements of paternalism and protest, may have a special appeal under such conditions.

The socialist and Christian Democratic movements are competing for the allegiance of the working class under relatively "historically equal" conditions, in the sense that both have become politically ascendant during the same relatively brief period and both have considerable organizational strength.[3] Chile, therefore, provides a unique opportunity to study the rela-

---

[2]For an analysis of the social contradictions within the Christian Democratic movement and the practice of the government it heads, see James Petras, *Chilean Christian Democracy: Politics and Social Forces* (Berkeley: Institute of International Studies, University of California, 1968).

[3]Of course, the socialists and communists had pockets of working-class support long before the emergence of the Christian Democrats as a significant movement. Since coming to power, on the other hand, the Christian Democrats have the organizational and patronage advantages accorded the government party. They came to power, moreover, with the full resources of virtually the entire spectrum of non-Marxian parties and social forces committed to their electoral victory.

tive appeal of the socialist and Christian Democratic movements to the working class.

The question of what class or classes form the base of the Marxian socialist parties compared to the Christian Democrats is, of course, of more than academic interest. Should the Christian Democrats really succeed in wresting the support of the working class from the socialists and communists—despite the historical strength of class consciousness and socialist ideology in that class—it would be a decisive political blow. The Marxian parties depend for their mass base on the workers and cannot expect any but marginal support in other classes or strata. What is more, it would be contrary to their very theoretical position as Marxists to expect otherwise.

Our analysis is based on the electoral returns of the presidential elections of 1958 and 1964 in Chile's 296 municipalities.[4] Chile is probably the only country in Latin America in which ecological analysis of election results is meaningful. We can assume minimal tampering with the vote, minimal coercion, and minimal distortion of the actual results in the elections under study. The question, put simply, is whether or not the workers of Chile were more likely to vote for Salvador Allende, the presidential candidate of the Communist-Socialist coalition, FRAP, than for the Christian Democratic candidate, Eduardo Frei. Did the majority of the workers vote for the *Frapistas* or Christian Democrats? Unfortunately, with electoral rather than survey research data, we cannot definitively answer this question. What we can do is discover whether there is a systematic relationship between the voting pattern and the social structures of the municipalities. Our hypothesis is that the typical worker of Chile voted for FRAP in 1958 and 1964. Therefore, in accordance with this hypothesis, we should expect to find that the greater the relative size of the working class in a municipality, the greater the likelihood of a high vote for Salvador Allende, the FRAP candidate.

Industry is predominantly located in the cities and towns and so, therefore, are the industrial workers, where they tend to live in densely populated working-class areas. Not only are the workers more likely to live in urban areas, but it is precisely in the conditions of life in the cities and industrial towns that the workers' class consciousness is more likely to develop, where, as Frederick Engels once put it, "the last vestiges of the old system of benevolent paternalism between masters and men" are eroded.[5] Here the workers are most likely to be integrated into a "compact group with its own ways of life and thought and its own outlook on society." Living in the same neighborhoods, associating with each other on the job and at home in their leisure hours, they are more likely to develop a common perspective and to recognize the community of interest they share with each other as opposed to the interests of the owning class. Workers from different locali-

---

[4]The percentages were calculated from raw figures given in the official reports: *Resultado Elección Presidencial, 4 de Septiembre de 1958*, and *Elección Presidencial, de Septiembre, 1964* (Santiago: Registro Electoral, 1958 and 1964), mimeo.

[5]*The Condition of the Working Class in England in 1848* (New York: Macmillan, 1958), pp. 137–138.

Table 36-1

Percent "High" Vote for Allende in Municipalities Classified by the Relative Size of the Urban Population, 1958 and 1964[a]

Percent urban	Men[b]		Women		Total		
	1958	1964	1958	1964	1958	1964	(N)
70 plus	75	90	46	39	63	68	(57)
50–69	51	69	15	26	44	51	(39)
30–49	47	53	13	24	38	53	(76)
10–29	37	52	8	13	29	37	(85)
Under 10	15	36	8	10	13	28	(39)

[a]We define a 'high' vote for Allende in 1958 as 30 percent (the national average) or over in the municipality, and 40 percent (the national average) or over in 1964.

[b]Men and women vote at separate polling places and their votes are counted separately.

ties are brought into contact with each other and their experiences are shaped under the impact of their common situation which, in turn, reinforces their sense of belonging to a nation-wide class with its own distinct interests. It is here, moreover that the contrast between their condition as a class and the lives of those in other classes is most strikingly revealed. For these reasons, we should expect to find that the greater the proportion of the municipality's population residing in urban areas, the greater the likelihood that Allende receives a high vote. This is precisely what we do find, in general, in both presidential elections, and among both men and women, as well as among all voters (men and women combined). The larger the relative size of the urban population, the greater the likelihood that Allende received a high vote (Table 1).

One of the major problems of ecological analysis is that we cannot know how the members of a given stratum actually vote from ecological data. We can only surmise this from the relationship between the vote and the relative concentration of the members of given strata in different areas. The more homogeneous the unit of analysis and the smaller it is, the greater our certainty about the actual behavior of the individuals involved. Using the relative percentage of urban residents in the municipality as an index of the relative concentration of urban *workers* compounds the problem even further, since not only the relative size of the working class tends to increase with urbanization, but so does the relative proportion of the middle strata. This is especially so in the larger towns and cities where the governmental bureaucracy and large firms employ great numbers of salaried personnel, and where centers of trade and commerce are located. Different political parties could be drawing on different strata, such as the workers and the middle strata, both of which are concentrated disproportionately in the larger urban areas, and both would, therefore, show a general positive relationship with urbanization.

Rather than relative urbanization, therefore, a more adequate measure of the relative size of the urban industrial working class is needed to discover how that class votes. Unfortunately, there are no data available on the occupational structure on the level of the municipality, which would probably be the most accurate indicator of the relative shape of the class structure in the municipality. However, there are systematic data on the level of the municipality on the employment of the economically active population by branch of the economy. (The terms labor force and economically active population are, for our purposes, interchangeable, though technically somewhat different.) These can be used in lieu of occupational data. The percent of the economically active population employed in manufacturing, mining, or construction—the so-called secondary sector—can serve as an index of industrialization[6] and of the relative size of the industrial working class. While this index also presents certain problems (there are nonmanual employees in these industries and there are

---

[6]Colin Clark, *The Conditions of Economic Progress* (London: Macmillan, 1951); Reinhard Bendix, *Work and Authority in Industry* (New York: John Wiley & Sons, 1956), pp. 254–255.

Table 36-2

Percent "High" Vote for Allende in Urban Municipalities[a] Classified by the Relative Size of the Working Class, 1958 and 1964

Percent of the labor force in manufacturing, mining, or construction	Men		Women		Total		(N)
	1958	1964	1958	1964	1958	1964	
40 plus %	96%	100%	83%	71%	92%	100%	(24)
30–39	71	87	25	21	58	63	(24)
20–29	52	70	17	22	35	43	(23)
10–19	42	67	4	17	33	37	(24)
Under 10	—	—	—	—	—	—	(1)

[a]Municipalities in which percent urban is 50 percent or more.

manual industrial workers in transportation and communication included in the tertiary sector), it is a far better index of the municipal class structure than urbanization, and the best we have available for Chile. Taking urban municipalities only (50 percent urban or over), and using the percent of the economically active population employed in the secondary sector, should ensure a reasonably accurate index of the relative size of the urban industrial working class.

We find (Table 2) that the larger the relative size of the working class in the municipality, the greater the likelihood in 1958 and 1964, among both sexes, and all voters combined, that Allende received a high vote. These findings support the view that the workers voted for the FRAP candidate.

There is, indeed, even more persuasive evidence for this view. So far we have used the high end of the voting spectrum as an index of the relative appeal of the political parties. When focusing on one political party at a time in order to analyze the variation in its strength in different social contexts this is a very useful and parsimonious index. However, we are interested here not only in how well a party does in different types of social contexts, but also how well it does in those contexts *compared to other parties.* What, in other words, is the ratio of the votes received by one party to the votes received by others in different contexts?[7] Here, the significant question is how well the Marxian coalition, FRAP (which should, according to the nature of its appeals and in accordance with its theory, receive the working-class vote), did in working-class areas compared to the Christian Democrats and the conservative coalition behind Allessandri. The answer is clear (Table 3). Generally, in 1958 and 1964, the larger the relative size of the working class in urban municipalities, the higher the mean ratio of Allende's vote to that of the other candidates. Among all voters in the 1964 election, when Allende and Frei virtually stood alone against each other as candidates, it is only in the municipalities where the working class is a substantial proportion (40 percent or more) of the labor force that Allende emerged victorious—by a mean ratio of 171 votes for every 100 Frei votes. It is not unreasonable to assume, therefore, that were we able to discover how members of the different classes actually voted, the Allende/Frei ratio within the working class alone would be far higher. It would be clear that the majority of the workers—men and women alike—voted for Allende, the Marxian candidate.

Given the consistency of all these findings, it is clear that the claim that "FRAP had failed in precisely those areas where it should have been strongest," and that the workers voted for Frei rather than Allende is incorrect. Given the nature of ecological data, we cannot prove that the overwhelming majority of the workers supported the candidate of the Marxian coalition, but our findings are very convincing indeed that they did. The Christian

---

[7]Of course, it is possible that two political parties, say, of the left, would draw their relative electoral support from the same types of municipalities, even though one were stronger than the other, and that, therefore, the ratio of their votes would tend to be constant in different types of municipalities.

Table 36-3

The Mean Ratio [a] of Allende Votes to the Votes of Other Presidential Candidates in Urban Municipalities Classified by the Relative Size of the Working Class, 1958 and 1964

Percent of the labor force in manufacturing, mining, or construction	Men			Women			Total		
	1958 Frei	Alessandri	1964 Frei	1958 Frei	Alessandri	1964 Frei	1958 Frei	Alessandri	1964 Frei
40 plus %	403	456	204	209	276	117	334	408	171
30–39	241	289	119	136	175	67	178	255	91
20–29	183	148	124	104	111	88	212	137	96
10–19	199	119	108	120	84	64	156	107	85
Under 10 [b]	–	–	–	–	–	–	–	–	–

[a] The number of Allende votes per 100 votes for the other candidate.

[b] Only one urban municipality falls in this category.

Democratic "alternative" failed (at least *before* its adherents gained *power*) to wrest the workers allegiances from the socialists and communists, with whom the workers have been identified throughout most of their struggles in this century.

The mass support of the Communist and Socialist parties in the working class gives those parties, especially when allied politically, a cohesive and strategically located social base that they can mobilize for political and social struggles that cannot be matched by the Christian Democrats, whose base is constituted of a heterogeneous mass of individuals of often contradictory values and interests.

Managers

37 The Industrialist and Labor

W. Paul Strassmann

Preserving the status quo with his labor force usually comes first on the industrialist's policy agenda. The industrialist does not enjoy the persistence of misery among his own or other workers, or the great differentials in living standards. If labor's share of a growing national income rises because skilled occupations are expanding faster than unskilled, he will not be alarmed. What harrows his soul and freezes his plans, to repeat once more, is uncertainty. Curtailment of credit or foreign exchange, increased taxes, or vigorous competition, while irritating, are yet somehow distant and impersonal. The enemy is outside the shop. But trouble with labor, which usually represents only 5 to 15 percent of costs, can disrupt operations at any time through strikes or sabotage, and when over, leaves the air poisoned with resentment. Even an acceptable change in the status quo initiated by labor shows that the status quo is changeable, and may lead to excessive requests, and thence to disagreement and loss of harmony. To forestall this trend is the objective of paternalism.

Among highly religious and tradition-minded industrialists, particularly those of Spanish American or Brazilian stock, paternalism fulfills a deeply conditioned sense of obligation. But would any industrialist be surprised to learn that industrial tranquillity has a pecuniary as well as a spiritual value? In extreme cases the firm supplies not only hospitalization, free transport to work, company stores, recreational facilities, low-cost housing, and social counseling, but also chapels, schools, and dormitories for single women, at times under the supervision of Catholic sisters. In the absence of detailed financial reports, one cannot say whether paternalism yields employers any benefits in addition to tranquillity. The possibility of keeping operations secret and under their own control, excluding government inspectors and minimizing reports, may itself be regarded as an advantage. Fragmentary replies in interviews at 51 Mexican plants suggest the combined wages and fringe benefits were no higher in paternalistic than other enterprises, and lower compared with foreign subsidiaries. But insofar as the differential means exploitation in the economic rather than moral sense, because of monopsony and immobility, it must be balanced against the protection afforded the worker from landlords, merchants, moneylenders,

Reprinted from "The Industrialist," by W. Paul Strassmann in *Continuity and Change in Latin America*, edited by John J. Johnson, with permission of the publishers, Stanford University Press. © 1964 by the Board of Trustees of the Leland Stanford Junior University.

and other potential exploiters. His lower pay may go further. For workers new to city life and used to rural paternalism, these practices of employers have often been regarded as helpful. I will not attempt to put a price tag on the elaborate spy systems and the danger of blacklisting for entire families that, whether legal or not, often afflict the employee of a paternalistic enterprise.

If in spite of all these arrangements the workers' sense of identification with the interests of the enterprise fades, the employer, not the worker, will probably want to eliminate paternalism. The employer's economic advantage, after all, lies in organizing production, not a cluster of welfare services. The inability of paternalism to guarantee employer domination of labor relations has led to its diminution in Chile, and may partly account for the unique, employer-financed and controlled, nationwide paternalism of Brazil.[1]

But the decline of paternalism has not generally meant a substantial increase in labor's power to bargain for itself. Such power leads to the pursuit of equity (on which minds never meet), which negates a poor society's priority for growth and creates the turbulence and uncertainty that smothers the candle of entrepreneurial daring. The 1951 report of the International Bank mission to Cuba implies that things had reached that point around 1950. Strikes were being called for comparatively trivial reasons; job tenure and seniority requirements were extreme; increased benefits were to be accompanied by shorter hours at lower productivity; and mechanization was staved off from tire-building to candy-wrapping and noodle-twisting.[2] To avert comparable labor problems, the Mexican Revolutionary party gave up much of its version of the class struggle after 1940.[3] By 1950 a large part of the labor movement itself had been brought into line, especially when Fidel Veláquez abandoned his former radicalism and gained official support for control of the Confederación de Trabajadores de México.[4]

---

[1]Robert J. Alexander, *Labor Relations in Argentina, Brazil, and Chile* (New York: McGraw-Hill, 1962), pp. 104–112 and 327–336. The paternalistic orientation of Brazilian workers did not give way to class-conscious militancy, as in Chile, but was diverted by Getulio Vargas, who "twisted the old patriarchal traditions to make himself patriarch of all Brazil." Alexander, p. 44.

[2]International Bank for Reconstruction and Development, *Report on Cuba: Findings and Recommendations of an Economic and Technical Mission* (Baltimore, 1951), pp. 136–148. Twelve years later an official Cuban study was quoted as finding that the mass of workers "appears in great part to have confused the purposes of the revolution and interpreted it as meaning they can work less." Communist indoctrination was recommended to combat absenteeism, irresponsibility, negligence, and lack of interest in work. (*New York Times*, August 3, 1962.) A few weeks later Labor Minister Augusto Martinez issued a decree instituting such penalties as one day's pay for six late arrivals or early departures. (*New York Times*, August 30, 1962.)

[3]John J. Johnson, *Political Change in Latin America: The Emergence of the Middle Sectors* (Stanford: Stanford University Press, 1956), pp. 148–149.

[4]Robert E. Scott, *The Mexican Government in Transition* (Urbana: University of Illinois Press, 1959), p. 163.

Except perhaps in Chile and Uruguay, the decline of paternalism has strengthened the state's hand more than labor's, and has led to the state's holding the balance of power in labor-management disputes. This development has been to the short-run disadvantage of workers, because government and industry in Latin America tend to agree in their emphasis on tranquillity and on minimizing consumer expenditures for the sake of capital accumulation and growth. In Brazil and Argentina, government still acts through the systems of labor courts established by Vargas and Perón. In Mexico union leadership is subject to government pressure, since the labor movement forms part of the structure of the official party and the personal ambitions of the leaders are apt to be primarily political. An industrialist dealing with a nationally affiliated union must therefore have a strategy toward labor that is, in large part, political.

38

Técnicos and Políticos: Managers in the Public Sector

Raymond Vernon

The Técnicos in Theory and Practice

In the development of nations, the economic technician is rapidly coming to be thought of as the indispensable man. By general agreement, such subjects as exchange-rate policy, fiscal and monetary policy, investment and saving policy, and similar esoteric matters can no longer be left entirely to the rough-and-ready ministrations of the politician. For one thing, the economic techniques have grown so complex that they are beyond the easy understanding of the amateurs; for another, the increasing flow of communications between nations and with international agencies on these subjects has demanded that every country develop a class of responsible officials which is capable of holding up its end in the interchange. In Mexico the economic technician has become an integral element in the decision-making process on issues affecting Mexico's development.

In many advanced countries, the distinction between the technician and the politician has come to be blurred and indistinct. Inside the Mexican government, however, there is still a reasonably clear line between the *técnicos* and the *políticos*. There have been times, of course, when a technician has jumped the fence into the higher and lusher pastures of the politicians, and these cases promise to be more common in the years ahead. But on the whole the division between the two groups is fairly well maintained.

This does not mean that all Mexican technicians tend to think alike on economic issues. There are some considerable doctrinal distinctions among them. A tiny minority, as nearly as any outside observer can tell, are doctrinaire Marxists; a much larger number are inclined to a mixed economy, with increased emphasis on the importance of the public sector. Within the latter group there are large differences over appropriate public policies. Some of the technicians connected with the Banco de México, for instance, tend to look on monetary and fiscal restraints as an indispensable instrument in ensuring a steady process of growth, while those in the investing and spending agencies tend to see such restraints as a handicap to growth. Economists in the industrializing agencies, such as Nacional Financiera,

Reprinted by permission of the publishers, from pp. 136–137 and 141–149 of Raymond Vernon, *The Dilemma of Mexico's Development* (Cambridge Mass.: Harvard University Press, 1963). Copyright 1963 by the President and Fellows of Harvard College.

tend to put a high priority on steel mills, while economists in the agricultural services place greater emphasis on irrigation and farm-to-market roads.

Nevertheless, as seen through the eyes of an outside observer, the similarities in viewpoint among Mexico's economic technicians, whatever their function in government may be, are more striking than the differences. They have a common ideology which, harnessed to the government apparatus, constitutes a strong force in shaping the behavior of the public sector in Mexico. True, at this stage in Mexico's governmental development, there is still only a limited amount of the relatively easy interchange between the official and the civil service levels that one finds in Canada, the United States, or Britain. Accordingly, the strength of the technicians lies not so much in their powers to shape policy directly as in their capacity to choose the technical alternatives which are presented to their political masters. But this is a very potent force in itself. And when the instructions from above are ambiguous or when the situation calls for technical action in the absence of instructions, the power of the technician is enhanced even further . . . .

One fundamental principle of the *técnicos* . . . is that Mexico must rapidly reduce her reliance on the exports of raw materials and on imports of manufactured products. There are various strands in the argument. Apart from the problems of the cyclical instability of demand, there is also the so-called "terms-of-trade" argument—the argument that nations reliant on exports of raw materials are forced over the long run to lower the prices of their exports in relation to the prices of their imports. On this assumption, if 500 pounds of copper ore could buy a refrigerator in 1940, it might take 700 or 800 pounds to buy the refrigerator in 1960.

The reasons for the assumption are various. In the long run, according to the argument, raw materials such as iron ore tend to be displaced by synthetic substitutes; this fact alone gives more buoyancy to the price of manufactured products than of raw materials. Besides, new exporters of raw materials tend to come into existence more readily than new producers of manufactured products, as each developing country expands its production first in the areas that are easiest. Beyond this, when labor-saving innovations occur in the production of raw materials for export, the reduction in cost usually gets passed on to the buyer in the form of reduced prices. The heavy competition among the unskilled laborers and the suppliers in the exporting countries means that the exporting economies are in no position to hold back a share of increased productivity in the form of higher wages or higher profits. As a result, increases in efficiency in the exporting countries simply lead to fewer jobs and greater unemployment, rather than to higher pay. Contrariwise, in the developed countries, according to the argument, labor unions and monopolies tend to hold on to the fruits of their cost reductions, either in shorter working hours, increased wages, or increased profits. The net effect of these tendencies is to raise the price of manufactured imports relative to raw material exports over the long run.

Apart from this so-called "terms-of-trade" argument, Mexico's *técnicos* assert other advantages in industrialization, advantages which will be familiar to any student of development theory. The *técnicos* maintain that increased industrialization leads to a more rapid increase in output per unit of manpower and capital than does the increased production of raw materials. This is due partly to the fact that, as factory installations grow in scale, their efficiency increases rapidly, more rapidly than the increase in efficiency of a growing mine or a growing farm. Besides, "*external* economies of scale" are more important in an industrial complex than in a materials-producing economy; the growth of a chemical industry, for instance, supports the expansion of an efficient electric generating system which then makes an efficient aluminum plant possible.

The argument goes further still. Industrialization, in which the worker learns new skills and disciplines, tends to upgrade the human resources of a nation in a way which mining and agriculture do not. Industrialization also tends to alter the distribution of income, so that it is easier to generate an increase in savings and investment; either the industrialist himself makes the increased savings and investment, or the state does the added savings and investment through increased taxation and public spending. Industrialization tends to relocate the population in compact centers so that it is easier and less costly to provide such public services as health and education—unless, of course, the population becomes too concentrated at one given point, such as Mexico City, in which case a certain rediffusion of population is called for. And so on.

Of late, the industrialization argument has grown a little more complex. In recent years, particularly in Mexico, there has been added emphasis on the point that, in the headlong rush to industrialize, agriculture should not be neglected. For, if agriculture is neglected, the price of foodstuffs remains high and the quantity of foodstuffs is limited. As a result, the industrial worker is forced to pay dearly for his subsistence and is forever being cheated of the advantages of his increased industrial productivity. Besides, agricultural workers represent over half of the labor force of Mexico. Unless they can increase their output per man, these workers will not be able to absorb the growing volume of industrial goods pouring out of Mexico's factories. Mexico's industrial sector, with half of its potential market stagnant, will be doomed to a stunted growth. So some sort of balance is the key. Agriculture must be stimulated—but primarily for the domestic market, and only secondarily for export.

The *técnico* is not only in wholehearted support of industrialization; he also is in favor of achieving that industrialization through the maximum use of domestic capital rather than foreign capital. There are many advantages to the use of domestic private capital, as he sees it. One such advantage is that the country's skills and manpower are upgraded faster; foreign firms, it is assumed, tend to hold the top management jobs for their own nationals, out of distrust for the ability or the "loyalty" of their indigenous employees. Foreign capital also drains a country's foreign-exchange reserves, it is argued; for though the inflow of capital may add to these reserves when the investment is first made, the remittances of company profits and foreign employee savings to the home country soon wipe out the temporary gain from the initial capital inflow.

Foreign investment involves other disabilities to the host country. If the investment is in manufacturing, it often represents the final stage in an assembly or processing operation. (For Mexico, of course, the classic case is its automobile assembly plants.) For various good and sufficient reasons, the foreign-owned subsidiary will be especially loath to buy its machinery and its intermediate products inside the host country; so there will be special resistances to completing the process of industrialization. If the foreign investment is in raw-material production, especially production for export, the problems will be even worse. Investments of this sort are usually made by firms which have a number of alternative sources of their materials. On any decline in world demand for the product, the foreigner will be free to decide which source of supply he wishes to shut off, thus leaving the domestic economy at the mercy of his decision.

Nor are these the only difficulties which face the host country. Foreign installations, according to the argument, represent a type of "unfair" competition to the incipient domestic competitor. The foreigner can fall back on his access to technology, his easier credit, and his management experience to crush domestic competition. Quite apart from the equity considerations which apply in such a situation, there are also the problems of generating monopolies inside the country and of slowing up the emergence of an indigenous entrepreneurial class.

The *técnicos* also have some fairly explicit ideas on the relative places of the public and the private sectors in domestic capital formation. First, of course, they ratify the idea, by now quite widely accepted, that certain types of investment cannot realistically be left to the private sector: projects whose financial needs are so large that they exceed the resources of any private group; projects whose financial outcome is subject to such uncertainty that they exceed the risk-taking propensities of any private group; and projects which, for welfare reasons, cannot pay out financially. Examples are a first experimental fertilizer plant, a school, a highway.

The *técnicos,* however, are inclined to go somewhat further in defining the appropriate role of the public sector. They begin by pointing to certain major reservations about the effectiveness of the price system in allocating resources. Take the division between investment in industry and investment in basic foodstuffs production; here, they are inclined to assume, monopoly pricing by the wholesale food merchants keeps agricultural profits so low that farm savings are held down and investment is discouraged. Accordingly, public investment in irrigation works, public assistance through easy credit, and public subsidies in the form of cheap fertilizer are seen as indispensable offsets to the effects of monopoly pricing.

The fertilizer case suggests another principle which most *técnicos* hold dear. According to their view, the achievement of the most rapid rate of development and of the most desirable distribution of income sometimes argues for the use of prices which are at variance with open-market prices. There are times when transport, power, or other basic products and services should be subsidized because of the stimulus which the lower rates will give to other branches of production or because of the effects of such subsidies on income distribution. The social gain to be derived from the altered rates is the real test, rather than the gain to the selling enterprise itself. In circumstances of this sort, public investment is sometimes the only possibility.

Still another element figures in the technician's views regarding the relative places of private and public capital investment. The technicians tend to share an ideological conception that capital formation in an unregulated private economy proceeds from trial and error. Monopolists in control of the market, so the argument runs, are not concerned with making a careful study of demand and of industrial locations. And where competition exists in the market, there is too much ignorance, haste, or ease of entry to make any careful study useful or possible. Where private investment decision-making prevails, therefore, extensive error is certain— error whose costs are borne by society through bankruptcy, high monopoly costs and prices, or chronic idle capacity.

By contrast, the *técnicos* think of public investment as proceeding from reason and study; and they assert that the reason and study are all the more likely to produce adequate results because in theory they can be integrated with all of the planning that goes on in other parts of the public sector. The *técnicos* are prepared to agree, indeed to insist, that the intervention of the *políticos* is sometimes a fly in the ointment of rational decision-making; but they see this as an imperfection, not as a fatal flaw, in the system.

These views of the Mexican technicians stem not only from their theoretical assumptions about the nature of the private economy in general but also from their evaluation of the attitudes and training of Mexican businessmen in particular. The *técnicos,* in general, have been drawn from schools of economics. To the extent that the businessmen are associated with any particular branch of professional training, it is with law or accounting. Though many of the *técnicos* are quick to agree that Mexico's schools of economics are far from providing an ideal training ground for market analysis, locational studies, and capital budgeting at the level of the individual firm, they tend to see themselves as well ahead of the private decision-maker in their training and preparation for activities involving industrial investment and management.

The programs and attitudes of the Mexican economic technicians are explained not only by their views but also by their current concerns about the nature of the roadblocks in Mexico's economic development. One of the worst, according to their view, is the nonegalitarian income distribution of the Mexican people. As they see it, this distribution prevents the development of mass demands for manufactured goods inside Mexico and prevents the growth of large-scale industry. The *técnicos,* therefore, tend to be strong supporters of measures which could lead to the redistribution of income. Some favor tax measures; some insist that wage boosts are the key; some concentrate on improvements in the pricing and marketing system of Mexico.

Because of their concern for the development of larger internal markets, practically all *técnicos* also tend to endorse the Latin American Free Trade Association, in hopes that the enlarged markets toward which the Association should lead over the next decade—though not necessarily altering the Mexican distribution of income—will offer Mexico some of the opportunities for large-scale production which its own internal markets do not. To charges that they may be attempting to exploit the less-developed countries of Latin America, using the very techniques that they impute to the foreign investors of the United States and Europe, they point to the provisions of the Association's treaty which seek to protect the laggard countries from the dominance of the senior partners in the Association.

A last point or two. Mexico's economic technicians are inclined to believe that Mexico has now developed its human resources and has now achieved a potential for domestic savings and investment to the point at which close contact with the more advanced countries is no longer indispensable to its growth; or, to put the case more modestly, that Mexico's remaining needs for foreign technology and capital are sufficiently limited that it can afford to bargain hard on the terms on which these needs should be provided. The ideal channel by which foreign technology should be brought into the country, in their view, is not through direct investment but through licensing agreements. And the ideal means by which foreign capital should be introduced into Mexico is likewise not through direct investment but through public loans in general support of Mexico's balance-of-payments position.

Most of the *técnicos* do not draw back from the implications of their particularistic approach to economic development. They do not flinch from the task of deciding in detail which investment should be made with public funds and which not, which product should be imported and which exported, which items should be relieved of taxes and which actually subsidized. For them, the word *dirigiste* has none of the invidious connotation which it usually carries in the French tongue. The *economía mixta,* according to their view, is the swiftest way to growth and social justice in the Mexican setting.

The views of the *técnicos* have had important implications for the policy lines to be followed by the Mexican government. In the range of proposals which the *técnicos* have formulated for the consideration of the *políticos,* it is unlikely that they have very often suggested a major relaxation of controls over the private sector; this possibility, we are safe in assuming, has not been a serious starter in the race among competing ideas within government councils.[1] It is equally improbable, however, that extremely

---

[1] A somewhat similar point is made regarding Latin American economic technicians in general by Daniel Cosío Villegas in his "Política y política económica en América Latina," *Foro Internacional* (April–June 1961). He says in part: ". . . the Latin American economist is not in general a man of deep convictions. . . . Besides, if one has to judge by what one sees directly in his own country, there are grounds for fear-

ambitious proposals in the opposite direction, such as proposals for a swift and drastic extension of government powers and government investment, have been pushed upward by the *técnico* group. Though an exceptional case occurs from time to time, it is not in the nature of most government technicians knowingly to propose a line of action which they believe the *políticos* are unlikely to accept. The *técnicos,* therefore, while tending to urge the continued extension of government powers in discrete and limited fashion, have not been a sufficient force to joggle the *políticos* off the "middle position" to which Mexican politics have slowly bound them.

---

ing that the great majority of the Latin American economists have been just as much opportunists as the politicians they serve . . ." (p. 510). Although this judgment is somewhat harsher than any to which I would subscribe with respect to the Mexican *técnicos,* it obviously supports the validity of the assumption in the text.

39

Management as a Bankrupt Power Factor

José Luis de Imaz

Why is it that industrialists [in Argentina] seem to have become incapable of articulating their interests with the ability and vigor with which they had done so before? Why do the various enterprises not agree to take great collective decisions? Why do they, despite their economic weight, their role in modernization, and the fact that they have been technological innovators, not have more weight within the life of the nation? What keeps the entrepreneurs from becoming a power factor similar to the armed forces? What inhibits them from articulating their interests with the same ability that the cattle-raisers of the Rural Society have shown? It is evident that there are many points demanding clarification.

First, the entrepreneurial sector may lack unity because it is relatively new. Even assuming that the entrepreneurs might really be a cohesive group, with group consciousness and norms, the organization of new groups is usually deficient, and their understanding of their own real interests is unclear and diffuse. In this sense the industrial sector is newer than the other groups constituted as power factors. But this does not explain everything. Its emergence antedates the emergence of labor union activity, yet the consciousness of unity which the labor unions display is incomparably more developed than that of the industrialists. Apparently, the labor unionists understand that numbers, unity of purpose and objectives, and organization give them strength, while their employers do not. The entrepreneurs continue to believe that each has his own strength, that each has his own objective, that each one should look out for his own personal profit and benefit, which do not precisely coincide with the interests of other entrepreneurs.

The second factor that seems to have had a negative influence on the adequate articulation of the entrepreneurs' interests is the diversity of the groups making up this sector. There are two different blocs of enterprises: the branch offices of international companies and the native entrepreneurs. . . . The former do not participate directly at the highest level of industrial organizations, partly because national production requirements do not always run parallel with their own. Thus, these large enterprises feel that their interests are relatively well represented within the

Reprinted from *Los Que Mandan* (*Those Who Rule*) by José Luis de Imaz, translated by Carlos A. Astiz, by permission of the State University of New York Press. Translation © 1970 by The Research Foundation of State University of New York. All rights reserved.

273

managerial organizations, and they go along with decisions, especially when the organizations present petitions on financial matters, on restrictions on imports, or on some government intervention to change the "free-play rules" of enterprises.

There is also the difference in size of industries. There are two industrial strata, almost without any intermediate levels: the large and economically powerful enterprises which employ a large labor force, and the 90 percent of the industrialists at the shop level which employ a permanent labor force of less than ten people. Because Argentina is still a pre-capitalist society, or, more properly, since capitalist development has not been harmonious, there are two entrepreneurial levels. The larger enterprises do not necessarily exert the greater influence on the control of common interests and business; sometimes quite the reverse is the case. It is generally the spokesmen for the intermediate or not-so-large enterprises who direct the entrepreneurial movement.

Third, unity is adversely affected because of personal and group conflicts and the different national origins among the entrepreneurs. . . . One of the many dividing lines that cuts through this entrepreneurial sector originates in the fact that different groups are structured around common values, norms, and social circles, and especially around common financial sources. All these groups are not aggregated; they are opposed to each other or, at best, suspicious of each other, usually because or ethnic differences and because of problems related to events outside Argentina. The situation does not create tension lines, but it does erect barriers to communication, which in this case are dysfunctional.[1]

Thus, though objectively entrepreneurs would seem to have common interests, such interests are not clearly perceived because the differences in form among the entrepreneurial groups are the first to be noticed.

There are old entrepreneurs, heirs of the founders, and there are also new entrepreneurs whose rapidly acquired fortunes are looked upon with suspicion by the old sectors because the latter consider the acquisition of these fortunes to be connected with politics. Besides the very large American, British, and German enterprises, there are national capital enterprises

---

[1]Perhaps the case closest to that of Argentina is that of Brazil. Fernando Enrique Cardoso, "O empresário industrial e o desenvolvimento econômico do Brazil" (São Paulo, 1963, mimeo.) sets forth some of the characteristics of the Brazilian sector as an independent stratum, which is more similar than different from the Argentine entrepreneurial group. For one thing, because of the speed with which that stratum was built up, as a result of the superimposing of groups whose industrial tradition is very recent, the "traditional industrialists" (the extreme cases) are those who can point to two generations in the business. Hence, according to the author, the "preindustrial" and recent origin of the group inhibits its acting as a class. In Brazil, together with an overwhelming majority of industrialists of immigrant background, a minority of "segments of the old seigneurial strata" are active, but the latter possess much more political influence than the former, as in the case in Argentina. In Cardoso's opinion, the Brazilian industrialists constitute a recent and heterogeneous social stratum, which makes it difficult to obtain the necessary maturity for elaborating uniform modes of thought, feeling, and action, and inhibits them from constructing an industrial ideology.

established around old English, German, and Italian national groups. There are traditional Belgian and French export enterprises, and there are also very new enterprises established by until recently unknown Arabs and Jews. Within the hypothetical bloc of the entrepreneurs, are traditional owners whose ways have not been brought up to date, new captains of industry motivated by a desire for instant profits, and the brand-new "corporate entrepreneurs" to whom the development of the enterprise means more than large short-term profits.

The potential causes for conflict are numerous: the different size of the enterprises, the length of time since they were established, the fact that they belong to different national groups, and the differences in behavior and motivation. These make the creation of group norms, cohesion, interests, objectives, and leadership difficult. No elements that could act as catalysts have yet appeared, and the differences still count far more than the similarities.

One of the clearest pieces of evidence that shows the lines of discord are stronger than those of agreement is that there are two entrepreneurial organizations, but what is even more significant is that it is precisely in the political arena that the final motivation for discord is found. Instead of the social factor of entrepreneurial economic power influencing the political field, it is the latter—traditional politization understood in its most simplistic terms—that is the framework for the former. The logical order is subverted and the political dichotomy of friend-enemy is institutionalized over and above common interests.

In politics, power is not held, but exercised. If it is not exercised, there is no political power despite all the economic and social power that may be possessed. Argentine entrepreneurs have not exhibited objective consciousness that power could be exercised or the desire to do so.[2] Entrepreneurs have been absorbed by the preoccupation of reaching the highest status possible, for the sole, exclusive, and personal benefit of themselves, their families, their group, their enterprise, but not for any entity, corps, institution, or social sector outside their own domain.

The former president of an entrepreneurial organization confidentially maintains that "entrepreneurs have never ceased to rule in Argentina," and he points out in favor of his thesis that "many decrees are drawn up in private offices and bureaus. . . . The entrepreneurs who, because of their political relations and contacts, impose their points of view on the others are to be found within a radius of fifteen blocks around the Presidential office." The writer feels that this is not true, that the entrepreneurs obtain benefits exclusively for their own enterprises, whether these benefits pertain to customs, tariffs, credit, or taxes. They negotiate, petition, and bring influence to bear until they get the favorable decision for themselves and their

---

[2]See the conclusions reached in E. Zalduendo, *El empresario industrial en la Argentina* (Buenos Aires: Instituto Torcuato Di Tella, Centro de Investigaciones Económicas, 1962), who after analyzing the results of his survey, maintains that the Argentine entrepreneur does not visualize the role he plays within society, and even less does he seem ready to face the dangers of command or power.

business, but not for the industry as a whole. The entrepreneurs do not rule as a unified sector vis-à-vis other sectors, even though hundreds of entrepreneurs individually and for their own exclusive benefit may obtain that favorable decision which interests them alone.[3] The entrepreneurs do not rule because, lacking solidarity, they have no other motivation than the manufacture of their own status. Since they are prestige seekers, their time is absorbed by the enterprise and then by the accumulation of all possible external trappings of prestige.

Economic power does not necessarily bring parallel political power.[4] What economic power does bring is the potential for political power if there is the intent, the understanding, and the vocation to exercise it. But if the largest enterprises are not interested in the exercise of leadership; if the entrepreneurs fear involvements which will take them away from their enterprises; if they are only motivated by concrete and obvious results (new status, more external symbols of prestige); if the group lacks maturity, if there is no objective group consciousness; if as a result of their experiences they believe that political activity is more likely to result in loss of prestige than in anything else, all this will lead to a vacuum between the economic power held and the political power which they do not wish to exercise.

Since they lack cohesion and have no frame of reference of their own, the members of the entrepreneurial bourgeoisie, as they have gone up the social scale, have been co-opted by the old upper class. They have lost a certain dynamic power, and, since they do not have the capacity to generate ideologies, they accept the prestige scale, the value system, and the stratifica-

---

[3]Cardoso ["O empresario industrial . . ."] reaches the same conclusions about the Brazilian entrepreneurs: "Lacking the necessary socialization to play the roles they should accept, the entrepreneurs only respond as an electoral 'maneuvering mass,' polarizing their interests around 'abstract vindications,' such as 'high cost of living,' or 'against inflation' and 'against the Government.'" The author maintains that the entrepreneurs seem to associate the government with all the evils that befall the country through a rationalization which is typical of the behavior of the middle classes. This is the reason why the isolated participation of industrialists and industrial groups in politics tends to be characterized by its individualism and, very often, by opportunism: "they act in order to achieve some degree of influence which will allow direct benefits for themselves or for their enterprises" (p. 205).

[4]In Argentina, the transfer of economic power from the agricultural to the industrial sectors begins to become discernible in 1945. At five-year intervals the figures show that, starting after World War II, the industrialists contributed more on a percentage basis to the gross national product than did the rural sectors. Nevertheless, the "political power" relation is exactly the opposite.

Contribution to the Gross National Product by the Economic Sectors

Five-Year Intervals	Percentage of GNP	
	Industrial	Rural
1935–1939	20.4%	24.3%
1940–1944	21.0	24.7
1945–1949	23.5	18.5
1950–1954	22.7	16.6

tion of the preceding social structure. Without even realizing it, they have adopted as their own the value framework of the traditional rural sector.

These entrepreneurs who moved up bought ranches once they had acquired enough capital, not only for economic diversification, but also to qualify under the old prestige norms. They had achieved wealth by a route other than ranching, traditional financing, or the practice of law. After having bought land, some entrepreneurs took a further step and became dairy ranchers, a complementing luxury. Instead of steadfastly defending their own interests, as they had done when their prestige was still marginal, they tried to identify with the ideas, points of view, and arguments of the rural sector. Even within entrepreneurial organizations, they sometimes disregarded their own interests in favor of the ones developed by the traditional rural elite.

There was also a leadership crisis among the entrepreneurs. From 1925 to 1946 Luis Colombo, the classical example of the self-made man, the perfect expression of his era, and the sort of personality then common among the entrepreneurs, exercised undisputed leadership. He was a leader who embodied the group's aspirations. His personal decline entailed that of the group. In 1946 he committed the great mistake of having the Industrial Union contribute heavily to the coffers of the candidate who eventually lost. As a result, the organization was placed under governmental control; and even though it continued to have a sort of latent life, it took many years to rebuild its leadership team.

The Argentine entrepreneur distinguished himself as long as he was led by an old fashioned *patrón,* and the group was composed of men who were themselves old-fashioned *patrones:* the leader embodied group reality. At the present time, the entrepreneurial group is partly made up of new corporate executives who are just part of a corporate hierarchy made up of impersonal managers. This impersonality is also present among the leadership of the entrepreneurial organizations.

The bureaucratization of the system precludes the possibility of personal leadership on the Colombo pattern and checks the impetus of strong personalities. This type of leadership is possible today only in party politics and in labor union activities, though it is not even possible in all the unions, but only in those with certain characteristics. It is no longer possible among the entrepreneurs where the existence of a ruling elite would not in itself be sufficient for the entrepreneurs to play a significant role. For them to do so, it is essential that the sector be boosted up as a whole, or at least that this be done to a whole set of innovating entrepreneurs who, because they head important enterprises, may be able to lead the way.

It is possible to ascertain the absence of a cohesive entrepreneurial elite, one authentically creative, since the leading industrial sectors[5] have been notorious for being behind the times, opposing governmental projects as well as those proposed by other groups. In such cases, these entrepreneurs have reacted by offering solutions which were based on orthodox principles

---

[5]Not all of them, but the very ones belonging to the most important organizations.

of economic dogma, rather than on the facts. This is a strange attitude for entrepreneurs to take since the personality type which is preponderant in these sectors is usually that of the executive accustomed to making decisions on the basis of facts, not abstract considerations. This is the type of personality that makes decisions on the basis of the events he himself sets in motion and not simply as a response to the stimuli presented by other groups.[6]

It is possible to be a "power factor" only to the extent that the power possessed is made effective in a coherent manner; that is, first it must be possible to do so, and then it must be done intelligently. The armed forces have no problem; when they want to act as a power factor what they must make effective is the direct exercise of force, or the threat of the use of force. Since this force comes from the state and resides in the use of a state instrument, there is no problem or complication.

But both the industrial forces and the large rural producers can only make effective the power that comes from money, from the amount they are ready to throw into the political arena, the direction they give the use of these funds, and where they concentrate them. The large rural landowners have no problem in donating money for political purposes since they are free to dispose of their own private funds, but it is a complicated matter for industrialists who manage the funds of others, of enterprises that are corporately owned. Besides, once the decision to do so is made, it must be done intelligently. As one of the top level leaders says, "on election eve, all the entrepreneurs play all the colors, just in case." This has been one of the two routes followed in the attempt to gain a number of momentary friends at election time.

The other route was that followed by some large entrepreneurs who on each occasion have consulted together and decided to support only one of the candidates, but unfortunately in the last fifteen years every time they have done so they have bet on the losing candidates. In the 1946 and 1951 elections they supported the presidential candidates who lost. In 1946 the Industrial Union went so far as to solicit financial support by a circular letter addressed to entrepreneurs and member organizations. In the 1957 elections for delegates to the constitutional convention, the entrepreneurs of the city of Buenos Aires supported a party which won only one delegate. In 1958 they were divided. In 1962, entrepreneurial groups in the province of Buenos Aires contributed to paying for the very costly propaganda campaign of the government candidate who lost, and the same thing happened in July, 1963, when in the new presidential elections "strong groups" backed a candidate who came in third.[7]

---

[6]See the Round Table of *Clarín* (special meeting of August 28, 1960) on the subject of "Argentine Industry: Its Improvement and Expansion," especially the contribution by Jorge A. Sábato.

[7]Hugo Berlatzky and Silvia Novick of the Department of Sociology of the School of Philosophy and Letters, University of Buenos Aires, have carried out a study on a theme on which nothing has previously been published in Argentina and which has been an important source for . . . [this chapter]: "Delimitación y análisis de los grupos

económicos en la Argentina" (unpublished monograph). Using the lists of directors of corporations and using the interlocking technique, they have classified eight groups to which they have given arbitrary names taken from some of the corporations included in the group. The results were as follows:

1) The *Tornquist* group, 38 industrial, banking, and insurance companies.
2) The *La Papelera* group, an Italian group.
3) *Bunge y Born*, import, export, and oils.
4) The *Dálmine* group, also Italian, metallurgy.
5) The *Siam* group.
6) *Braun Menéndez*, a Patagonian agricultural, commercial, industrial, and shipping group.
7) The *Italo* group, electrical and diversified.
8) The *Williams* group, Swedish and British capital.

The existence of these "groups" breaks the pattern of industrial concentration in Argentina, since the majority in Argentina are shops employing up to 10 workers (85 percent of enterprises in the 1946 census). In the 1954 census this percentage rose to 90 percent. These figures, which imply a reversal of the world-wide trend toward economic concentration, have, with reference to what is of interest here, an adverse effect, the existence of two levels of stratification: a) The great corporations as the entrepreneurial minority; b) The overwhelming majority at the shop level. This greatly hampers the creation of a homogeneous entrepreneurial elite and also the leadership of the large enterprises. The intermediate stratum, which would be the next following, is very small. Yet, it is from that entrepreneurial intermediate stratum that the leaders of the two management organizations emerge.

40 The Politics of Organizational Underdevelopment: Chile

Stanley M. Davis

"If men define situations as real they are real in their consequences."

W. I. Thomas.

This study is an attempt to help understand the problem of organizational underdevelopment.* It deals with the political, cultural, and moral conditions of economic organization. It examines the factors which impede modernization of industrial corporations in a country desperately needing more effective and efficient enterprise. Looking specifically at the case of Chile, it suggests an answer to the question of why so many industrial organizations fail to modernize despite their continual efforts in such a direction.

The explanation offered is in terms of the highly politicized nature of Chilean economic enterprise and the negative effect of this on organizational development. Emphasis will be placed on the ideological beliefs of Chilean businessmen about their country's political economy and on the implications these beliefs have on their organizational actions. Since our focus is on industrial organization, it will be helpful, first, to know something about the extent of the unit under study.[1]

The first industrial census in Chile (taken in 1927) reported 8,585 establishments employing 97,832 workers. Almost 40 percent of these, however, were one-man shops and about 75 percent employed fewer than five workers. A very small number of companies employed the majority of the country's industrial labor force.

The most recent industrial census (1957) reported 5,854 establishments of five or more workers employing over 216,000 persons.[2] Only 13 percent

Reprinted from *Industrial and Labor Relations Review*, Vol. 24, No. 1 (October 1970). Copyright © 1970 by Cornell University. All rights reserved.

The author expresses thanks to Maria-Louisa Zapata T. and Luis Valencia R. for their assistance in the research on which this article is based.

[1]The study is based on a series of 75 interviews and some participant observation in 14 locally owned companies (of the 121 large firms) in the Santiago area. Eleven of the firms were engaged in industrial manufacturing, one in retailing, one in construction, and one in publishing. Wherever possible, the top manager and his immediate subordinates were interviewed, meetings were attended, and daily routines were observed. The research was carried on during a 7-month period in 1968.

[2]"III Censo Nacional de Manufacturas" (Direccion de Estadistica y Censos), published in 1960. On the basis of data furnished by University of Chile Economic Institute, Frederick Harbison and Charles A. Myers report that in 1956 (about the

of these companies (755) employed more than fifty people, but they accounted for 67 percent (about 145,000) of the total industrial labor force. Only 161 firms, or slightly less than 3 percent of the total, employed over 200 persons. This small minority, however, employed 44 percent of the industrial labor force, represented 50 percent of the sales, and generated 56 percent of the total value of industrial output. Seventy-five percent of the firms were located in the Santiago area.[3] The next two sections will sketch some of Chile's major development problems and some usual explanations of them.

Traditional and Modern Chile

Chile cannot be classified neatly according to standard measures of development. In many senses it represents a paradox of high social, political, and economic indexes of development which do not reflect realities. Chile lives between traditional and modern worlds, not as a country which is moving dynamically from the old to the new but as a nation which has attained many of the features of a modern society without discarding traditional patterns which stand in the way of development. Thus, Chile is, simultaneously, a land of promise and frustration: a symbol of potential immobilized by contradictions. The contradictions are evident in its political, social, and economic institutions.

Politically, Chile has been a symbol of civic restraint and respect for constitutional stability in a continent more renowned for dictatorship and *coups d'état*. There is a wide respect for rule by law, legitimate election, and orderly succession of officials. Even the revolutionary left and the reactionary right have stayed within legal and constitutional bounds. The military does not interfere in politics, and corruption is kept to a minimum.

It is in Chile's multiparty system that the political contradictions between traditional and modern Chile can be seen most clearly, for there are two parties within each of the three major positions of right, left, and center— one bound by custom and tradition and the other committed to change and development.

Socially, Chile seems to have the earmarks of a fairly developed society. The literacy rate is 80 percent. The country is rather urbanized: six out of

time of the last census) Chilean manufacturing industry employed 20 percent of the total labor force. Mining accounted for about 4 percent, commerce and services 34 percent, agriculture 28 percent, and others (including government) 14 percent. *Management in the Industrial World* (New York: McGraw-Hill, 1959), p. 170.

[3] On the basis of the 1957 Industrial Census, the United Nations Organization for Industrial Development estimated that the number of companies employing over 200 persons had increased to 190 by 1963, but no breakdown by sector was provided and no estimates given for later years. The median number of employees in these firms was estimated to be 521. *El desarrollo industrial de america latina: Chile* (Athens, Greece: Organization de las Naciones Unidas para el Desarrollo Industrial, 1967, ID/CONF. 1/R.B.P./3/Add. 7), pp. 25–26.

every ten people live in the cities, and one out of four lives in or around the capital city, Santiago. The complex social security system provides old age, medical, and family allowances for all employees; and labor laws provide for bonuses, profit sharing, and housing allowances. Only about a third of all Chileans in the labor force work in agriculture; about one of every five has a white-collar or professional occupation, many in services, and this figure jumps to one out of three in Santiago.

In contrast to these optimistic indexes, however, the most important characteristic of the Chilean social structure is the wide gulf which separates the lower classes from middle- and upper-class persons. Traditional societies are often characterized by a small aristocratic class and a large mass of peasants. Modernization creates new middle sectors composed of an industrial working class and a middle class of industrial and commercial entrepreneurs, civil servants, and white-collar professionals. This increase in the range of social strata, according to general social theory, is paralleled by a number of other changes: there is greater mobility between strata; social distinctions are not so sharp; and the distribution of income, status, and power is more equalitarian than in the past. These conditions have not developed in Chile.

Despite its increasingly modern profile, Chile's social structure has maintained many dysfunctional traditional rigidities.

Economic Frustration. Economically, Chile passed through a period of rapid growth in the 1930s and 1940s and then lapsed into a stagnation in the 1950s from which it has not recovered. Performance in agriculture has been disappointing and a constant sore point in political debate. Agrarian reform is needed badly, and agricultural production barely has kept up with the galloping population growth rate of 2.5 percent a year. Mining is another important area of the economy, and copper, the country's largest export, is subject to extreme price fluctuation in the world market. Chile, therefore, has had little control over its major means of earning critical foreign exchange. In a response to economic nationalism, however, the government recently moved to "Chileanize" the copper companies, hammering out an agreement with Anaconda to acquire 51 percent ownership and majorities on the boards of two joint companies in January 1970.

It is in industry that the results of economic frustration have been most obvious. The Depression of 1929 and World War II, as well as internal factors, spurred Chile in the development of import-substituting industries. Between 1930 and 1964 industrial production increased 94 percent, mainly from the growth of small firms producing light consumer goods. Large-scale production of iron, steel, chemicals, pharmaceuticals, paper, cellulose, and petroleum and its derivatives began between 1946 and 1953. This industrialization was supposed to lead to a growing and self-generating economy, but since 1953 there has been an unarrested drought of effective demand, and Chilean industry has remained virtually stagnant.[4] Increase in

---

[4]The reasons for Chile's economic stagnation have been the subject of endless discus-

real GNP reached a low of 1.1 percent in 1967 and is estimated to have reached only 2 to 3 percent last year.

The Chilean economy may be described as traditional in its unproductive and semifeudal agricultural system and in its lack of autonomy vis-à-vis fluctuations in world economic conditions. However, it also has developed the shell of modern industry and has made strenuous, if unproductive, efforts at stability and growth through diversification and import substitution. The contradictions between traditional and modern Chile may be found in its economic, as well as in its social and political, institutions. Here, too, Chile suffers from both the inadequacies of a traditional society and from the inabilities of a stagnant industrial one. Why has local industrial enterprise been unable to overcome the contradictions and the frustrations?

Common Explanations. Six answers usually were offered by Chilean businessmen for the paucity of effective and efficient industrial organization. Each answer has a strong appeal and has been mentioned frequently by those who have studied Chile.

1. Chile has a small market size. Of the nine million people in the country, only a fifth to a quarter of that number are actually part of the national economy and social life. A small domestic market inhibits economies of scale. The country's geography increases costs and fractionalizes the market further.

2. Most Chilean manufacturers lack export opportunities. They are unable to compete in foreign markets because of Chile's lack of any comparative advantage in the manufacturing sector. Copper, the country's major earner of foreign exchange, is subject to severe and uncontrollable fluctuations, and Chile lacks buying power for its purchase of major imports.

3. Moderate short-term periods of inflation often act as a stimulus to economic growth, but Chile has suffered from the most severe rises in the level of prices in all of Latin America. While a few powerful groups have been able to grow rich in the process, the overall effect on the economy has been devastating. The price index rose an average of 18 percent annually in the 1940s, 36 percent in the 1950s, and 25 percent in the 1960s. Chile's persistent bout with inflation is one of the major retarders of its economic growth.

---

sion and controversy. For a treatment of this subject, see Jorge Ahumada, *En vez de la miseria* (Santiago: Editorial del Pacifico, 1958); David Felix, "Chile," in Pepelasis Adamantios, Leon Mears, and Irma Adelman, *Economic Development: Analysis and Case Studies* (New York: Harper, 1961); Albert O. Hirschman, *Journeys Toward Progress* (New York: Twentieth Century Fund, 1963), and *Latin American Issues, Essays and Comments* (New York: Twentieth Century Fund, 1961); *Instituto de Economia de Chile en el periodo 1950–1963*, 2 vols. (Santiago: Universidad de Chile, Instituto de Economia, 1963); Milton D. Lower, "Institutional Basis of Economic Stagnation in Chile," *Journal of Economic Issues* 3 (March 1969); Oscar E. Muñoz, "An Essay on the Process of Industrialization in Chile Since 1914," *Yale Economic Essays* 8 (Spring 1968); Aníbal Pinto Santa Cruz, *Chile: Un economía deficil* (Mexico: Fondo de Cultural Economica, 1964), and *Chile: Un caso de desarrollo frustrado* (Santiago: Editorial Universitaria, 1959).

4. Chilean enterprise lacks sufficient capital. Chronic inflation has discouraged savings as a potential source of capital, and low rates of return on investment have dried up another source. In their efforts to control the country's financial instability and to provide greater social benefits to large numbers of people, the government has tied up a third source by imposing tough credit restrictions. The absence of medium- and long-term credit has obliged businesses to finance their investment needs through short-term credit, foreign loans (which increase the economy's external dependency), not providing for depreciation of plant and equipment, and retention of profits. Many smaller companies argue that the Central Bank, which administers the credit system, is subject to favoritism and personal influences. The result is an increase in perceived risk in long-term investment and a sense of permanent financial insecurity.

5. The government has instituted price controls. This was done for several reasons: to curb inflation, to reduce deficit spending, to direct productive resources to determined areas, to protect national industry, to facilitate redistribution of the national income, and to inculcate in the consumer an anti-inflationary attitude. The businessman's argument is that price controls do not curb inflation but do cut profit margins and put industries at a competitive disadvantage, particularly in the world market, because price-fixing reduces the incentive to produce.

6. Bureaucratic regulations and restrictions have become so abundant that the idea of working through the *trámites* (red-tape procedures) is enough to discourage any new and innovative activities. Since information is often incomplete and systems for storage and retrieval are often cumbersome and slow, as is common in most developing countries, decisions frequently are made on the basis of faulty and inadequate data.

Validity of Popular Explanations. Organizational underdevelopment and economic stagnation are interrelated phenomena, but these explanations too often confuse cause with effect. There is some truth in each of them; but while each describes the situation which confronts Chilean private enterprise, it cannot explain or predict the inadequate organizational response in specific circumstances.

The size of Chile's market is small, to be sure, but the country is experiencing extremely rapid population growth (2.5 percent annually), and the majority of this growth is located in the cities where people do take part in the goods and services of an industrial economy. As the economies of Denmark, Israel, and Switzerland suggest, population is certainly not the only or even the major factor in limiting market size.

Many practical problems stand in the way of realizing a Latin American common market, and Chilean businessmen cannot plan on the basis of the distant dreams of politicians and development economists. What is most striking, however, is their belief that their industrial organization is so inefficient that their protected position within the country would be lost if free trade prevailed. Their attitudes tell more than do the tactical problems about the causes of organizational underdevelopment.

Because of inflation, many members of the nation's middle class have the attitude, "To save money in Chile you must buy things as fast as you can." While this helps perpetuate the inflation which victimizes the consumer, it certainly does not discourage manufacturers from supplying various consumer goods. Inflation can be blamed for many things, but holding it responsible for inefficiencies in the operation of enterprise is stretching the point too far. At best, the relationship is indirect.

The Chilean businessman's problem with capital shortage is like the plain girl's problem in attracting men: it's not what you have but the way that you use it. If lack of funds keeps business organizations from developing, then those with the highest capitalization ought to be the most profitable and fastest growing. This is not always the case.

The same argument holds true for price control: it cannot entirely explain why two manufacturers of a product selling for the same price have different unit costs. Managers do not like price control; they say it wipes out their profits and reduces their incentives. What it actually does is to redirect incentive and motivate managers to look for new ways of earning profits by circumventing or getting a readjustment of price levels. The main point is that incentives are psychological phenomena and managers' motivations are oriented defensively toward changing political policy rather than directed offensively toward implementing effective economic ideas.

The last argument, that bureaucratic red tape reduces motivation and organizational effectiveness, applies more to the rules and procedures of government administration than to the internal operation of private enterprise. Dealing with a government ministry can be a trying and complicated affair, but it does not *ipso facto* produce confusion and inefficiency within private business organizations.

If some of these theories give only a partial answer, confuse cause with effect, and describe the facts but do not explain or predict them—then what alternative explanation can make intelligible the underdevelopment of organizational behavior in Chilean private enterprise?

Politics of Organizational
Underdevelopment

An alternative hypothesis is, simply, that the behavior of Chilean businessmen and the consequences of this behavior for organizational development are both intelligible and predictable because Chilean businessmen act on the belief that

> the private enterprise system (capitalism) is struggling for survival.

The purpose here is not to show how many entrepreneurs and managers believe that capitalism is struggling to survive in Chile nor to test the truth or falsity of this hypothesis.[5] The purpose is to show the effect of actions based on such a belief. Some logical implications of the belief are set forth below. It will be seen that these describe the facts of organizational under-development in much of Chilean industry. The concurrence of theory and fact does not "prove" the theory, but it does demonstrate that the theory will clarify and predict behavior. The hypothesis is not meant to suggest a single-factor explanation nor is it meant to describe a solely Chilean phenomenon.

(1) Survival replaces profit-making as the predominant orientation. The most elemental goal of the businessman is profits. An essential prerequisite for attaining this goal is survival. To the extent this prerequisite is threat-ened, all his time, energy, and effort are diverted to survival at the expense of fulfilling his goal. The means become an end in themselves. The most frequent response to questions about how organizations modernize and develop was "How can I worry about development when I am trying to survive?"

The national election at the end of 1970 is going to be the third one in Chile to decide whether or not the government becomes communist. Each time you wonder how much longer we can hold out.
Of course socialism is very much a matter of emotional ambience and very difficult to measure; but if you use national investments in the public sector as an index, then it is quite obvious that socialism has been increasing significantly here, in Chile, over many years.

Survival, according to this belief, will come from election results which shy away from the left and from reprieves from public-sector spending but not from efforts concentrated on the growth and development of corporate organization.
The focus on survival also contains elements of fatalism and passivity. It is basically a defensive and security-seeking orientation: to hold out against the seemingly inexorable onslaught of those who would abolish the private enterprise system entirely. Since Chilean businessmen certainly are not a monolithic group, there is a range of attitudes about the role of capitalism in the future of Chile; but all feel that their system and ideology are under attack, and in only two cases did a respondent take the approach that "a good offense is the best defense." All of them believe that private enter-prise "could make a substantial contribution" to the development of the country, as obviously expected, but their talk suggested doubts as to whether it would have the chance to demonstrate this.

(2) The focus of competition shifts from profits to power, and economic organizations become highly politicized. The struggle for existence of one economic system vis-à-vis another is basically a fight for power, not profit.

---

[5]A few of the organizations studied were highly developed, according to our definition, and quite successful, if measured by profits and growth.

The businessman who operates according to the belief that capitalism is fighting for survival in Chile sees the struggle as political, not economic, in nature. Increased profits, he argues, will not improve his chances for survival if the private enterprise system is abolished; but survival of the system at least will enable him to operate. He believes that in theory there is a direct relationship between the effective direction of private corporate organization and the strength of the private enterprise system; but in practice he does not apply this belief to planning, coordinating, and appraising the organization's activities. In other words, effective economic management is not sufficient, and it even may not be necessary.

The politicized quality of management has increased greatly in recent years, although it remains a reaction orientation rather than an initiating one. It is not that ownership and policy positions are held on the basis of political affiliation, but that the policies and decisions reached are more and more influenced by political issues.

(3) The time horizon of the manager is determined by changes in the political system more than by the economic conditions of the market or of his enterprise. The approach of the politicized manager to the elections is that the outcome of the national election, which occurs every six years, will be the best indicator not so much of his chances for profit as of his chances for survival. After such an election there is a period of from six months to a year during which business, as well as the rest of the country, watches to see how the strengths of the new president develop, what his policies are, and whether he is able to implement them through control of Congress. There usually follows a three- to four-year period in which planning and major decision-making are resumed and then a one- to three-year period when people again begin to put off decisions until after the next presidential election.

It is not difficult to see why economic organizations remain underdeveloped when systematic planning on the basis of anticipated requirements is replaced by the suspension of major decision-making and planning on the basis of an unpredictable political environment. Planning for the efficient expenditure of resources is not likely to develop when it is not considered to bear any relation to profit-making, when the future seems so uncertain and when there is extreme difficulty securing long-term credit.

(4) Internal operations are believed to be less relevant to achieving organizational goals than is influence in the surrounding environment. The Chilean industrial elite are educated in what they call "modern methods of business administration," but they find them of secondary importance, at most, for accomplishing their goals. Two typical statements from business leaders were

I have learned about computers and market analysis, human relations and financial forecasting, but in making a profit all of these are less important than having the ear of government ministers and other key officials.

For me to run my company successfully, I have to spend my time in places like the Ministry of Economics, the Central Bank, and the Chamber of Industry and Commerce, not in my office or in my factory.

Senior managers indicated they spent between a third and half of their working time in and around government offices.

In sum, the pressures to justify their position and needs to the public (and to its officials in government) supersedes the pressures to coordinate, control, and direct the activities of their workers and employees.

To the believer in this ideological struggle, his efforts must be devoted to saving the private enterprise system as much as to saving his own particular company; this also diverts his attention from developing more efficient administrative practices. In addition to the manager's focus on his own company's government relations, therefore, the heads of enterprise who were interviewed also reported they devote between a quarter and a third of their time to voluntary associations whose major purposes are to promote the interest of private enterprise as a whole, or its various subsectors and specific industries. According to the responses, then, the presidents and general managers of major Chilean corporations spend around 60 to 80 percent of their time in matters either external to or only indirectly related to the organization of their companies. There is little time to subject corporate policies to self-conscious scrutiny and organization structure to systematic design.

(5) The board of directors of enterprise plays a very powerful role, whereas senior executives are of little consequence. Connection, not competence, determines performance. Decision-making power within the enterprise will lie with those people who deal most directly with the power-determining elements in the political environment outside the firm. As one of the leading Chilean management consultants explained,

The board treats top executives, here in Chile, like you treat middle-level managers in the United States. The general manager is really nothing more than a watchdog. He is picked so that he won't run away with the dishes. [A Chilean expression comparable to "rob you blind."] The general manager is picked by the board, and the board is generally dominated by the president, who is everything. The general manager, however, is picked to be a person who is neat, not too ambitious, and who displays an almost servile attitude. In Chile, managers are refined and intelligent serfs.

Except for a few highly developed firms, this judgment seems as true as it is harsh. In addition to major policy decisions, most presidents and their boards also oversee the implementation of these decisions through simultaneous administrative control of operational activities. Not only will a board decide on a new plant installation, for example, but it also plays the major role in securing necessary loans and permits, determines the plans and designs for its construction, and often makes periodic on-site inspection of the progress and process. When long-term planning is considered difficult, if not impossible, then top managers find themselves spending more time in day-to-day administration. Also, when the head of an enterprise believes the life and growth of his company depends on external political affiliations, and not on strategic planning or on operational efficiency, then he does not consider his executive personnel very important, and he will develop neither them nor the system in which they function. In the politics of organizational underdevelopment, management is a frill.

In the choice of a governing board, connection is more important than competence. The primary function of the board is not to have legal responsibility for the control and maintenance of the organization; nor is it to plan goals and policies, allocate resources, and coordinate and appraise the work of the enterprise. Although it may concern itself with these functions, its main task is to influence the strategic power centers in the environment: banks and government agencies.

(6) Daily activities become radicalized, and normal conflicts become polarized. The result is a zero-sum approach to problem solving. Since Chile has institutionalized democratic political processes more successfully than most other Latin American republics, few businessmen believe that leftist forces will take over control of the government by illegal means. The fear is, however, that if the left should win power through the electoral process it would then nationalize companies of any significant size. The fight for political power is seen as a battle for the right to establish a different brand of essentially economic principles as official.

The normal conflict involved in everyday behavior therefore becomes heightened by the idea that literally everything is at stake. A question as to whether the screw on a machine should be tightened or loosened becomes not just a difference of opinion between a manager and a worker but a confrontation of two ideological systems which are fundamentally opposed. The tension on the screw is no longer susceptible to rational determination, because the issue of confrontation involves a politicized struggle which cannot be resolved on nonideological grounds.

The perceived struggle for survival can be described best in terms of a zero-sum game. In a zero-sum game, winning and losing are in inverse relation to one another; one side wins only to the extent that the other side loses. In a nonzero-sum (or positive-sum) game, winning is relative to an independent criterion: one side may be gaining more than, but not necessarily at the expense of, the other side. In economic terms, the rich get richer and the poor get poorer in a zero-sum approach, whereas some get richer faster than others in a nonzero-sum situation. "There is cooperation in increasing the pie and competition in sharing it"[6] in positive-sum orientations. Positive-sum game orientations are impossible when political ideologies are polarized. Public decisions then must rest on absolute principles and

---

[6]Kenneth E. Boulding, *Conflict and Defense* (New York: Harper, 1962), p. 192. Also see Thomas Schelling, *The Strategy of Conflict* (Cambridge: Harvard University Press, 1960), chap. iv.

cannot be based on compromise. Under these conditions, management-labor disputes are more likely to lead to strikes (as has been the case in Chile) than to mediation. Also, there are negative attitudes toward investment because of a fear of expropriation.

(7) The private enterprise system and managerial decisions made within it become sacred. If a specific private company fails, a tendency develops to see this demise as proof of a threat to the existence of the entire enterprise system, whether the particular company in question was managed poorly or not. To the believer in the struggle, it is difficult not to see increased government control over industry as an attempt to "take over everything." That point is well put by Anthony Jay when he says,

> To renounce Christianity for Islam in the Middle Ages was not to make a private decision about your own worship, it was to threaten the security of your fellow men who were busy keeping (or failing to keep) the armed forces of Islam out of their fields and towns. You might have no thoughts of treachery but you would have a job to prove it, just as American communists have a job proving that they are loyal to the state they belong to despite subscribing to the opposing political theory.[7]

The stakes involved in the struggle are not merely two different sets of economic or organizational principles but an entire "way of life." The potential harm of strikes and credit restrictions is not limited to a man's business and his freedom to administer it as he sees fit: it is also a threat to his family, his friends, and to the likelihood that he will continue to live in that country. His economic good fortune must be legitimated on moral grounds, particularly when it is threatened. In this atmosphere there is little room for a reasoned analysis in order to make the optimum choice of available alternatives. "Those are the kinds of words that come from North American textbooks on economics and administration," said several managers, "but they are of no help to us here." Indeed, the writings of Machiavelli and Luther make more sense of their perceived situation than do the works of Peter Drucker and Chester Barnard.

On September 4, 1970, almost three million Chileans voted in the presidential election.[8] The winning candidate was Dr. Salvador Allende, a Marxist who is backed by a left-wing coalition that has its organizational core in the Chilean Communist and Socialist parties. Allende received 36.3 percent of the votes, a victory margin of 39,000 votes, or 1.4 percent of the total, over the right-wing candidate, Jorge Alessandri. The Christian-Democratic candidate ran a poor third.

This is the first time in Latin American politics that a Marxist revolutionary candidate and program have won in a free and orderly election. Dr. Allende's victory is all the more significant because he has promised to destroy the right wing's economic base by fully nationalizing all basic

---

[7]*Management and Machiavelli* (London: Hodder & Stoughton, 1967), pp. 50–51.
[8]The following three paragraphs were added to the article for inclusion in this volume.
—Eds.

industry (including U.S. copper, iron, nitrate, and other interests with an estimated value of over $500 million), banks, and communications systems; and by taking over all large private farms and turning them into peasant cooperatives. At the time this book went to press, the Chilean business community, as well as many others, believed that this election would seal the fate of private enterprise in Chile. The answer remains to be seen.

What is clear, however, is that politicized management will take precedence over professional management in both the public and private sectors in Chile for some time to come.

Theory and Ideologies of Management in the Third World

An ideology is a set of ideas, more or less shared by a social group, which articulates a certain picture of reality and sets up desirable values or goals for the group to strive for or (as in the case of Chile) preserve. In this concluding section, a brief look at managerial ideologies in today's lesser-developed countries can help answer the initial question: Why do some societies retain traditional forms of organization whereas others are able to organize themselves effectively and efficiently in order to help build a modern society?

During early periods of industrialization in both capitalist Europe and pre-communist Russia, the ideologies of management were concerned primarily with the justification of industrial activity and of its leaders to the society at large. As the industrial way of life became accepted, the focus of this ideology shifted from "the effort to win public acceptance *for* the economic activities with which the employers were identified" to "the problems of coordination and direction *in* large-scale enterprises."[9] In other words, the consideration of management as an organizational problem, internal to the enterprise, did not belong to the early phase of the industrial era. Instead, the ideological focus was external to the organization, reflecting the conflict between social classes brought about by industrialization.

In modern industry of both the capitalist and communist world, the earlier ideological focus of management on justifying its existence has been relegated to "the important, but separate, task of developing the public relations between the enterprise and the community."[10] The ideologies of management in the industrial world concern themselves with justifying their systems of organization in which a few command and many obey.

Today managers in developing countries do not have to justify their existence in terms of an industrial way of life which they seek to create, for this is already a universal goal. Yet, in many of these countries, the heads of enterprise are not free to turn their attention to the ideological and practical problems of internal management within their organizations. Their

---

[9]Reinhard Bendix, *Work and Authority in Industry* (New York: Harper, 1963); p. 9, emphasis added.
[10]Ibid.

ideological focus is still external to principles of organizations because the society has not yet decided between the capitalist path of the first industrialized nations, the communist road of the second group of modernized countries, or on an appropriate and specific mix between the two.

In the developing and unaligned third world, managers of private enterprise often feel they have not justified their position in *society* to a sufficient degree that they may turn their ideological focus to their position in the *organization*. This is exactly the problem which confronts the Chilean businessman. Until the society determines whether or not private enterprise has a permanent future in the nation's political economy, he will continue to seek to preserve that system in the face of perceived threats to its survival. In his reaction to this perceived situation, he is unwittingly helping to make it real in its consequences. The resolution of this question, however, will not be made at any one moment in time, but will be the result of continual and complex changes in the structure of Chilean society. Thus, unfortunately, it is probable that the politics of organizational underdevelopment will continue to characterize Chile's stagnating industrial enterprise.

41

Authority and Control in Mexican Enterprise

Stanley M. Davis

If management is to control and direct the activities of its workers and employees, it must have a strategy of organization and a system of values to support it. As societies develop and industrialization takes place, organizations grow in both size and complexity. The task of enterprise management increases proportionately and becomes a full-time concern. The coordination of men and machines by administration requires an ordering of positions and duties, an integration of a variety of functions in order to achieve a more or less defined set of goals. Sufficient managerial resources are therefore necessary in order to accomplish this task.

Since organization involves more than one person, it also means the delegation of various functions to different people throughout the organizational hierarchy. The larger and more complex the organizational structure, the more delegation there must be. Delegation may be either of tasks or of authority; it may refer to the increased division of labor and the specialization of job functions, or to the chain of command by which orders are passed down. Delegation of authority, or the decentralization of decision-making, involves a strategy of organization which gives increased discretion to subordinates and has often been considered a logical consequence of organizational development. In this light, we turn to an examination of the system of authority within Mexican business organizations, to the characteristics of its development, the problems which it creates, and its relation to social change and the development of managerial resources.

Centralization

. . . The most characteristic feature of the authority system is its centralization. In the more traditional Mexican firms, it is the centralization of *all* power in the one top man who is simultaneously organizer, owner, manager, and sole decision-maker. Here, management is a person, not a position, concept, or function. Authority likewise resides in this person and is not spread throughout a managerial organization, for indeed no such organization exists.

Reprinted from Stanley M. Davis, "Managerial Resource Development in Mexico," in *Latin American Management: Development and Performance*, ed. Robert R. Rehder (Reading, Mass.: Addison-Wesley Publishing Co., 1968), pp. 166–179, by permission of the publisher.

The traditional entrepreneur of a small enterprise runs an operation in which the only division of labor is between himself and a few workers. Above this barest minimum, the introduction of an intermediate status creates the rank of *empleado de confianza* (trusted employee). *Maestros,* skilled senior workers, are usually among the first such *confiados.* The growing structural complexity, here, is an unplanned consequence of industrial expansion. These early *confiados* are tomorrow's supervisors and department heads, and the important point is that their personal merits are established before their positions are defined.

Seen positively, the result is stability in the organization's structure, a general absence of the *empleado-obrero* (employee/worker) barrier, and little tension regarding the foreman role. Seen negatively, such entrepreneurially run firms tend to develop along lines of an increased differentiation from below, but with slight development, differentiation, or access to the top. Despite the natural evolution of an increased division of labor, however, all ranks are still subordinate to the top. What little authority *is* delegated is done so on the basis of *confianza,* not competence: you do not entrust a man with any authority simply because he has had training and is skilled at his job.

William F. Whyte and Graciela Flores report on this attitude in Peru as the reflection of a general cultural sentiment:

The prevailing system of centralization of control seems to be based upon beliefs that you cannot trust your subordinates to do the right things unless you watch them closely. Delegation of authority and responsibility requires a degree of faith in people that is not common in Peru.

. . . The suspicious point of view [manifested by the Peruvian] would suggest that you had better not do something for the other fellow because he will just interpret that as a sign of weakness and take advantage of you in the future.[1] [Trans. S.M.D.]

In family-owned firms, fathers sometimes display this attitude of suspicion toward their sons, especially during periods of succession when the transfer of authority is a major issue. This may manifest itself in several ways. In one type, effective authority is completely denied to the son and is viewed as a threat to the power of the father. In a second pattern, authority is given to the son to carry on in his father's footsteps but not to expand on his own initiative; the ultimate authority still rests with the father. A third type of centralization involves the attempts of one branch in a family firm to wrest power away from another family group.[2]

The unwillingness to grant legitimate power to hire employees is even

---

[1] William F. Whyte and Graciela Flores, "Los valores y el crecimiento económico en el Perú," in *La industrialización en América Latina,* Joseph A. Kahl, ed. (México: Fondo de Cultura Económica, 1965), p. 228. For similar reports on delegation in Argentine industry, see Tomás R. Fillol, *Social Factors in Economic Development: The Argentine Case* (Cambridge, Mass.: The M.I.T. Press, 1964), pp. 18–21.

[2] For a complete discussion of these three patterns, see Stanley M. Davis, "Entrepreneurial Succession," *Administrative Science Quarterly* 13 (December 1968).

stronger than the hesitancy to delegate authority to other family members. This is most apparent in the firms which apply the more literal and traditional meaning of *empleado de confianza,* the small number of nonrelated employees who can be trusted.[3] Even when these individuals are given responsibility, however, they are less often given authority, and while they may formally be considered part of management, they have no decision-making powers. This prompted one observer to describe a Mexican manager as a man who "would delegate work but not authority."

No matter how highly placed a traditional employee may be, he still lacks the functional perquisite of his office, namely, authority of his own. This is because of the intimate bond between ownership and authority in Mexican enterprise. The notion was well expressed by one engineer who simply said, "If the men who give the orders were not the owners, they could not give the orders." The owner is the ultimate, and often only, source of authority in the firm; hired management is there to carry out his directives. Thus, there is a distinct separation between the owner of a firm and his employee underlings. Charles Myers reports on the same distinctions in Chile:

Few top operating managers are members of boards, for there is still a social distinction between the director of a firm and its hired manager. The latter is considered an "employee"—no matter how highly placed.[4]

When one Mexican worker was asked about the difference between the owners and the top-ranking employee in his firm, he said, "The differences are great. The *patrones* are *patrones,* but Sanchez is a servant, like me."

The same gap seems to exist between the few above and the many below in Brazilian enterprise. Pereira reports that this gap creates strong disparities between production and managerial systems:

Often, we find side-by-side the most modern machines and the oldest systems of management. More expressive, however, is the conflict within the typical small- or medium-sized family enterprise, closed, paternalistic, working at a relatively low level of productivity, but using modern techniques, electricity, assembly line, [and] modern equipment. . . . In other words, the forms of ownership and management of the enterprises are generally backward when compared to the productive system.[5]

Speaking of Latin America in general, Lauterbach sees the concentration of authority in Latin management as due to the fact that

---

[3]Fernando H. Cardoso describes this same situation in Brazil and its negative effect on expansion and investment due to limited executive and administrative capabilities. *El empresario industrial en América Latina: Brazil* (Mar del Plata: Naciones Unidas Comisión Económica para América Latina, 1963), E/CN.12/642/Add. 2, pp. 25–26.
[4]Frederick Harbison and Charles A. Myers, *Management in the Industrial World* (New York: McGraw-Hill Book Company, 1959), p. 178.
[5]L. C. Bresser Pereira, "The Rise of Middle Class and Middle Management in Brazil," *Journal of Inter-American Studies,* Vol. IV, No. 3 (July 1962), pp. 322–323.

. . . without the top man's political links and family standing little could be achieved in the conduct of *any* of these firms, and informal conversations with friends or influential people take up a very substantial part of the top man's activity. Since the latter thus occupies a unique and authoritarian position, delegation of his major activities is considered impossible by himself and the others.[6]

* * *

The conjunction of ownership and management plays a critical role in determining the authority system in Mexican enterprise, but it cannot neatly be logged into the traditional category of one-man-rule companies. Among entrepreneurs heading large, complex, and modern industrial firms, some are characteristic of their traditional counterparts in smaller companies, while others hardly differ from executive employees heading operations of all sizes. With the growth of an enterprise, and an increase in its division of labor, the tendency to concentrate authority in one's own hands also develops among middle-level management. The extent of this development depends upon the nature of the man or men in the top position(s); the more they are willing to delegate authority, the stronger becomes the control of the department heads. Foreign firms, invariably headed by executive management, show a marked tendency toward this development of departmental autocracy. Unlike management in the German firm, there are two loci of centralization: one at the top and the other at the middle.

In Mexico, the tendency of department heads to concentrate their authority in their own hands, rather than delegate some of it to subordinates, is in part a reaction to their lack of ownership. In an attempt to legitimize their positions, middle-level managers will sometimes turn to their technical competence as justification for their holding of power. In all cases, and especially when the expertise is lacking, department heads often attempt to impose a personal cast on everything within their domain; they may try to create their own little kingdoms.

One observer described the situation in his factory by showing me an article from a Mexican magazine, entitled "Win Over Your Employees." At the top was a cartoon in which a man with a crown on his head stood like a conqueror with his hands crossed over his puffed-out chest, and with one foot on top of a worker. To the right was another worker bowing down to the crowned man, and behind the man was a third worker sticking out his tongue and waving his hands from his ears. The respondent pointed to the drawing and said, "This is the problem we have here; the middle managers all want to be kings."

In a foreign company employing close to 1,000 people and having sixteen department heads, the general manager described his problem with centralization at the middle:

---

[6]Albert Lauterbach, *Enterprise in Latin America* (Ithaca: Cornell University Press, 1966), pp. 8–9. This distinction between owner management and executive management, as it relates to authority within the firm, is perhaps strongest in Germany. . . .

We have to restrain the tendency of the departmental managers to make their own little kingdoms because they may do something which sets a precedent. For instance, if the sweeper in their department comes to them and says, "I need more money," and they say, "Sure, I'll give you fifty *centavos* an hour more." Their attitude is that we've only got two sweepers, so that's only costing eight *pesos* a day, which can't affect the firm. But that would immediately mean that everyone in the plant had to have fifty *centavos* more. But they don't see it that way. They feel, "Why do I have to consult with the Personnel Office on the matter of fifty *centavos* an hour? It's taking away my dignity to have to tell a man I can't decide, myself on such a minor matter."

The middle-level manager is interested in protecting and enhancing every bit of authority that has been granted to him. The more authority he has, the more secure he feels in his position. The result is to create a hoarding effect:[7] the more authority you accumulate, the more indispensable you are; and as a corollary, abide by the rule not to grant authority to anyone when you can take care of the matter yourself. One of the key values of good management in the United States is the ability to delegate. In North America, the junior executive who is able to delegate authority is on his way *up*; in Mexico, however, the popular interpretation would be that this man is on his way out.[8]

Thus, for both owner management at the top and executive management at middle levels, hoarding of authority is part of the *modus operandi* of Mexican enterprise. Even in countries where decentralization is considered a positive managerial value, however, its implementation is proportionate to an increase in problems of control. Whether seen as a philosophy of management or as a logical part of industrial development, the delegation of authority involves a major paradox: "The more top management tries to decentralize decision-making, the more it must centralize its control of decisions."[9] Mexican management sees little efficacy in this distinction because it is the very fear of loss of control which prevents any decentralization from taking place. Authority and control are seen as identities. There is little or no distinction made between the two because of the feeling that you cannot maintain control unless you also maintain complete authority, and vice versa.

It should be noted, however, that centralization of one's business and of one's authority are not the same thing. Oriol Pi-Sunyer has shown how the heads of industrial enterprise in a rural region of Mexico prefer to diversify their business holdings in order to better maintain control:

---

[7]Since "centralize" means to concentrate in *one* place, the term "hoarding" is used when authority is concentrated at different levels and among different individuals.

[8]See Michel Crozier, *The Bureaucratic Phenomenon* (Chicago: University of Chicago Press, 1964) for similar remarks about the French tendency to visualize authority as something which must be complete to be effective. It is not something to share, as in the U.S. view.

[9]Editors of *Fortune, The Eexcutive Life* (New York: Doubleday & Company, Inc., 1956), p. 139.

Rather than expand existing business to a size that would permit them to operate beyond the confines of the regional market, Zamora entrepreneurs prefer to launch another enterprise designed to tap a further segment of the regional market; expansion takes the form of multiplication.[10]

He goes on to suggest that:

. . . [the local] technique of multiplying the units of production rather than expanding a given unit is an attempt on the part of the entrepreneurs to increase total holdings while still retaining the organizational advantages accruing from small units of production.[11]

A central part of these organizational advantages involves the system of authority. Zamoran entrepreneurs decentralize their business holdings *in order to* maintain better control, and at the same time increase profits by tapping other segments of the market. Diversification within a regional market, moreover, helps create enough places for relatives to hold positions of authority without jeopardizing too large a financial investment at any one time, in case the relative proves incompetent. Entering the national market, on the other hand, would require increases in size per unit and perhaps vertical integration. Besides concentrating the financial risk, this would increase pressures to establish middle layers of management, and thus threaten the direct control which the entrepreneurs can maintain within the regional context.[12]

*   *   *

Responsibility and Bypassing

The centralization of authority above creates problems of responsibility below. One of the most prevalent complaints by superiors about their subordinate personnel is the latter's unwillingness to accept any responsibility. In owner-managed firms, this complaint is often directed at middle-level executive management, if there is any; and when centralization occurs at

---

[10]Oriol Pi-Sunyer, "A Regional Coalition Economy in Mexico: An Historical Ethnography of Zamora, Michoacan" (doctoral dissertation, Harvard University, 1962), p. 354.

[11]Ibid., p. 364.

[12]A corollary of this restrictive control and family-centered outlook is the "reluctance to merge with other enterprises even when the separate units are much too small for optimum efficiency," and even an unwillingness to "promote joint action on industry-wide problems." W. Paul Strassmann, "The Industrialist," in *Continuity and Change in Latin America*, ed. John J. Johnson (Stanford, Calif.: Stanford University Press, 1964), p. 168 (R9); and Thomas C. Cochran, *The Puerto Rican Businessman* (Philadelphia: University of Pennsylvania Press, 1959), p. 108 (R10). Frederick Harbison and Eugene Burgess report similar occurrences among family-centered firms in France, Belgium, and Italy in "Modern Management in Western Europe," *American Journal of Sociology*, Vol. LX, No. 1 (July 1954), pp. 15–23. It is worth noting here that Torcuato Di Tella (R10), the great Argentine entrepreneur, faced these same problems, but resolved them differently. The history of Di Tella and his company, S.I.A.M., are the exception in Latin American entrepreneurial development.

the middle level, the complaint is usually directed at the foreman. Ordinary workers are almost universally charged with a lack of responsibility by management in Mexico.

One personnel manager described a typical problem involving responsibility. He said that if a department head gave an incorrect order to a supervisor, the supervisor would carry it out without saying anything, even if he knew the order was wrong. Later, when his department head would ask why he had carried out the order, he would answer that he had been told to do so. A general manager in another company reported the same phenomenon, saying:

I have to be very careful what I say to people. If I say "do something" and I haven't thought it out well, they will often go and do it, even though they know that it hasn't been too well thought out. There aren't many people here who would argue with me. I don't mean because they're unwilling to, or because they're afraid of me; they just feel that this is my factory and I can do what I like in it. And it's very difficult to get that attitude out of people.

An observer in another company reported that workers and employees had adopted the attitude "knowledge is power."[13] Even if someone knew how to do something which was expected of him, he would not do it unless he was explicitly told to do so. A clear definition of job responsibility, in this case, would have established amounts of authority: no one was willing to do this, especially at the top, and the result was a continual power struggle which pervaded all levels.

In a third firm, a delivery date had to be decided. The department head in charge of the product in question said that delivery could not be made within a week, but the planning manager told the general manager that it could be done within five days. The boss was pleased with the early promised delivery date and displeased with the department head's estimate. After the meeting, the planning manager said to the department head: "Why did you tell him that? You know he wants to be happy. It would have been better to tell him we can have it in five days and then, when the time is up, tell him the machine is overloaded, or something like that."

While these examples reflect only part of reality, they are quite common, and hence influence behavior.[14] To the extent that the absence of responsibility does exist, it is largely a consequence of centralization at the top. When superiors are unwilling to delegate authority, subordinates do not want to accept responsibility. To the extent that the lack of responsibility at lower levels exists independently of management's efforts to centralize, however, it does reinforce tendencies in that direction. When subordinates are unwilling to accept responsibility, management will be hesitant to grant

---

[13]The respondent, here, actually used the verb *conocer*, which has the implication "to know someone," rather than the verb *saber*, "to know how to do something." In the context, he was referring to the latter kind of knowledge, but his choice of verb also stresses the importance of the personal element involved in carrying out an order.
[14]For similar findings, see John Fayerweather, *The Executive Overseas* (Syracuse, N.Y.: Syracuse University Press, 1959).

them any authority. Speaking of this vicious circle as common in most developing countries, Albert Waterson states that "a general reluctance to take responsibility on one hand and failure to delegate authority on the other lead to overcentralization and delays in decision making."[15]

Another critical effort of the centralization of authority is bypassing. A major principle of organization theory is the necessity of an orderly transmission of information up and down the organization's hierarchy, through the maintenance of an explicit line of authority. According to this principle, effective control can be maintained only if an order from above is filtered through all successively subordinate positions until it reaches its intended recipient. In other words, if the director of a company orders a certain product to be made, he does not give the order directly to the workers who will make it. Instead, he transmits to his general manager, who in turn passes it on to the appropriate department head, who then gives the order to the foreman, who sees that the workers carry out the original order. The same is true, holds the theory, for all upward communication. Bypassing occurs when one or more levels in the organization hierarchy are jumped in the process.

Bypassing is an extremely common phenomenon in Mexican organizations. It is particularly widespread in traditional systems of enterprise, which are small in size, and characterized by an informal and personal system of management. Here, it is easy for the head of the company to communicate directly with someone at any level, without the implication of thereby criticizing his immediate subordinate(s). This is especially true in a family firm, when his subordinate is a son or cousin. The informal and largely unstructured quality of lines of authority depends almost entirely on the discretion of the man at the top and his subordinates' personal loyalty to him.

Under the conditions described above, bypassing is rarely a problem. Formal lines of authority are seldom defined and both superiors and subordinates have direct and frequent access to one another. What few individuals there are who occupy middle positions do so, as we have said, because of their personal connections with the owner. The relationship between a *patrón* and his workers is not something that they are about to tamper with by trying to impose themselves as intermediary.

This relationship between the owner or owning family at the top and the workers at the bottom, and the consequent bypassing of intermediates, is something desired by both parties. When it is not desired, then bypassing becomes a problem, and this change is usually instigated at the top.

The owner-manager of a very centralized and very authoritarian firm permitted frequent upward bypassing among his 150 personnel, but refused to reciprocate by taking any direct action himself. His office was in a secluded corner of the company, yet all sorts of people were continually walking right in for various reasons. When queried about this constant traffic, he replied:

[15]Albert Waterson, *Development Planning: Lessons of Experience* (Baltimore: Johns Hopkins Press, 1965), p. 290.

I let anyone come in. They don't even have to knock; you noticed that. They can walk right in, because if you always have the door closed, and they have to ask, they think you are too high up and that no one can talk to you. Even the guy who washes the car outside can come and talk to me. They know I can't decide anything. They tell me everything, but I'm just a wall. They tell me they want a raise in salary, they've been fired, they want some money; they tell me all sorts of things. I always write down everything they want and then I go through the ranks and say, "So and so came to me and told me all of this; what's it all about?"

In one family firm of several hundred people, the owners both desired and encouraged frequent bypassing. The general manager, eldest son of the owner, said:

When there's trouble inside the factory, say, if someone gets hurt, well, they don't go and see anyone else. They come right here to us and we take care of them. They have the personal feeling that we help them better than if they go to the one that is head of their department, their immediate supervisor.

This practice was looked upon favorably and encouraged by the production chief, a first cousin of the general manager: "The workers will not tell their *encargado* [foreman], but prefer to come to me because they have more *confianza* in me. This has developed after so many years that they prefer to jump the *encargado* and come directly to me."

In this organization, workers were required to come directly to the family managers for even the smallest request, such as a Band-Aid. Immediately after one worker came in with such a request, the researcher asked why this was done, and the family manager replied: "They like us and that's why they come. When they have a problem, we feel we should help them because they're not completely capable of doing these things themselves." A similar occurrence took place while speaking with the production chief, and he said: "This is done so the workers can feel that the factory feels a responsibility for them, and also so they can acquire responsibility toward the factory." In actuality, this centralized and very paternal control discouraged independent action and developed a sense of loyalty and attachment to a set of persons, not principles.

The practice of dealing directly with the owners is often initiated by the workers, without any encouragement from those at the top. This was the case in a small factory, where an *obrero* was discussing why he liked working there. One of his reasons was "because here the owners and managers are the same people, so if you have a problem you can go and get it resolved right away, while this is not so when there is an intermediary." Middle managers, for him, blocked rather than helped a worker with his problems. Managers, therefore, bypass middle levels in order to centralize their control, while workers prefer to bypass middle levels because they feel that only the owner can take direct action.

The phenomenon of bypassing is not solely limited to internal relations. It is also found in relations between the enterprise and the general community, and the latter's influence on the authority system within the enterprise. The sales manager, son of an owning partner in a large firm, described the following situation:

We have a man whose job is to sell products at list prices. We found ourselves with a situation that whenever a customer went to him for some orders, *before* leaving the building he would come into my office and ask me to check the prices personally to make sure that he was getting the best deal. This happens in 99 percent of all sales, even though we will not change our prices. . . . [As a result] salesmen will generally come up to me, leave the order on my desk, and ask me to call the customer and verify the price.

This manager then went on to make a more general statement:

People in Mexico have a very special feeling: they always want to talk to the *patrón,* you know. They always want to talk to the owner; a general sales manager is not enough. That, of course, helps me because when [someone] walks in here, he knows that I'm his last resort. . . . That is very typical in Latin countries. People here are not accustomed to talking to an administrator, or a supervisor, or anybody like that. They want to talk to the man who owns the business because they feel they are important enough, regardless of their size, so that they should be taken care of by the boss.

The growth of enterprise reflects a growing gap in education and cultural background between management and labor. To date, this gap still reflects a strong hiatus between department heads, above the major stratifying line, and foremen, below it. Because middle management view foremen as only glorified *obreros,* they are unwilling to entrust them with more than minimal responsibilities and will only delegate authority to them for routine operations. Given these attitudes, it is not surprising to find a department head bypassing his foreman in order to deal directly with his workers.

The middle manager is likely to practice and encourage bypassing of the foreman with his workers if he makes few distinctions between the cultural and technical backgrounds of those beneath him, and if he feels a great separation between himself and all his subordinates in this regard. Likewise, if he is unsure of his position or his authority with respect to those above him, he is more prone to attempt to hoard his authority and control. He generally does this by establishing ties of personal loyalty to himself among the rank and file in his department. When this is accomplished, workers will carry out an order because it comes directly and personally from him, but are more reluctant to do so simply because it has come down an impersonal chain of command. Workers, therefore, more often bypass the foreman on personal matters than on technical ones. Criticizing this development of departmental fiefdoms in his company, the general manager of a Canadian-owned firm said:

A good manager anywhere will try to give the impression to the workers and everybody else that he's available to discuss their personal problems when everything else has failed. But he can take damn good care that that never happens.

When the foreman is bypassed, however, this is not always done at the initiation of those immediately above or below him. If the foreman is unwilling to take responsibility, he often initiates the bypassing himself. In the same Canadian-owned firm, this caused the general manager to comment:

There's also a certain encouragement to bypass responsibility. [This occurs] when a man comes to a supervisor with a problem and the supervisor says, "Hell, I don't dare touch that; I'd get chopped down about it. Why don't you go and see the departmental manager?" Now, the bypassing is being done there by the foreman, not by the worker. It's quite a strong tendency for everybody. One of the things you have to learn when you become a manager is to make sure not to bypass things to the man above you.

In sum, the tendency of upper- and middle-level management to centralize control discourages the acceptance of responsibility at lower levels and encourages the practice of bypassing authority. This bypassing occurs in both directions, and its locus depends upon such factors as the size of the firm, whether or not ownership and management are separate, and the particular personalities of the individuals involved. While the North American student of social theory and business administration classifies them as either traditional forms of organization or deviations from modern organizational requirements, the Mexican manager and worker are apt to consider them natural and legitimate features of the authority system in an organization's hierarchy.

About the Contributors

Manuel Barrera—Professor, Department of Industrial Relations, Instituto de Organización y Administración, Universidad de Chile, Santiago, Chile.

Frank Brandenburg—Counsel for Latin American and American Chambers of Commerce in Brazil, Rio de Janeiro, Brazil.

Guillermo Briones—Professor of Sociology, Instituto de Sociologia, Universidad de Concepción, Concepción, Chile.

Fernando H. Cardoso—Director, Centro Brasileiro de Anális e Planejamento, Sao Paulo, Brazil.

David Chaplin—Associate Professor of Sociology, University of Wisconsin, Madison, Wisconsin.

Christopher Clague—Assistant Professor of Economics, University of Maryland, College Park, Maryland.

Thomas C. Cochran—Professor of History, University of Pennsylvania, Philadelphia, Pennsylvania.

Stanley M. Davis—Sociologist and Associate Professor of Business Administration, Harvard University, Boston, Massachusetts.

Jose Luis de Imaz—Professor, Catholic University of Buenos Aires, Buenos Aires, Argentina.

Flavia Derossi—Centro di Ricerche Industrialie Sociali, Turin, Italy.

Peter Evans—Assistant Professor of Sociology, Brown University, Providence, Rhode Island.

Carlos Fuentes—renowned Mexican novelist.

N. N. Franklin—International Labor Office, Geneva, Switzerland.

Louis Wolf Goodman—Assistant Professor of Sociology, Yale University, New Haven, Connecticut.

Wendell C. Gordon—Professor of Economics, University of Texas, Austin, Texas.

Charles S. Green—Assistant Professor of Sociology and Anthropology, University of Virginia, Charlottesville, Virginia.

Everett E. Hagen—Professor of Economics and Political Science, Massachusetts Institute of Technology, Cambridge, Massachusetts.

Gavin W. Jones—Staff Associate, The Population Council, New York City, New York.

Edgardo Jurgensen—Instituto de Organización y Administración, Universidad de Chile, Santiago, Chile.

Joseph A. Kahl—Professor of Sociology, Cornell University, Ithaca, New York.

Henry A. Landsberger—Professor of Sociology, University of North Carolina, Chapel Hill, North Carolina.

Albert Lauterbach—Professor of Economics, Sarah Lawrence College, Bronxville, New York.

Oscar Lewis—Late Professor of Anthropology, University of Illinois, Urbana, Illinois.

Aaron Lipman—Professor of Sociology, University of Miami, Coral Gables, Florida.

Alfredo Mallet—International Labor Office, Geneva, Switzerland.

Carmelo Mesa-Lago—Associate Professor of Economics, University of Pittsburgh, Pittsburgh, Pennsylvania.

James O. Morris—Associate Professor, New York State School of Industrial and Labor Relations, Cornell University, Ithaca, New York.

James Petras—Assistant Professor of Political Science and Public Administration, Pennsylvania State University, University Park, Pennsylvania.

Jose Luis Reyna—Investigador, Colegio de Mexico, Mexico, D.F.

Zygmunt Slawinski—Economic Development and Research Division, Economic Commission for Latin America.

W. Paul Strassmann—Professor of Economics, Michigan State University, East Lansing, Michigan.

Abel Toro—Instituto de Organización y Administración, Universidad de Chile, Santiago, Chile.

Raymond Vernon—Professor, Graduate School of Business Administration, Harvard University, Cambridge, Massachusetts.

Lawrence K. Williams—Professor, New York State School of Industrial and Labor Relations, Cornell University, Ithaca, New York.

William F. Whyte—Professor of Organizational Behavior, Cornell University, Ithaca, New York.

Harry K. Wright—Area Counsel for Latin America, Texaco, Inc.

Maurice Zeitlin—Associate Professor of Sociology, University of Wisconsin, Madison, Wisconsin.